The McAfee House in Mercer County, Kentucky, Built about 1790 by James McAfee

PRESIDENTIAL EDITION

THE WINNING OF THE WEST

BY

THEODORE ROOSEVELT

VOLUME THREE

THE FOUNDING OF THE TRANS-ALLEGHANY
COMMONWEALTHS
1784–1790

WITH MAP

Introduction to the Bison Book Edition
by Michael N. McConnell

University of Nebraska Press
Lincoln and London

Introduction to the Bison Book Edition © 1995
by the University of Nebraska Press

⊖ The paper in this book meets the minimum requirements
of American National Standard for Information Sciences—
Permanence of Paper for Printed Library Materials,
ANSI Z39.48-1984.

First Bison Book printing: 1995
Most recent printing indicated by the last digit below:
10   9   8   7   6   5   4   3   2   1

Library of Congress Cataloging-in-Publication Data
Roosevelt, Theodore, 1858–1919.
The winning of the West / by Theodore Roosevelt—Presidential
ed.
p. cm.
Includes index.
Originally published: New York: G. P. Putnam's Sons, 1894.
Contents: v. 1. From the Alleghanies to the Mississippi, 1769–
1776—v. 2. From the Alleghanies to the Mississippi, 1777–
1783—v. 3. The founding of the trans-Alleghany common-
wealths, 1784–1790—v. 4. Louisiana and the Northwest, 1791–
1807.
ISBN 0-8032-8958-8 (set)—ISBN 0-8032-8954-5 (v. 1)—
ISBN 0-8032-8955-3 (v. 2)—ISBN 0-8032-8956-1 (v. 3)—
ISBN 0-8032-8957-X (v. 4)
1. United States—Territorial expansion.   2. Northwest, Old—
History.   3. West (U.S.)—History.   I. Title.
E179.5.R66   1995
976—dc20
94-46645   CIP

The four-volume set of *The Winning of the West* was copyrighted
and published between 1889 and 1896 by G. P. Putnam's Sons,
New York. This Bison Book is a reprint of volume 3, © 1894. The
title-page designation of Presidential Edition and the fron-
tispiece illustration were added later, but in all other respects
this is the original edition.

THIS BOOK IS DEDICATED, WITH HIS PERMISSION

TO

FRANCIS PARKMAN

TO WHOM AMERICANS WHO FEEL A PRIDE IN THE PIONEER HISTORY OF
THEIR COUNTRY ARE SO GREATLY INDEBTED

INTRODUCTION
Michael N. McConnell

The Founding of the Trans-Alleghany Commonwealths
carries Theodore Roosevelt's history of the West into the
post-Revolutionary era. Having won independence from
Great Britain, the fragile American republic faced daunt-
ing challenges, not least in the trans-Appalachian territories ceded to the nation as part of the peace settlement of
1783. Far from being distant and unimportant, the West
became ever more important to the nation between 1783
and 1790.

During the Revolution thousands of settlers continued
to pour into western lands, especially in the Tennessee Valley and Kentucky. Far removed from eastern political and
economic centers, these new settlements became increasingly alienated from state and national governments too
weak and divided to offer the protection and economic assistance the westerners demanded. As a remedy, some in
the West seriously considered joining the British or Spanish colonial empires. Moreover, while the War for Independence ended in 1783, the chronic hostilities between American settlers and Indian societies continued unabated.
These conditions and more left the future of the western
territories in doubt at a time when mounting debt, postwar
depression, and political division made it difficult for the
American government to assert its authority west of the
Appalachians.

Roosevelt viewed these seven years as a crucial period in
the country's history. In his mind, the struggle for the nation's first frontier would determine "whether we should be
a mighty nation" or remain a "mere snarl of weak and

quarrelsome little commonwealths" and, indeed, "whether the victory [over Britain] was or was not worth winning" (xvii, 329). In fact, Roosevelt found in this phase of western history the playing out of two great themes in American history. The first, of recent origin, was for Roosevelt of great importance: the contest between localism—what he characterized as "the spirit of sedition, or lawlessness, and of wild individualism and separatism"—and the development of a strong, centralized federal union. (329).

The second theme had roots deep in the nation's colonial past: the conflict between Indians and settlers for control of the land. This was a struggle that for Roosevelt and his generation could only be understood in terms of a universal conflict between savagery and western civilization.

Thus, for Roosevelt and his readers the winning of the West was more than an exciting story of real-life heroes like George Rogers Clark, intriguers such as John Sevier and Don Diego Gardoqui, and villains like James Wilkinson. It was also an object lesson in the triumph of civilization and of nationalism, lessons that carried special meaning for Americans living in the "Gilded Age" of the late-nineteenth century.

Roosevelt's choice of subject and the way in which he portrayed the history of the West were heavily influenced by his own times and experiences. Born in 1858, on the eve of the Civil War, Roosevelt was, like his generation, profoundly affected by this defining moment in American history.[1] It is no accident, therefore, that his story of the West emerges as a struggle between separatism and an evolving national union that would become "the greatest of all Republics" (53, 96). He thus directed much of this volume to the rise and fall of independence movements in the West, notably the State of Franklin, and the organization of the Northwest Territory. Each symbolized the contending forces in the West. Of particular importance was the development of the Northwest, which Roosevelt identified as a triumph of nationalism, expressed in the now-famous Land Ordinances of 1785 and 1787.

This theme of a struggle between particularism and nationalism is also reflected in Roosevelt's treatment of those who populate his historical landscape. His heroes are men who were able to transcend private and local interests for the good of the nation: the "rifle bearing freemen" who were ultimately able to reconcile "personal liberty and national union," and the settlers of the Old Northwest, whose efforts represented the "triumph of an intelligent collectivism" (xviii, 242). These stood in stark contrast to the "insurrectionary" leaders of Franklin and men like Sevier, men whose actions defied what Roosevelt saw as the self-evident virtues of national union which alone could guarantee the country's "mighty future" (190, 152).

Throughout the book, Roosevelt hammered home the connection between the triumph of the nation in the West and America's subsequent achievement of enormous wealth and place among the world's leading nations. It was a message easily accepted by a nation recently torn apart by civil war and now coming to terms with an industrial economy, waves of immigrants, and its new-found place in a global economy—challenges that Roosevelt would later confront as president. But if events in his own times help explain how he approached the history of the West, so too did prevailing intellectual trends, especially within the young field of American history.

Roosevelt was among the last of a group of "patrician historians"—gentleman scholars who dominated the writing of American history for much of the nineteenth century.[2] Indeed, by the time *The Winning of the West* appeared, the field of history was already falling under the sway of university-trained professionals; within a generation they, not the amateurs, would dominate the writing of history in America.[3]

The greatest of the patrician historians was Francis Parkman, whose epic account of the Anglo-French struggle for North America began to appear in 1851, just seven years before Roosevelt's birth. Roosevelt saw in Parkman the ideal historian, consciously attempted to emulate his style, his thorough use of the available primary evidence, and dedicated *The Winning of the West* to his intellectual idol. Parkman's generation of historians greatly influenced the way in which Americans viewed their past, in large measure because they were master storytellers, skillfully using words to paint dramatic portraits of great men and events. These historians, including Roosevelt, strongly believed that history was a form of literature and an art and the high quality of their prose guaranteed that they would reach the ever-growing literate public.[4]

Equally important was the message that these historians conveyed. The gentleman amateurs were dedicated nationalists who defined their principal task as fostering respect for and pride in the nation by recounting how the United States was forged out of diverse European peoples and settlements. They consciously worked against sectional prejudices, and their histories emphasized the common ground that all Americans shared and those characteristics that defined a unique and powerful society.[5]

Roosevelt's history of the West is an accurate reflection of this way of viewing the past, as is his emphasis on the *inevitability* of the processes he described. He, like his fellow historians, read their own times back into the past and saw history as the deliberate—even divinely ordained—unfolding of events that would lead to the present (1). It was this assumption that allowed Roosevelt to castigate men like Wilkinson and Sevier: their actions were wrong precisely because subsequent events (which these men could not have foreseen) made them wrong.

A view of history as the story of the inevitable triumph of a great nation also determined how Roosevelt would treat the other great theme of his story: the contest between Indians and white Americans for control of the West. Like most Americans of his day, Roosevelt viewed native peoples as racially inferior, as savages, and a hindrance to the advance of civilization—people easily enough written out of history since they were bound to lose their struggle with the American nation. The inevitability of Indian defeat

(Roosevelt wrote as the Plains Indian wars were coming to an end) was strongly influenced by Social Darwinism that further reinforced the picture of American expansion and Indian defeat as the natural outcome of a collision between superior and inferior peoples (46).

Thus, for Roosevelt and his audience, the struggle for the West was a war between two incompatable races, one civilized, the other "warlike . . . wild and squalid" savages, a conflict that was, by definition, "eternal" (2, 41). Moreover, this was a conflict in which the ends easily justified the means. Roosevelt asserted that how white Americans took the West, whether "by treaty . . . armed conquest, or . . . a mixture of both," mattered "comparatively little, so long as the land was won." That civilization should prevail over savagery was, to Roosevelt, "all important" since the winning of the West would ultimately benefit all mankind (44). He also hastened to remind his readers that "the most ultimately righteous of all wars is a war with savages" (45).

Recently, historians have reexamined the history of the Revolutionary frontier. In some respects their work supports the interpretations first put forward in *The Winning of the West*. Roosevelt understood that the fundamental tension between the East and the raw frontier setlements was basic to an understanding of the separatist movements that occurred in the West. Recent work on the Ohio Valley shows just how alienated westerners had become from distant and unresponsive governments. By 1794 farmers were actively resisting a federal excise tax on locally made whiskey that threatened the region's fragile economy.[6] This "Whiskey Rebellion," while a failure, underscored the weakness of western allegiance to the new national government that grew from the government's inability to meet the needs of western citizens. Roosevelt clearly saw the relationship between governmental authority and the winning of the West. Both historians and historical geographers have continued to explore this theme and have added to our understanding of the period from 1783 to 1790 by studying the impact of physical distance, poor communications, land speculation, and national politics on the development of the nation's western frontier.[7]

The conflict between a new national government and the many local interests that surfaced in the West also affected Indian relations, and it is on this aspect of frontier history that modern scholarship has most clearly departed from Roosevelt's interpretation. Historians now agree that the hostility between Indian societies and the new United States was rooted not in any inherent racial incompatability but in a long history shaped especially by the complex struggle between native peoples, the French, and the British for control of the trans-Appalachian region. The emergence of the new American republic marked only the latest phase of that struggle as the nation attempted to secure its title to western lands whose development meant a growing national economy and a sound national treasury—both badly needed in the uncertain years that followed the Revolution.

Setting aside the racial assumptions and the belief in the inevitability of "civilization's" triumph over "savagery," historians now understand the frontier to have been not so much a place as a complex and creative meeting of peoples defined by their cultures, not race. In such a view, Indians as well as settlers were active participants in events, behaving according to rational appraisals of needs and opportunities.

This way of looking at the frontier offers valuable new insight into long-familiar events. The years after 1783 were as crucial to Indians in the West as for the United States. Indeed, from 1783 through the 1790s, Indian societies faced a major crisis as they struggled to maintain their independence and cultural autonomy in the face of an expanding American society. Western Indians had counted on the British to contain colonial settlements and, during the Revolution, some nations, including the Senecas, Shawnees, and Delawares, had entered the war as British allies.

Britain's defeat dramatically altered the balance of power throughout the West as much of the region was ceded to the United States. Continued warfare after 1783 arose both from Indian efforts to retain control of their lands and from the American government's lack of a coherent Indian policy and inability to curb the excessive land-hunger of western settlers.[8] The border warfare that resulted did indeed become, as Roosevelt insisted, more vicious and atrocity-ridden on both sides. However, this development grew out of a long and bloody history of frontier warfare that began during the Seven Years' War. Americans rejected accommodation with native societies that were now seen as obstacles to expansion. It was this increasingly bitter warfare that generated the racial stereotypes that would become an article of faith for Roosevelt's generation.[9]

While it dominated the histories of men like Roosevelt who were drawn to military history, warfare between Indians and the American republic was not the only problem facing western Indians.[10] Disease as well as fighting took its toll on Indian populations and threatened the very fabric of native societies, while trade and the American settlers' ongoing transformation of the land itself reinforced the growing technological dependence of Indians and produced an ecological crisis that ultimately forced native communities to give up traditional economies in favor of new—and often unsettling—strategies borrowed from the increasing numbers of white settlers.[11]

These challenges remind us that the triumphant American conquest of the West came at a stiff price to Indian societies as well as to the often besieged homesteaders who figured most prominently in Roosevelt's story. Yet, recent work also makes clear that, unlike Roosevelt's "savages," real Indians did not vanish before the onrushing tide of white civilization. Instead, they drew on reserves of individual and collective strength and persisted by selectively adapting when necessary and by finding renewed purpose and spiritual power through revitalization movements that reaffirmed collective identities which have survived despite defeat and dispossession.[12]

New interest in and better understanding of the nature of the frontier reminds us that the study of history is an evolving process, a dialogue between the historian's time and the past. Roosevelt's *Winning of the West* reflects, as all history does, the issues and values that shaped the times in which it was written. Roosevelt's work, therefore, represents an effort to understand the present by reference to the past. Thus, while his assumptions about the historical process may be in many respects dated, his work remains of considerable importance as an historical artifact in its own right, an avenue into the man and his age.

NOTES

1. Theodore Roosevelt, *Theodore Roosevelt, An Autobiography* (New York: The MacMillan Company, 1916), 5.

2. John Higham, *History: The Development of Historical Studies in the United States* (Englewood Cliffs NJ: Prentice-Hall, 1965), 20.

3. Ibid., 7, 104; Harvey Wish, ed., *American Historians, A Selection* (New York: Oxford University Press, 1962), 142.

4. Allan Nevins, *The Gateway to History* (New York: Doubleday & Company, 1962), 32; Wish, *American Historians*, 5.

5. Higham, *History*, 148, 150.

6. Thomas Slaughter, *The Whiskey Rebellion: Frontier Epilogue to the American Revolution* (New York: Oxford University Press, 1986).

7. For example, see Reginald Horsman, *The Frontier in the Formative Years, 1783–1815* (Albuquerque: University of New Mexico Press, 1975); Malcomb J. Rorabaugh, *The Trans-Appalachian Frontier: People, Societies, and Institutions, 1775–1850* (New York: Oxford University Press, 1978); D. W. Meinig, *The Shaping of America: A Geographical Perspective on 500 Years of History*, vol. 1: *Atlantic America, 1492–1800* (New Haven: Yale University Press, 1986), esp. 338–454.

8. Reginald Horsman, *Expansion and American Indian Policy, 1783–1812* (Norman: University of Oklahoma Press, 1967), chaps. 1–6; Francis Paul Prucha, *American Indian Policy in the*

Formative Years: The Indian Trade and Intercourse Acts, 1790–1834 (Lincoln: University of Nebraska Press, 1963), chaps. 2–3.

9. Richard White, *The Middle Ground: Indians, Empires, and Republics in the Great Lakes Region, 1650–1815* (New York: Cambridge University Press, 1991), esp. chaps. 6–11; R. David Edmunds, *The Shawnee Prophet* (Lincoln: University of Nebraska Press, 1983); Randolph C. Downes, *Council Fires on the Upper Ohio: A Narrative of Indian Affairs in the Upper Ohio Valley to 1795* (Pittsburgh: University of Pittsburgh Press, 1969), chaps. 12–13.

10. Higham, *History,* 153–54.

11. On trade, see Kathryn E. Holland Braund, *Deerskins and Duffels: Creek Indian Trade with Anglo-America, 1680–1815* (Lincoln: University of Nebraska Press, 1993); on ecological issues, Richard White, *The Roots of Dependency: Subsistence, Environment, and Social Change among the Choctaws, Pawnees, and Navajos* (Lincoln: University of Nebraska Press, 1983), chaps. 1–5; see also James H. Merrell, *The Indians' New World: Catawbas and Their Neighbors from European Contact through the Era of Removal* (Chapel Hill: University of North Carolina Press, 1989), esp. chaps. 5–6; Anthony F. C. Wallace, *The Death and Rebirth of the Seneca* (New York: Random House, 1972); J. Leitch Wright, *Creeks and Seminoles: The Destruction and Regeneration of the Muscogulge People* (Lincoln: University of Nebraska Press, 1986), chap. 5.

12. On cultural and spiritual renewal, see Edmunds, *The Shawnee Prophet;* Gregory Evans Dowd, *A Spirited Resistance: The North American Indian Struggle for Unity, 1745–1815* (Baltimore: The Johns Hopkins University Press, 1992); Joel W. Martin, *Sacred Revolt: The Muscogee's Struggle for a New World* (Boston: Beacon Press, 1991).

PREFACE TO THIRD VOLUME.

THE material used herein is that mentioned in the preface to the first volume, save that I have also drawn freely on the Draper Manuscripts, in the Library of the State Historical Society of Wisconsin, at Madison. For the privilege of examining these valuable manuscripts I am indebted to the generous courtesy of the State Librarian, Mr. Reuben Gold Thwaites; I take this opportunity of extending to him my hearty thanks.

The period covered in this volume includes the seven years immediately succeeding the close of the Revolutionary War. It was during these seven years that the Constitution was adopted, and actually went into effect; an event if possible even more momentous for the West than the East. The time was one of vital importance to the whole nation; alike to the people of the inland frontier and to those of the seaboard. The course of events during these years determined whether we should become a mighty nation, or a mere snarl of weak and quarrelsome little commonwealths, with a history as bloody and meaningless as that of the Spanish-American states.

At the close of the Revolution the West was peopled by a few thousand settlers, knit by but the slenderest ties to the Federal Government. A remarkable inflow of population followed. The warfare with the Indians, and the quarrels with the British and Spaniards over boundary questions, reached no decided issue. But the rifle-bearing freemen who founded their little republics on the western waters gradually solved the question of combining personal liberty with national union. For years there was much wavering. There were violent separatist movements, and attempts to establish complete independence of the eastern States. There were corrupt conspiracies between some of the western leaders and various high Spanish officials, to bring about a disruption of the Confederation. The extraordinary little backwoods state of Franklin began and ended a career unique in our annals. But the current, though eddying and sluggish, set towards Union. By 1790 a firm government had been established west of the mountains, and the trans-Alleghany commonwealths had become parts of the Federal Union.

THEODORE ROOSEVELT.

SAGAMORE HILL, LONG ISLAND,
   October, 1894.

CONTENTS.

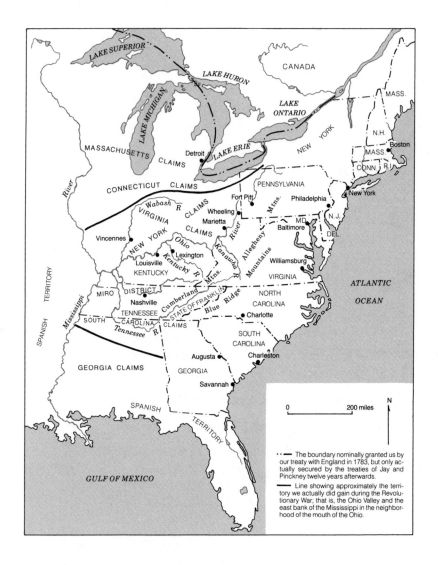

The Western Land Claims at the Close of the Revolution. Showing also the state of Franklin, Kentucky, and the Cumberland Settlements, or Miro District. *Source:* Based on a map by G. P. Putnam's Sons, New York and London.

THE WINNING OF THE WEST.

CHAPTER I.

THE INRUSH OF SETTLERS, 1784–1787.

AT the beginning of 1784 peace was a definite fact, and the United States had become one among the nations of the earth; a nation young and lusty in her youth, but as yet loosely knit, and formidable in promise rather than in actual capacity for performance.

On the western frontier lay vast and fertile vacant spaces; for the Americans had barely passed the threshold of the continent predestined to be the inheritance of their children and their children's children. For generations the great feature in the nation's history, next only to the preservation of its national life, was to be its westward growth; and its distinguishing work was to be the settlement of the immense wilderness which stretched across to the Pacific. But before the land could be settled it had to be won.

The valley of the Ohio already belonged to the Americans by right of conquest and of armed possession; it was held by rifle-bearing backwoods

The Western Frontier.

farmers, hard and tenacious men, who never lightly
yielded what once they had grasped.   North and
south of the valley lay warlike and powerful Indian confederacies, now at last thoroughly alarmed
and angered by the white advance; while behind
these warrior tribes, urging them to hostility, and
furnishing them the weapons and means wherewith
to fight, stood the representatives of two great European nations, both bitterly hostile to the new
America, and both anxious to help in every way the
red savages who strove to stem the tide of settlement.   The close alliance between the soldiers and
diplomatic agents of polished old-world powers
and the wild and squalid warriors of the wilderness
was an alliance against which the American settlers
had always to make head in the course of their long
march westward.   The kings and the peoples of the
old world ever showed themselves the inveterate
enemies of their blood-kin in the new; they always
strove to delay the time when their own race should
rise to wellnigh universal supremacy.   In mere
blind selfishness, or in a spirit of jealousy still
blinder, the Europeans refused to regard their kinsmen who had crossed the ocean to found new realms
in new continents as entitled to what they had
won by their own toil and hardihood.   They persisted in treating the bold adventurers who went
abroad as having done so simply for the benefit of
the men who stayed at home; and they shaped
their transatlantic policy in accordance with this
idea.   The Briton and the Spaniard opposed the
American settler precisely as the Frenchman had

done before them, in the interest of their own merchants and fur-traders. They endeavored in vain
to bar him from the solitudes through which only
the Indians roved.

All the ports around the Great Lakes were held
by the British ;[1] their officers, military and civil, still
kept possession, administering the government of the
scattered French hamlets, and preserving their old-
time relations with the Indian tribes, whom they
continued to treat as allies or feudatories. To the
south and west the Spaniards played the same part.
They scornfully refused to heed the boundary established to the southward by the treaty between England and the United States, alleging that the former
had ceded what it did not possess. They claimed
the land as theirs by right of conquest. The territory
which they controlled stretched from Florida along
a vaguely defined boundary to the Mississippi, up
the east bank of the latter at least to the Chickasaw
Bluffs, and thence up the west bank ; while the
Creeks and Choctaws were under their influence.
The Spaniards dreaded and hated the Americans
even more than did the British, and they were right;
for three fourths of the present territory of the
United States then lay within the limits of the
Spanish possessions.[2]

Thus there were foes, both white and red, to be
overcome, either by force of arms or by diplomacy,
before the northernmost and the southernmost por-

[1] State Dep. MSS., No. 150, vol. ii., March, 1788. Report of Secretary
Knox.
[2] State Dep. MSS., No. 81, vol. ii., pp. 189, 217. No. 120, vol. ii., June
30, 1786.

tions of the wilderness lying on our western border
could be thrown open to settlement. The lands
lying between had already been conquered, and yet
were so sparsely settled as to seem almost vacant.
While they offered every advantage of soil and climate to the farmer and cultivator, they also held out
peculiar attractions to ambitious men of hardy and
adventurous temper.

With the ending of the Revolutionary War the
rush of settlers to these western lands assumed striking proportions. The peace relieved the
The Rush pressure which had hitherto restrained this
of Settlers. movement, on the one hand, while on the
other it tended to divert into the new channel of
pioneer work those bold spirits whose spare energies
had thus far found an outlet on stricken fields. To
push the frontier westward in the teeth of the forces
of the wilderness was fighting work, such as suited
well enough many a stout soldier who had worn the
blue and buff of the Continental line, or who, with
his fellow rough-riders, had followed in the train of
some grim partisan leader.

The people of the New England States and of
New York, for the most part, spread northward and
westward within their own boundaries ; and Georgia
likewise had room for all her growth within her
borders ; but in the States between there was a stir
of eager unrest over the tales told of the beautiful
and fertile lands lying along the Ohio, the Cumberland, and the Tennessee. The days of the early
pioneers, of the men who did the hardest and
roughest work, were over ; farms were being laid out
and towns were growing up among the felled forests

from which the game and the Indians had alike been
driven.   There was still plenty of room for the rude
cabin and stump-dotted clearing of the ordinary
frontier settler, the wood-chopper and game hunter.
Folk of the common backwoods type were as yet
more numerous than any others among the settlers.
In addition there were planters from among the
gentry of the sea-coast ; there were men of means
who had bought great tracts of wild land ; there
were traders with more energy than capital ; there
were young lawyers ; there were gentlemen with a
taste for an unfettered life of great opportunity ; in
short there were adventurers of every kind.

All men who deemed that they could swim in
troubled waters were drawn towards the new country.   The more turbulent and ambitious spirits saw
roads to distinction in frontier warfare, politics, and
diplomacy.   Merchants dreamed of many fortunate
ventures, in connection with the river trade or the
overland commerce by packtrain.   Lawyers not only
expected to make their living by their proper calling,
but also to rise to the first places in the commonwealths, for in these new communities, as in the
older States, the law was then the most honored of
the professions, and that which most surely led to
high social and political standing.   But the one great
attraction for all classes was the chance of procuring
large quantities of fertile land at low prices.

To the average settler the land was the prime
source of livelihood.   A man of hardihood, thrift,
perseverance, and bodily strength could
surely make a comfortable living for him-   **Value of
the Land.**
self and his family, if only he could settle

on a good tract of rich soil; and this he could do if he went to the new country. As a matter of course, therefore, vigorous young frontiersmen swarmed into the region so recently won.

These men merely wanted so much land as they could till. Others, however, looked at it from a very different standpoint. The land was the real treasury-chest of the country. It was the one commodity which appealed to the ambitious and adventurous side of the industrial character at that time and in that place. It was the one commodity the management of which opened chances of procuring vast wealth, and especially vast speculative wealth. To the American of the end of the eighteenth century the roads leading to great riches were as few as those leading to a competency were many. He could not prospect for mines of gold and of silver, of iron, copper, and coal; he could not discover and work wells of petroleum and natural gas; he could not build up, sell, and speculate in railroad systems and steamship companies; he could not gamble in the stock market; he could not build huge manufactories of steel, of cottons, of woollens; he could not be a banker or a merchant on a scale which is dwarfed when called princely; he could not sit still and see an already great income double and quadruple because of the mere growth in the value of real estate in some teeming city. The chances offered him by the fur trade were very uncertain. If he lived in a sea-coast town, he might do something with the clipper ships that ran to Europe and China. If he lived elsewhere, his one chance of acquiring great wealth, and his best chance to acquire even moderate wealth without long and plodding labor, was to speculate in wild land.

Accordingly the audacious and enterprising business men who would nowadays go into speculation in stocks, were then forced into speculation in land. Sometimes as individuals, some- Land Speculators.
times as large companies, they sought to procure wild lands on the Wabash, the Ohio, the Cumberland, the Yazoo. In addition to the ordinary methods of settlement by, or purchase from private persons, they endeavored to procure grants on favorable terms from the national and State legislatures, or even from the Spanish government. They often made a regular practice of buying the land rights which had accrued in lieu of arrears of pay to different bodies of Continental troops. They even at times purchased a vague and clouded title from some Indian tribe. As with most other speculative business investments, the great land companies rarely realized for the originators and investors anything like what was expected; and the majority were absolute failures in every sense. Nevertheless, a number of men made money out of them, often on quite a large scale; and in many instances, where the people who planned and carried out the scheme made nothing for themselves, they yet left their mark in the shape of settlers who had come in to purchase their lands, or even in the shape of a town built under their auspices.

Land speculation was by no means confined to those who went into it on a large scale. The settler without money might content himself with staking out an ordinary-sized farm; but the new-comer of any

means was sure not only to try to get a large estate for
his own use, but also to procure land beyond any immediate need, so that he might hold on to it until it
rose in value.   He was apt to hold commissions to
purchase land for his friends who remained east of
the mountains.   The land was turned to use by private individuals and by corporations ; it was held for
speculative purposes ; it was used for the liquidation
of debts of every kind.   The official surveyors, when
created, did most of their work by deputy ; Boone
was deputy surveyor of Fayette County, in Kentucky.[1] Some men surveyed and staked out their own
claims ; the others employed professional surveyors,
or else hired old hunters like Boone and Kenton,
whose knowledge of woodcraft and acquaintance
with the most fertile grounds enabled them not only
to survey the land, but to choose the portions best
fit for settlement.   The lack of proper government
surveys, and the looseness with which the records
were kept in the land office, put a premium on fraud
and encouraged carelessness.   People could make
and record entries in secret, and have the land surveyed in secret, if they feared a dispute over a title ;
no one save the particular deputy surveyor employed
needed to know. [2] The litigation over these con-
fused titles dragged on with interminable tedious-
ness.   Titles were often several deep on one "loca-
tion," as it was called ; and whoever purchased land

[1] Draper MSS. ; Boone MSS.   Entry of August court for 1783.
[2] Draper MSS. in Wisconsin State Hist. Ass.   Clark papers.   Walter
Darrell to Col. William Fleming, St. Asaphs, April 14, 1783.   These valuable Draper MSS. have been opened to me by Mr. Reuben Gold Thwaites,
the State Librarian ; I take this opportunity of thanking him for his generous courtesy, to which I am so greatly indebted.

too often purchased also an expensive and uncertain lawsuit.

The two chief topics of thought and conversation, the two subjects which beyond all others engrossed and absorbed the minds of the settlers, were the land and the Indians. We have already seen how on one occasion Clark could raise no men for an expedition against the Indians until he closed the land offices round which the settlers were thronging. Every hunter kept a sharp lookout for some fertile bottom on which to build a cabin. The volunteers who rode against the Indian towns also spied out the land and chose the best spots whereon to build their blockhouses and palisaded villages as soon as a truce might be made, or the foe driven for the moment farther from the border. Sometimes settlers squatted on land already held but not occupied under a good title; sometimes a man who claimed the land under a defective title, or under pretence of original occupation, attempted to oust or to blackmail him who had cleared and tilled the soil in good faith; and these were both fruitful causes not only of lawsuits but of bloody affrays. Among themselves, the settlers' talk ran ever on land titles and land litigation, and schemes for securing vast tracts of rich and well watered country. These were the subjects with which they filled their letters to one another and to their friends at home, and the subjects upon which these same friends chiefly dwelt when they sent letters in return.[1] Often well-to-do men visited

[1] Clay MSS. and Draper MSS., *passim : e. g.*, in former, J. Mercer to George Nicholas, Nov. 28, 1789 ; J. Ware to George Nicholas, Nov. 29, 1789 ; letter to Mrs. Byrd, Jan. 16, 1786, etc., etc., etc.

the new country by themselves first, chose good sites
for their farms and plantations, surveyed and purchased them, and then returned to their old homes,
whence they sent out their field hands to break the
soil and put up buildings before bringing out their
families.

The westward movement of settlers took place
along several different lines.   The dwellers in what
is now eastern Tennessee were in close
Lines Fol-
lowed in the touch with the old settled country; their
Western farms and little towns formed part of the
Movement. chain of forest clearings which stretched
unbroken from the border of Virginia down the valleys of the Watauga and the Holston.   Though
they were sundered by mountain ranges from the
peopled regions in the State to which they belonged,
North Carolina, yet these ranges were pierced by
many trails, and were no longer haunted by Indians.
There were no great obstacles to be overcome in
moving in to this valley of the upper Tennessee.
On the other hand, by this time it held no very
great prizes in the shape of vast tracts of rich and
unclaimed land.   In consequence there was less
temptation to speculation among those who went to
this part of the western country.   It grew rapidly,
the population being composed chiefly of actual settlers who had taken holdings with the purpose of
cultivating them, and of building homes thereon.
The entire frontier of this region was continually
harassed by Indians; and it was steadily extended
by the home-planting of the rifle-bearing backwoodsmen.

The danger from Indian invasion and outrage was, however, far greater in the distant communities which were growing up in the great bend **The Cum-** of the Cumberland, cut off, as they were, **berland** by immense reaches of forest from the sea- **Country.** board States. The settlers who went to this region for the most part followed two routes, either descending the Tennessee and ascending the Cumberland in flotillas of flat-boats and canoes, or else striking out in large bodies through the wilderness, following the trails that led westward from the settlements on the Holston. The population on the Cumberland did not increase very fast for some years after the close of the Revolutionary War; and the settlers were, as a rule, harsh, sturdy backwoodsmen, who lived lives of toil and poverty. Nevertheless, there was a good deal of speculation in Cumberland lands; great tracts of tens of thousands of acres were purchased by men of means in the old districts of North Carolina, who sometimes came out to live on their estates. The looseness of the system of surveying in vogue is shown by the fact that where possible these lands were entered and paid for under a law which allowed a warrant to be shifted to new soil if it was discovered that the first entry was made on what was already claimed by some one else.[1]

Hamlets and homesteads were springing up on the left bank of the upper Ohio, in what is now West Virginia; and along the streams flowing into it from the east. A few reckless adventurers were

[1] Clay MSS., Jesse Benton to Thos. Hart, April 3, 1786.

building cabins on the right bank of this great river. Others, almost as adventurous, were pushing into the neighborhood of the French villages on the Wabash and in the Illinois. At Louisville men were already planning to colonize the country just opposite on the Ohio, under the law of the State of Virginia, which rewarded the victorious soldiers of Clark's famous campaign with grants in the region they had conquered.

The great growth of the west took place in Kentucky. The Kentucky country was by far the most widely renowned for its fertility; it was much more accessible and more firmly held, and its government was on a more permanent footing than was the case in the Wabash, Illinois, and Cumberland regions. In consequence the majority of the men who went west to build homes fixed their eyes on the vigorous young community which lay north of the Ohio, and which already aspired to the honors of statehood.

Movement of Settlers to Kentucky.

The immigrants came into Kentucky in two streams, following two different routes—the Ohio River, and Boone's old Wilderness Trail. Those who came overland, along the latter road, were much fewer in number than those who came by water; and yet they were so numerous that the trail at times was almost thronged, and much care had to be taken in order to find camping places where there was enough feed for the horses. The people who travelled this wilderness road went in the usual backwoods manner, on horseback, with laden packtrains, and often with

The Wilderness Road to Kentucky.

their herds and flocks.   Young men went out alone
or in parties; and groups of families from the same
neighborhood often journeyed together. They struggled over the narrow, ill-made roads which led from
the different back settlements, until they came to
the last outposts of civilization east of the Cumberland Mountains;   scattered block-houses, whose
owners were by turns farmers, tavern-keepers, hunters, and Indian fighters.   Here they usually waited
until a sufficient number had gathered together to
furnish a band of riflemen large enough to beat off
any prowling party of red marauders; and then set
off to traverse by slow stages the mountains and
vast forests which lay between them and the nearest Kentucky station.   The time of the journey depended, of course, upon the composition of the travelling party, and upon the mishaps encountered; a
party of young men on good horses might do it in
three days, while a large band of immigrants, who
were hampered by women, children, and cattle, and
dogged by ill-luck, might take three weeks.   Ordinarily six or eight days were sufficient.   Before
starting each man laid in a store of provisions for
himself and his horse; perhaps thirty pounds of
flour, half a bushel of corn meal, and three bushels
of oats.   There was no meat unless game was shot.
Occasionally several travellers clubbed together and
carried a tent; otherwise they slept in the open.
The trail was very bad, especially at first, where it
climbed between the gloomy and forbidding cliffs
that walled in Cumberland Gap.   Even when undisturbed by Indians, the trip was accompanied by

much fatigue and exposure; and, as always in frontier travelling, one of the perpetual annoyances was
the necessity for hunting up strayed horses.[1]

The chief highway was the Ohio River; for to
drift down stream in a scow was easier and quicker,
The Travel and no more dangerous, than to plod
down the through thick mountain forests. More-
Ohio. over, it was much easier for the settler
who went by water to carry with him his household
goods and implements of husbandry; and even such
cumbrous articles as wagons, or, if he was rich and
ambitious, the lumber wherewith to build a frame
house. All kinds of craft were used, even bark
canoes and pirogues, or dugouts; but the keel-boat,
and especially the flat-bottomed scow with square
ends, were the ordinary means of conveyance. They
were of all sizes. The passengers and their live
stock were of course huddled together so as to take
up as little room as possible. Sometimes the immigrants built or bought their own boat, navigated it
themselves, and sold it or broke it up on reaching
their destination. At other times they merely hired
a passage. A few of the more enterprising boat
owners speedily introduced a regular emigrant service, making trips at stated times from Pittsburg or
perhaps Limestone, and advertising the carriage
capacity of their boats and the times of starting.
The trip from Pittsburg to Louisville took a week
or ten days; but in low water it might last a
month.

The number of boats passing down the Ohio,

[1] Durrett MSS. Journal of Rev. James Smith, 1785.

laden with would-be settlers and their belongings, speedily became very great. An eye-wit-   Numbers of ness stated that between November 13th   the Immi- and December 22d, of 1785, thirty-nine   grants. boats, with an average of ten souls in each, went down the Ohio to the Falls; and there were others which stopped at some of the settlements farther up the river.[1] As time went on the number of immigrants who adopted this method of travel increased; larger boats were used, and the immigrants took more property with them. In the last half of the year 1787 there passed by Fort Harmar 146 boats, with 3196 souls, 1371 horses, 165 wagons, 191 cattle, 245 sheep, and 24 hogs.[2] In the year ending in November, 1788, 967 boats, carrying 18,370 souls, with 7986 horses, 2372 cows, 1110 sheep, and 646 wagons,[3] went down the Ohio. For many years this great river was the main artery through which the fresh blood of the pioneers was pumped into the west.

There are no means of procuring similar figures for the number of immigrants who went over the Wilderness Road; but probably there were not half as many as went down the Ohio. Perhaps from ten to twenty thousand people a year came into Kentucky during the period immediately succeeding the close of the Revolution; but the net gain to the

---

[1] Draper MSS., *Massachusetts Gazette*, March 13, 1786 ; letter from Kentucky, December 22, 1785.

[2] Harmar Papers, December 9, 1787.

[3] *Columbian Magazine*, January, 1789. Letter from Fort Harmar, November 26, 1788. By what is evidently a clerical error the time is put down as one month instead of one year.

population was much less, because there was always a smaller, but almost equally steady, counter-flow of men who, having failed as pioneers, were struggling wearily back toward their deserted eastern homes.

The inrush being so great Kentucky grew apace. In 1785 the population was estimated at from **Kentucky's** twenty [1] to thirty thousand; and the lead- **Growth.** ing towns, Louisville, Lexington, Harrods- burg, Booneboro, St. Asaph's, were thriving little hamlets, with stores and horse grist-mills, and no longer mere clusters of stockaded cabins. At Louis- ville, for instance, there were already a number of two-story frame houses, neatly painted, with veran- dahs running the full length of each house, and fenced vegetable gardens alongside [2]; while at the same time Nashville was a town of logs, with but two houses that deserved the name, the others being mere huts.[3] The population of Louisville amounted to about 300 souls, of whom 116 were fighting men [4]; between it and Lexington the whole country was well settled; but fear of the Indians kept settlers back from the Ohio.

The new-comers were mainly Americans from all the States of the Union; but there were also a few people from nearly every country in Europe, and even from Asia.[5] The industrious and the adven- turous, the homestead winners and the land specu-

---

[1] " Journey in the West in 1785," by Lewis Brantz.

[2] " Lettres d'un cultivateur américain," St. John de Créve Cœur. Sum- mer of 1784.

[3] Brantz.

[4] State Department MSS. Papers Continental Congress, No. 150, vol. ii., p. 21.   Letter from Major W. North, August 23, 1786.

[5] Letter in *Massachusetts Gazette*, above quoted.

lators, the criminal fleeing from justice, and the honest man seeking a livelihood or a fortune, all alike prized the wild freedom and absence of restraint so essentially characteristic of their new life; a life in many ways very pleasant, but one which on the border of the Indian country sank into mere savagery.

Kentucky was "a good poor man's country"[1] provided the poor man was hardy and vigorous. The settlers were no longer in danger of starvation, for they already raised more flour than they could consume. Neither was there as yet anything approaching to luxury. But between these two extremes there was almost every grade of misery and well-being, according to the varying capacity shown by the different settlers in grappling with the conditions of their new life. Among the foreign-born immigrants success depended in part upon race; a contemporary Kentucky observer estimated that, of twelve families of each nationality, nine German, seven Scotch, and four Irish prospered, while the others failed.[2] The German women worked just as hard as the men, even in the fields, and both sexes were equally saving. Naturally such thrifty immigrants did well materially; but they never took any position of leadership or influence in the community until they had assimilated themselves in speech and customs to their American neighbors. The Scotch were frugal and industrious; for good or for bad

---

[1] State Department MSS. Madison Papers. Caleb Wallace to Madison, July 12, 1785.

[2] "Description of Kentucky," 1792, by Harry Toulmin, Secretary of State.

they speedily became indistinguishable from the native-born. The greater proportion of failures among the Irish, brave and vigorous though they were, was due to their quarrelsomeness, and their fondness for drink and litigation; besides, remarks this Kentucky critic, "they soon take to the gun, which is the ruin of everything." None of these foreign-born elements were of any very great importance in the development of Kentucky; its destiny was shaped and controlled by its men of native stock.

In such a population there was of course much loosening of the bands, social, political, moral, and religious, which knit a society together. A great many of the restraints of their old life were thrown off, and there was much social adjustment and readjustment before their relations to one another under the new conditions became definitely settled. But there came early into the land many men of high purpose and pure life whose influence upon their fellows, though quiet, was very great. Moreover, the clergyman and the school-teacher, the two beings who had done so much for colonial civilization on the seaboard, were already becoming important factors in the life of the frontier communities. Austere Presbyterian ministers were people of mark in many of the towns. The Baptist preachers lived and worked exactly as did their flocks; their dwellings were little cabins with dirt floors and, instead of bedsteads, skin-covered pole-bunks; they cleared the ground, split rails, planted corn, and raised hogs on equal

Character of the Frontier Population.

terms with their parishioners.[1] After Methodism
cut loose from its British connections in 1785, the
time of its great advance began, and the circuit-
riders were speedily eating bear meat and buffalo
tongues on the frontier.[2]

Rough log schools were springing up everywhere,
beside the rough log meeting-houses, the same building often serving for both purposes. The school-
teacher might be a young surveyor out of work for
the moment, a New Englander fresh from some academy in the northeast, an Irishman with a smatter-
ing of learning, or perhaps an English immigrant of
the upper class, unfit for and broken down by the
work of a new country.[3] The boys and girls were
taught together, and at recess played together—
tag, pawns, and various kissing games. The rod
was used unsparingly, for the elder boys proved
boisterous pupils. A favorite mutinous frolic was
to " bar out " the teacher, taking possession of the
school-house and holding it against the master with
sticks and stones until he had either forced an en-
trance or agreed to the terms of the defenders.
Sometimes this barring out represented a revolt
against tyranny; often it was a conventional, and
half-acquiesced-in, method of showing exuberance of
spirit, just before the Christmas holidays. In most
of the schools the teaching was necessarily of the
simplest, for the only books might be a Testament,
a primer, a spelling book, and a small arithmetic.

[1] " History of Kentucky Baptists," by J. H. Spencer.
[2] " History of Methodism in Kentucky," by John B. McFerrier.
[3] Durrett MSS.   " Autobiography of Robert McAfee."

In such a society, simple, strong, and rude, both
the good features and the bad were nakedly promi-
Frontier   nent; and the views of observers in refer-
Society.   ence thereto varied accordingly as they were
struck by one set of characteristics or another.   One
traveller would paint the frontiersmen as little better
than the Indians against whom they warred, and
their life as wild, squalid, and lawless; while the
next would lay especial and admiring stress on their
enterprise, audacity, and hospitable openhandedness.
Though much alike, different portions of the frontier
stock were beginning to develop along different
lines.   The Holston people, both in Virginia and
North Carolina, were by this time comparatively
little affected by immigration from without those
States, and were on the whole homogeneous; but the
Virginians and Carolinians of the seaboard considered them rough, unlettered, and not of very good
character.   One travelling clergyman spoke of them
with particular disfavor; he was probably prejudiced by their indifference to his preaching, for he
mentions with much dissatisfaction that the congregations he addressed "though small, behaved extremely bad." [1]   The Kentuckians showed a mental
breadth that was due largely to the many different
sources from which even the predominating American elements in the population sprang.   The Cumberland people seemed to travellers the wildest and
rudest of all, as was but natural, for these fierce and
stalwart settlers were still in the midst of a warfare

---

[1] Durrett MSS. Rev. James Smith, "Tour in Western Country," 1785.

as savage as any ever waged among the cave-dwellers of the Stone Age.

The opinion of any mere passer-through a country is always less valuable than that of an intelligent man who dwells and works among the people, and who possesses both insight and sympathy. At this time one of the recently created Kentucky judges, an educated Virginian, in writing to his friend Madison, said: "We are as harmonious amongst ourselves as can be expected of a mixture of people from various States and of various Sentiments and Manners not yet assimilated. In point of Morals the bulk of the inhabitants are far superior to what I expected to find in any new settled country. We have not had a single instance of Murder, and but one Criminal for Felony of any kind has yet been before the Supreme Court. I wish I could say as much to vindicate the character of our Land-jobbers. This Business has been attended with much villainy in other parts. Here it is reduced to a system, and to take the advantage of the ignorance or of the poverty of a neighbor is almost grown into reputation."[1]

Of course, when the fever for land speculation raged so violently, many who had embarked too eagerly in the purchase of large tracts became land poor; Clark being among those The Gentry. who found that though they owned great reaches of fertile wild land they had no means whatever of getting money.[2] In Kentucky, while much land was taken up under Treasury warrants, much was also

[1] Wallace's letter, above quoted.

[2] Draper MSS. G. R. Clark to Jonathan Clark, April 20, 1788.

allotted to the officers of the Continental army; and the retired officers of the Continental line were the best of all possible immigrants. A class of gentle-folks soon sprang up in the land, whose members were not so separated from other citizens as to be in any way alien to them, and who yet stood sufficient-ly above the mass to be recognized as the natural leaders, social and political, of their sturdy fellow-freemen. These men by degrees built themselves comfortable, roomy houses, and their lives were very pleasant; at a little later period Clark, having abandoned war and politics, describes himself as living a retired life with, as his chief amusements, reading, hunting, fishing, fowling, and corresponding with a few chosen friends.[1] Game was still very plen-tiful: buffalo and elk abounded north of the Ohio, while bear and deer, turkey, swans, and geese,[2] not to speak of ducks and prairie fowl swarmed in the immediate neighborhood of the settlements.

The gentry offered to strangers the usual open-handed hospitality characteristic of the frontier, with **The Army** much more than the average frontier refine-**Officers.** ment; a hospitality, moreover, which was never marred or interfered with by the frontier sus-piciousness of strangers which sometimes made the humbler people of the border seem churlish to travellers. When Federal garrisons were established along the Ohio the officers were largely dependent for their social pleasures on the gentle-folks of the

[1] *Do.*, letter of Sept. 2, 1791.
[2] *Magazine of American History*, I. Letters of Laurence Butler from Kentucky, Nov. 20, 1786, etc.

neighborhood.   One of them in his journal gives
several rather curious glimpses of the life of the
time.[1]   He mentions being entertained by Clark at
"a very elegant dinner,"[2] a number of gentlemen
being present.   After dinner the guests adjourned
to the dancing school, "where there were twelve or
fifteen young misses, some of whom had made considerable improvement in that polite accomplish-
ment, and indeed were middling neatly dressed
considering the distance from where luxuries are to
be bought and the expense attending the purchase
of them here"—for though beef and flour were
cheap, all imported goods sold for at least five times
as much as they cost in Philadelphia or New York.
The officers sometimes gave dances in the forts, the
ladies and their escorts coming in to spend the night;
and they attended the great barbecues to which the
people rode from far and near, many of the men
carrying their wives or sweethearts behind them on
the saddle.   At such a barbecue an ox or a sheep, a
bear, an elk, or a deer, was split in two and roasted
over the coals; dinner was eaten under the trees;
and there was every kind of amusement from horse-
racing to dancing.

Though the relations of the officers of the regular
roops with the gentry were so pleasant there was
always much friction between them and
the ordinary frontiersmen; a friction which
continued to exist as long as the frontier
itself, and which survives to this day in

*Friction
with the
Back-
woodsmen.*

---

[1] Major Erkuries Beattie.   In the *Magazine of Am. Hist.*, I., p. 175.
[2] Aug. 25, 1786.

the wilder parts of the country. The regular army officer and the frontiersman are trained in fashions so diametrically opposite that, though the two men be brothers, they must yet necessarily in all their thoughts and instincts and ways of looking at life, be as alien as if they belonged to two different races of mankind. The borderer, rude, suspicious, and impatient of discipline, looks with distrust and with a mixture of sneering envy and of hostility upon the officer; while the latter, with his rigid training and his fixed ideals, feels little sympathy for the other's good points, and is contemptuously aware of his numerous failings. The only link between the two is the scout, the man who, though one of the frontiersmen, is accustomed to act and fight in company with the soldiers. In Kentucky, at the close of the Revolution, this link was generally lacking; and there was no tie of habitual, even though half-hostile, intercourse to unite the two parties. In consequence the ill-will often showed itself by acts of violence. The backwoods bullies were prone to browbeat and insult the officers if they found them alone, trying to provoke them to rough-and-tumble fighting; and in such a combat, carried on with the revolting brutality necessarily attendant upon a contest where gouging and biting were considered legitimate, the officers, who were accustomed only to use their fists, generally had the worst of it; so that at last they made a practice of carrying their side-arms—which secured them from molestation.

Besides raising more than enough flour and beef to keep themselves in plenty, the settlers turned

their attention to many other forms of Pursuits of the Settlers.
produce. Indian corn was still the leading
crop; but melons, pumpkins, and the like
were grown, and there were many thriving orchards;
while tobacco cultivation was becoming of much importance. Great droves of hogs and flocks of sheep
flourished in every locality whence the bears and
wolves had been driven; the hogs running free in the
woods with the branded cattle and horses. Except in
in the most densely settled parts much of the beef was
still obtained from buffaloes, and much of the bacon
from bears. Venison was a staple commodity. The
fur trade, largely carried on by French trappers,
was still of great importance in Kentucky and Tennessee. North of the Ohio it was the attraction
which tempted white men into the wilderness. Its
profitable nature was the chief reason why the British
persistently clung to the posts on the Lakes, and
stirred up the Indians to keep the American settlers
out of all lands that were tributary to the British
fur merchants. From Kentucky and the Cumberland country the peltries were sometimes sent east
by packtrain, and sometimes up the Ohio in bateaus
or canoes.

In addition to furs, quantities of ginseng were
often carried to the eastern settlements at this
period when the commerce of the west Boone's Trading Ventures.
was in its first infancy, and was as yet
only struggling for an outlet down the
Mississippi. One of those who went into this trade
was Boone. Although no longer a real leader in
Kentucky life he still occupied quite a prominent

position, and served as a Representative in the
Virginia Legislature,[1] while his fame as a hunter
and explorer was now spread abroad in the United
States, and even Europe. To travellers and new-
comers generally, he was always pointed out as the
first discoverer of Kentucky; and being modest,
self-contained and self-reliant he always impressed
them favorably. He spent most of his time in
hunting, trapping, and surveying land warrants for
men of means, being paid, for instance, two shillings
current money per acre for all the good land he
could enter on a ten-thousand acre Treasury warrant.[2] He also traded up and down the Ohio
River, at various places, such as Point Pleasant and
Limestone; and at times combined keeping a tavern
with keeping a store. His accounts contain much
quaint information. Evidently his guests drank as
generously as they ate; he charges one four pounds
sixteen shillings for two months' board and two
pounds four shillings for liquor. He takes the note
of another for ninety-three gallons of cheap corn
whiskey. Whisky cost sixpence a pint, and rum
one shilling; while corn was three shillings a
bushel, and salt twenty-four shillings, flour, thirty-
six shillings a barrel, bacon sixpence and fresh pork
and buffalo beef threepence a pound. Boone procured for his customers or for himself such articles
as linen, cloth, flannel, corduroy, chintz, calico, broad-
cloth, and velvet at prices varying according to the
quality, from three to thirty shillings a yard; and

[1] Draper's MSS., Boone MSS., from Bourbon Co. The papers cover the years from 1784 on to '95.
[2] *Do.*, certificate of G. Imlay, 1784.

there was also evidently a ready market for "tea ware," knives and forks, scissors, buttons, nails, and all kinds of hardware. Furs and skins usually appear on the debit sides of the various accounts, ranging in value from the skin of a beaver, worth eighteen shillings, or that of a bear worth ten, to those of deer, wolves, coons, wildcats, and foxes, costing two to four shillings apiece. Boone procured his goods from merchants in Hagerstown and Williamsport, in Maryland, whither he and his sons guided their own packtrains, laden with peltries and with kegs of ginseng, and accompanied by droves of loose horses. He either followed some well-beaten mountain trail or opened a new road through the wilderness as seemed to him best at the moment.[1]

Boone's creed in matters of morality and religion was as simple and straightforward as his own character. Late in life he wrote to one of his kinsfolk : " All the religion I have is to love and fear God, believe in Jesus Christ, do all the good to my neighbors and myself that I can, and do as little harm as I can help, and trust on God's mercy for the rest." The old pioneer always kept the respect of red man and white, of friend and foe, for he acted according to his belief. Yet there was one evil to which he was no more sensitive than the other men of his time.

Among his accounts there is an entry recording his purchase, for another man, of a negro woman for the sum of ninety pounds.[2] There **Negro** was already a strong feeling in the western **Slavery.**

[1] *Do., passim.*   [2] *Do.*, March 7, 1786.

settlements against negro slavery,[1] because of its
moral evil, and of its inconsistency with all true
standards of humanity and Christianity, a feeling
which continued to exist and which later led to
resolute efforts to forbid or abolish slave-holding.
But the consciences of the majority were too dull,
and, from the standpoint of the white race, they
were too shortsighted to take action in the right
direction.   The selfishness and mental obliquity
which imperil the future of a race for the sake of
the lazy pleasure of two or three generations prevailed; and in consequence the white people of the
middle west, and therefore eventually of the southwest, clutched the one burden under which .they
ever staggered, the one evil which has ever warped
their development, the one danger which has ever
seriously threatened their very existence.   Slavery
must of necessity exercise the most baleful influence
upon any slave-holding people, and especially upon
those members of the dominant caste who do not
themselves own slaves.   Moreover, the negro, unlike
so many of the inferior races, does not dwindle away
in the presence of the white man.   He holds his own;
indeed, under the conditions of American slavery
he increased faster than the white, threatening to
supplant him.   He actually has supplanted him in
certain of the West Indian islands, where the sin of
the white in enslaving the black has been visited
upon the head of the wrongdoer by his victim with
a dramatically terrible completeness of revenge.
    What has occurred in Hayti is what would

[1] See Journals of Rev. James Smith.

eventually have occurred in our own semi-tropical States if the slave-trade and slavery had continued to flourish as their shortsighted advocates wished. Slavery is ethically abhorrent to all right-minded men ; and it is to be condemned without stint on this ground alone.   From the standpoint of the master caste it is to condemned even more strongly because it invariably in the end threatens the very existence of that master caste.   From this point of view the presence of the negro is the real problem ; slavery is merely the worst possible method of solving the problem.   In their earlier stages the problem and its solution, in America, were one. There may be differences of opinion as to how to solve the problem ; but there can be none whatever as to the evil wrought by those who brought about that problem ; and it was only the slave-holders and the slave-traders who were guilty on this last count. The worst foes, not only of humanity and civilization, but especially of the white race in America, were those white men who brought slaves from Africa, and who fostered the spread of slavery in the States and territories of the American Republic.

CHAPTER II.

THE INDIAN WARS, 1784–1787.

AFTER the close of the Revolution there was a short, uneasy lull in the eternal border warfare be-
Lull in the Border War. tween the white men and the red. The Indians were for the moment daunted by a peace which left them without allies; and the feeble Federal Government attempted for the first time to aid and control the West by making treaties with the most powerful frontier tribes. Congress raised a tiny regular army, and several companies were sent to the upper Ohio to garrison two or three small forts which were built upon its banks. Commissioners (one of whom was Clark himself) were appointed to treat with both the northern and southern Indians. Councils were held in various places. In 1785 and early in 1786 utterly fruitless treaties were concluded with Shawnees, Wyandots, and Delawares at one or other of the little forts.[1]

About the same time, in the late fall of 1785, another treaty somewhat more noteworthy, but
Treaty of Hopewell. equally fruitless, was concluded with the Cherokees at Hopewell, on Keowee, in

[1] State Department MSS., No. 56, p. 333, Letter of G. Clark, Nov. 10, 1785; p. 337, Letter of G. Clark to R. Butler, etc.; No. 16, p. 293; No. 32, p. 39.

South Carolina. In this treaty the Commissioners promised altogether too much. They paid little heed to the rights and needs of the settlers. Neither did they keep in mind the powerlessness of the Federal Government to enforce against these settlers what their treaty promised the Indians. The pioneers along the upper Tennessee and the Cumberland had made various arrangements with bands of the Cherokees, sometimes acting on their own initiative, and sometimes on behalf of the State of North Carolina. Many of these different agreements were entered into by the whites with honesty and good faith, but were violated at will by the Indians. Others were violated by the whites, or were repudiated by the Indians as well, because of some real or fancied unfairness in the making. Under them large quantities of land had been sold or allotted, and hundreds of homes had been built on the lands thus won by the whites or ceded by the Indians. As with all Indian treaties, it was next to impossible to say exactly how far these agreements were binding, because no persons, not even the Indians themselves, could tell exactly who had authority to represent the tribes.[1] The Commissioners paid little heed to these treaties, and drew the boundary so that quantities of land which had been entered under regular grants, and were covered by the homesteads of the frontiersmen, were declared to fall within the Cherokee line. Moreover, they even undertook to drive all settlers off these lands.

Of course, such a treaty excited the bitter anger

[1] American State Papers, Public Lands, I., p. 40, vi.

of the frontiersmen, and they scornfully refused to
obey its provisions. They hated the Indians, and,
as a rule, were brutally indifferent to their rights,
while they looked down on the Federal Government
as impotent. Nor was the ill-will to the treaty confined to the rough borderers. Many men of means
found that land grants which they had obtained in
good faith and for good money were declared void.
Not only did they denounce the treaty, and decline
to abide by it, but they denounced the motives of the
Commissioners, declaring, seemingly without justification, that they had ingratiated themselves with the
Indians to further land speculations of their own.[1]

As the settlers declined to pay any heed to the
treaty the Indians naturally became as discontented
Violation   with it as the whites. In the following
of the   summer the Cherokee chiefs made solemn
Treaty.   complaint that, instead of retiring from the
disputed ground, the settlers had encroached yet
farther upon it, and had come to within five miles of
the beloved town of Chota. The chiefs added that
they had now made several such treaties, each of
which established boundaries that were immediately
broken, and that indeed it had been their experience
that after a treaty the whites settled even faster on
their lands than before.[2] Just before this complaint was
sent to Congress the same chiefs had been engaged
in negotiations with the settlers themselves, who advanced radically different claims. The fact was that
in this unsettled time the bond of Governmental

---

[1] Clay MSS. Jesse Benton to Thos. Hart, April 3, 1786.

[2] State Department MSS., No. 56. Address of Corn Tassel and Hanging
Maw, Sept. 5, 1786.

authority was almost as lax among the whites as among the Indians, and the leaders on each side who wished for peace were hopelessly unable to restrain their fellows who did not. Under such circumstances, the sword, or rather the tomahawk, was ultimately the only possible arbiter.

The treaties entered into with the northwestern Indians failed for precisely the opposite reason. The treaty at Hopewell promised so much to the Indians that the whites refused to abide by its terms. In the councils on the Ohio the Americans promised no more than they could and did perform; but the Indians themselves broke the treaties at once, and in all probability never for a moment intended to keep them, merely signing from a greedy desire to get the goods they were given as an earnest. They were especially anxious for spirits, for they far surpassed even the white borderers in their crazy thirst for strong drink. " We have smelled your liquor and it is very good; we hope you will give us some little kegs to carry home," said the spokesmen of a party of Chippewas, who had come from the upper Great Lakes.[1] These frank savages, speaking thus in behalf of their far northern brethren, uttered what was in the minds of most of the Indians who attended the councils held by the United States Commissioners. They came to see what they could get, by begging, or by promising what they had neither the will nor the power to perform. Many of them, as in the case of the Chippewas, were from lands so re-

Treaties with Northwestern Indians.

---

[1] *Do.*, Letters of H. Knox, No. 150, vol. i., p. 445.

mote that they felt no anxiety about white encroachments, and were lured into hostile encounter with the Americans chiefly by their own overmastering love of plunder and bloodshed.

Nevertheless, there were a few chiefs and men of note in the tribes who sincerely wished peace. One of these was Cornplanter, the Iroquois. The power of the Six Nations had steadily dwindled; moreover, they did not, like the more western tribes, lie directly athwart the path which the white advance was at the moment taking. Thus they were not drawn into open warfare, but their continual uneasiness, and the influence they still possessed with the other Indians, made it an object to keep on friendly terms with them. Cornplanter, a valiant and able warrior, who had both taken and given hard blows in warring against the Americans, was among the chiefs and ambassadors who visited Fort Pitt during the troubled lull in frontier war which succeeded the news of the peace of 1783. His speeches showed, as his deeds had already shown, in a high degree, that loftiness of courage, and stern, uncomplaining acceptance of the decrees of a hostile fate, which so often ennobled the otherwise gloomy and repellent traits of the Indian character. He raised no plaint over what had befallen his race; "the Great Spirit above directs us so that whatever hath been said or done must be good and right," he said in a spirit of strange fatalism well known to certain creeds, both Christian and heathen. He was careful to dwell on the fact that in addressing the representatives of "the Great Council who watch the Thirteen Fires and

keep them bright," he was anxious only to ward off
woe from the women and little ones of his people
and was defiantly indifferent to what might personally be before him. " As for me my life is short, 't is
already sold to the Great King over the water," he
said. But it soon appeared that the British agents
had deceived him, telling him that the peace was a
mere temporary truce, and keeping concealed the
fact that under the treaty the British had ceded to
the Americans all rights over the Iroquois and
western Indians, and over their land. Great was
his indignation when the actual text of the treaty
was read him, and he discovered the double-dealing
of his far-off royal paymaster. In commenting on it
he showed that, like the rest of his race, he had been
much impressed by the striking uniforms of the
British officers. He evidently took it for granted
that the head of these officers must own a yet more
striking uniform ; and treachery seemed doubly
odious in one who possessed so much. " I assisted
the great King," he said, " I fought his battles, while
he sat quietly in his forts; nor did I ever suspect
that so great a person, one too who wore a red coat
sufficient of itself to tempt one, could be guilty of
such glaring falsehood." [1] After this Cornplanter
remained on good terms with the Americans and
helped to keep the Iroquois from joining openly in
the war. The western tribes taunted them because
of this attitude. They sent them word in the fall
of 1785 that once the Six Nations were a great
people, but that now they had let the Long Knife

[1] State Dept. MSS., No. 56, March 7, 1786, p. 345, also p. 395.

throw them ; but that the western Indians would set them on their feet again if they would join them ; for "the western Indians were determined to wrestle with Long Knife in the spring."[1]

Some of the Algonquin chiefs, notably Molunthee the Shawnee, likewise sincerely endeavored to bring about a peace.   But the western tribes as a whole were bent on war.   They were constantly excited and urged on by the British partisan leaders, such as Simon Girty, Elliot, and Caldwell.   These leaders took part in the great Indian councils, at which even tribes west of the Mississippi were represented ; and though they spoke without direct authority from the British commanders at the lake posts, yet their words carried weight when they told the young red warriors that it was better to run the risk of dying like men than of starving like dogs.   Many of the old men among the Wyandotes and Delawares spoke against strife ; but the young men were for war, and among the Shawnees, the Wabash Indians, and the Miamis the hostile party was still stronger. A few Indians would come to one of the forts and make a treaty on behalf of their tribe, at the very moment that the other members of the same tribe were murdering and ravaging among the exposed settlements or were harrying the boats that went down the Ohio.   All the tribes that entered into the treaties of peace were represented among the different parties of marauders.   Over the outlaw bands there was no pretence of control ; and their

Failure of the Treaties.

[1] *Do.,* No. 150, vol. i., Major Finley's Statement, Dec. 6, 1785.

successes, and the numerous scalps and quantities of plunder they obtained, made them very dangerous examples to the hot-blooded young warriors every- where. Perhaps the most serious of all obstacles to peace was the fact that the British still kept the lake posts.[1]

The Indians who did come in to treat were sullen, and at first always insisted on impossible terms. They would finally agree to mutual concessions, would promise to keep their young men from marauding, and to allow surveys to be made, provided the settlers were driven off all lands which the In- dians had not yielded ; and after receiving many gifts, would depart. The representatives of the Federal Government would then at once set about performing their share of the agreement, the most important part of which was the removal of the settlers who had built cabins on the Indian lands west of the Ohio. The Federal authorities, both military and civil, disliked the intruders as much as they did the Indians, stigmatizing them as "a ban- ditti who were a disgrace to human nature." There was no unnecessary harshness exercised by the troops in removing the trespassers; but the cabins were torn down and the sullen settlers themselves were driven back across the river, though they protested and threatened resistance. Again and again this was done ; not alone in the interest of the Indians, but in part also because Congress wished to reserve the lands for sale, with the purpose of paying off

[1] *Do.*, Letters of H. Knox, No. 150, vol. i., pp. 107, 112, 115, 123, 149, 243, 269, etc.

the public debt. At the same time surveying
parties were sent out. But in each case, no sooner
had the Federal Commissioners and their subordinates begun to perform their part of the agreement, than they were stopped by tidings of fresh
outrages on the part of the very Indians with whom
they had made the treaty; while the surveying
parties were driven in and forced to abandon their
work.[1]

The truth was that while the Federal Government
sincerely desired peace, and strove to bring it about,
Both Sides the northwestern tribes were resolutely
Bent on bent on war; and the frontiersmen them-
War.   selves showed nearly as much inclination
for hostilities as the Indians.[2] They were equally
anxious to intrude on the Government and on the
Indian lands; for they were adventurous, the lands
were valuable, and they hated the Indians, and
looked down on the weak Federal authority.[3] They
often made what were legally worthless " tomahawk
claims," and objected almost as much as the Indians
to the work of the regular Government surveyors.[4]
Even the men of note, men like George Rogers
Clark, were often engaged in schemes to encroach on
the land north of the Ohio; drawing on themselves
the bitter reproaches not only of the Federal authorities, but also of the Virginia Government, for their
cruel readiness to jeopardize the country by incurring

[1] State Dept. MSS., No. 30, p. 265 ; No. 56, p. 327 ; No. 163, pp. 416,
418, 422, 426.
[2] *Do.*, Indian Affairs. Letter of P. Mühlenberg, July 5, 1784.
[3] *Do.*, Report of H. Knox, April, 1787.
[4] *Do.*, 150, vol. ii., p. 548.

the wrath of the Indians.[1] The more lawless whites
were as little amenable to authority as the Indians
themselves; and at the very moment when a peace
was being negotiated one side or the other would
commit some brutal murder. While the chiefs and
old Indians were delivering long-winded speeches to
the Peace Commissioners, bands of young braves
committed horrible ravages among the lonely settlements.[2] Now a drunken Indian at Fort Pitt murdered an innocent white man, the local garrison of
regular troops saving him with difficulty from being
lynched[3]; now a band of white ruffians gathered to
attack some peaceable Indians who had come in to
treat[4]; again a white man murdered an unoffending
Indian, and was seized by a Federal officer, and
thrown into chains, to the great indignation of his
brutal companions[5]; and yet again another white
man murdered an Indian, and escaped to the woods
before he could be arrested.[6]

Under such conditions the peace negotiations
were doomed from the outset. The truce on the
border was of the most imperfect descrip- Bloodshed
tion; murders and robberies by the In- Begun.
dians, and acts of vindictive retaliation or aggression by the whites, occurred continually and steadily
increased in number. In 1784 a Cherokee of note,
when sent to warn the intruding settlers on the

[1] Draper MSS. Benj. Harrison to G. R. Clark, August 19, 1784.
[2] State Dept. MSS., No. 56, pp. 279 and 333 ; No. 60, p. 297, etc.
[3] Denny's Journal, p. 259.
[4] State Dept. MSS., No. 56, p. 255.
[5] *Do.*, No. 150, vol. ii., p. 296.
[6] Draper MSS. Clark, Croghan, and Others to Delawares, August 28,
1785.

French Broad that they must move out of the land,
was shot and slain in a fight with a local militia captain.   Cherokee war bands had already begun to
harry the frontier and infest the Kentucky Wilderness Road.[1]   At the same time the northwestern
Indians likewise committed depredations, and were
only prevented from making a general league against
the whites by their own internal dissensions—the
Chickasaws and Kickapoos being engaged in a desperate war.[2]   The Wabash Indians were always
threatening hostilities.   The Shawnees for some
time observed a precarious peace, and even, in
accordance with their agreement, brought in and
surrendered a few white prisoners; and among the
Delawares and Wyandots there was also a strong
friendly party; but in all three tribes the turbulent
element was never under real control, and it gradually got the upper hand.   Meanwhile the Georgians
and Creeks in the south were having experiences of
precisely the same kind—treaties fraudulently procured by the whites, or fraudulently entered into
and violated by the Indians; encroachments by
white settlers on Indian lands, and bloody Indian
forays among the peaceful settlements.[3]

The more far-sighted and resolute among all the
Indians, northern and southern, began to strive for a
general union against the Americans.[4]   In 1786 the

[1] State Dept. MSS., No. 48, p. 277.

[2] *Do.*, Mühlenberg's Letter.

[3] *Do.*, No. 73, pp. 7, 343.   Gazette of the State of Georgia, Aug. 5, 1784,
May 25, June 1, Nov. 2, Nov. 30, 1786.

[4] *Do.*, No. 20, pp. 321 and 459; No. 18, p. 140 ; No. 12, vol. ii., June
30. 1786.

northwestern Indians almost formed such a union.
Two thousand warriors gathered at the Shawnee
towns and agreed to take up the hatchet against the
Americans ; British agents were present at the council ; and even before the council was held, war parties
were bringing into the Shawnee towns the scalps
of American settlers, and prisoners, both men and
women, who were burned at the stake.[1]   But the
jealousy and irresolution of the tribes prevented the
actual formation of a league.

The Federal Government still feebly hoped for
peace ; and in the vain endeavors to avoid irritating
the Indians forbade all hostile expeditions into the
Indian country—though these expeditions offered
the one hope of subduing the savages and preventing their inroads.   By 1786 the settlers generally,
including all their leaders, such as Clark,[2] had become convinced that the treaties were utterly futile,
and that the only right policy was one of resolute
war.

In truth the war was unavoidable.   The claims
and desires of the two parties were irreconcilable.
Treaties and truces were palliatives which   The War
did not touch the real underlying trouble. Inevitable.
The white settlers were unflinchingly bent on seizing
the land over which the Indians roamed but which
they did not in any true sense own or occupy.   In
return the Indians were determined at all costs and
hazards to keep the men of chain and compass, and
of axe and rifle, and the forest-felling settlers who

---

[1] *Do.*, No. 60, p. 277, Sept. 13, 1786.
[2] *Do.*, No. 50, p. 279.   Clark to R. H. Lee.

followed them, out of their vast and lonely hunting-grounds. Nothing but the actual shock of battle could decide the quarrel. The display of overmastering, overwhelming force might have cowed the Indians; but it was not possible for the United States, or for any European power, ever to exert or display such force far beyond the limits of the settled country. In consequence the warlike tribes were not then, and never have been since, quelled save by actual hard fighting, until they were overawed by the settlement of all the neighboring lands.

Nor was there any alternative to these Indian wars. It is idle folly to speak of them as being the fault of the United States Government; and it is even more idle to say that they could have been averted by treaty. Here and there, under exceptional circumstances or when a given tribe was feeble and unwarlike, the whites might gain the ground by a treaty entered into of their own free will by the Indians, without the least duress; but this was not possible with warlike and powerful tribes when once they realized that they were threatened with serious encroachment on their hunting-grounds. Moreover, looked at from the standpoint of the ultimate result, there was little real difference to the Indian whether the land was taken by treaty or by war. In the end the Delaware fared no better at the hands of the Quaker than the Wampanoag at the hands of the Puritan; the methods were far more humane in the one case than in the other, but the outcome was the same in both. No treaty could be satisfactory to the whites, no treaty served the needs of humanity and civilization, unless it gave the land to the Americans as unreservedly as any successful war.

As a matter of fact, the lands we have won from the Indians have been won as much by treaty as by war; but it was almost always war, or else the menace and possibility of war, that secured the treaty. In these treaties we *Our Dealings with the Indians.* have been more than just to the Indians; we have been abundantly generous, for we have paid them many times what they were entitled to ; many times what we would have paid any civilized people whose claim was as vague and shadowy as theirs. By war or threat of war, or purchase we have won from great civilized nations, from France, Spain, Russia, and Mexico, immense tracts of country already peopled by many tens of thousands of families; we have paid many millions of dollars to these nations for the land we took; but for every dollar thus paid to these great and powerful civilized commonwealths, we have paid ten, for lands less valuable, to the chiefs and warriors of the red tribes. No other conquering and colonizing nation has ever treated the original savage owners of the soil with such generosity as has the United States. Nor is the charge that the treaties with the Indians have been broken, of weight in itself; it depends always on the individual case. Many of the treaties were kept by the whites and broken by the Indians; others were broken by the whites themselves; and sometimes those who broke them did very wrong indeed, and sometimes they did right. No treaties, whether between civilized nations or not, can ever be regarded as binding in perpetuity ; with changing conditions, circumstances may arise which render it not only expedient, but imperative and honorable, to abrogate them.

Whether the whites won the land by treaty, by armed conquest, or, as was actually the case, by a

Necessity of the Conquest. mixture of both, mattered comparatively little so long as the land was won. It was all-important that it should be won, for the benefit of civilization and in the interests of mankind. It is indeed a warped, perverse, and silly morality which would forbid a course of conquest that has turned whole continents into the seats of mighty and flourishing civilized nations. All men of sane and wholesome thought must dismiss with impatient contempt the plea that these continents should be reserved for the use of scattered savage tribes, whose life was but a few degrees less meaningless, squalid, and ferocious than that of the wild beasts with whom they held joint ownership. It is as idle to apply to savages the rules of international morality which obtain between stable and cultured communities, as it would be to judge the fifth-century English conquest of Britain by the standards of to-day. Most fortunately, the hard, energetic, practical men who do the rough pioneer work of civilization in barbarous lands, are not prone to false sentimentality. The people who are, are the people who stay at home. Often these stay-at-homes are too selfish and indolent, too lacking in imagination, to understand the race-importance of the work which is done by their pioneer brethren in wild and distant lands;

and they judge them by standards which would only
be applicable to quarrels in their own townships and
parishes. Moreover, as each new land grows old, it
misjudges the yet newer lands, as once it was itself
misjudged. The home-staying Englishman of Britain
grudges to the Africander his conquest of Matabele-
land; and so the home-staying American of the Atlantic States dislikes to see the western miners and
cattlemen win for the use of their people the Sioux
hunting-grounds. Nevertheless, it is the men actually
on the borders of the longed-for ground, the men
actually in contact with the savages, who in the end
shape their own destinies.

The most ultimately righteous of all wars is a war
with savages, though it is apt to be also the most
terrible and inhuman. The rude, fierce Righteous-
settler who drives the savage from the ness of
land lays all civilized mankind under a the War.
debt to him. American and Indian, Boer and
Zulu, Cossack and Tartar, New Zealander and Maori,
—in each case the victor, horrible though many of
his deeds are, has laid deep the foundations for
the future greatness of a mighty people. The
consequences of struggles for territory between
civilized nations seem small by comparison. Looked
at from the standpoint of the ages, it is of little
moment whether Lorraine is part of Germany or
of France, whether the northern Adriatic cities
pay homage to Austrian Kaiser or Italian King;
but it is of incalculable importance that America,
Australia, and Siberia should pass out of the hands
of their red, black, and yellow aboriginal owners,

and become the heritage of the dominant world races.

Yet the very causes which render this struggle between savagery and the rough front rank of civilization so vast and elemental in its consequence to the future of the world, also tend to render it in certain ways peculiarly revolting and barbarous. It is primeval warfare, and it is waged as war was waged in the ages of bronze and of iron. All the merciful humanity that even war has gained during the last two thousand years is lost. It is a warfare where no pity is shown to non-combatants, where the weak are harried without ruth, and the vanquished maltreated with merciless ferocity. A sad and evil feature of such warfare is that the whites, the representatives of civilization, speedily sink almost to the level of their barbarous foes, in point of hideous brutality. The armies are neither led by trained officers nor made up of regular troops—they are composed of armed settlers, fierce and wayward men, whose ungovernable passions are unrestrained by discipline, who have many grievous wrongs to redress, and who look on their enemies with a mixture of contempt and loathing, of dread and intense hatred. When the clash comes between these men and their sombre foes, too often there follow deeds of enormous, of incredible, of indescribable horror. It is impossible to dwell without a shudder on the monstrous woe and misery of such a contest.

The men of Kentucky and of the infant Northwest would have found their struggle with the In-

dians dangerous enough in itself; but there was an
added element of menace in the fact that
back of the Indians stood the British. It was   **The Lake Posts.**
for this reason that the frontiersmen grew
to regard as essential to their well-being the possession of the lake posts; so that it became with them
a prime object to wrest from the British, whether by
force of arms or by diplomacy, the forts they held
at Niagara, Detroit, and Michilimakinac. Detroit
was the most important, for it served as the head-
quarters of the western Indians, who formed for the
time being the chief bar to American advance. The
British held the posts with a strong grip, in the
interest of their traders and merchants. To them
the land derived its chief importance from the fur
trade. This was extremely valuable, and, as it
steadily increased in extent and importance, the consequence of Detroit, the fitting-out town for the fur
traders, grew in like measure. It was the centre of
a population of several thousand Canadians, who
lived by the chase and by the rude cultivation of
their long, narrow farms; and it was held by a garrison of three or four hundred British regulars, with
auxiliary bands of American loyalist and French
Canadian rangers, and, above all, with a formidable
but fluctuating reserve force of Indian allies.[1]

It was to the interest of the British to keep
the American settlers out of the land ; and   **The British
Aid the
Indians.**
therefore their aims were at one with
those of the Indians. All the tribes between the Ohio and the Missouri were subsidized

[1] Haldimand Papers, 1784, 5, 6.

by them, and paid them a precarious allegiance.
Fickle, treacherous, and ferocious, the Indians at
times committed acts of outrage even on their allies,
so that these allies had to be ever on their guard;
and the tribes were often at war with one another.
War interrupted trade and cut down profits, and the
British endeavored to keep the different tribes at
peace among themselves, and even with the Americans. Moreover they always discouraged barbarities,
and showed what kindness was in their power to
any unfortunate prisoners whom the Indians happened to bring to their posts. But they helped the
Indians in all ways save by open military aid to
keep back the American settlers. They wished a
monopoly of the fur trade; and they endeavored
to prevent the Americans from coming into their
settlements.[1] English officers and agents attended
the Indian councils, endeavored to attach the tribes
to the British interests, and encouraged them to
stand firm against the Americans and to insist upon
the Ohio as the boundary between the white man
and the red.[2] The Indians received counsel and advice from the British, and drew from them both
arms and munitions of war, and while the higher
British officers were usually careful to avoid committing any overt breach of neutrality, the reckless
partisan leaders sought to inflame the Indians
against the Americans, and even at times accompanied their war parties.

[1] *Do.* John Hay to Haldimand, Aug. 13, 1784 ; James McNeil, Aug. 1,
1785.

[2] *Do.* Letter of A. McKee, Dec. 24, 1786 ; McKee to Sir John Johnson,
Feb. 25, 1786 ; Major Ancrum, May 8, 1786.

The life led at a frontier post like Detroit was
marked by sharp contrasts. The forest round about
was cleared away, though blackened stumps still
dotted the pastures, orchards, and tilled
fields. The town itself was composed   Life at a
mainly of the dwellings of the French   Frontier
                                           Post.
habitans; some of them were mere hovels,
others pretty log cottages, all swarming with black-
eyed children; while the stoutly-made, swarthy men,
at once lazy and excitable, strolled about the streets
in their picturesque and bright-colored blanket suits.
There were also a few houses of loyalist refugees;
implacable Tories, stalwart men, revengeful, and
goaded by the memory of many wrongs done and
many suffered, who proved the worst enemies of
their American kinsfolk. The few big roomy buildings, which served as storehouses and residences for
the merchants, were built not only for the storage of
goods and peltries, but also as strongholds in case
of attack. The heads of the mercantile houses were
generally Englishmen; but the hardy men who trav-
ersed the woods for months and for seasons, to procure furs from the Indians, were for the most part
French. The sailors, both English and French,
who manned the vessels on the lakes formed another class. The rough earthworks and stockades
of the fort were guarded by a few light guns.
Within, the red-coated regulars held sway, their
bright uniforms varied here and there by the dingy
hunting-shirt, leggings, and fur cap of some Tory
ranger or French partisan leader. Indians lounged
about the fort, the stores, and the houses, begging,

or gazing stolidly at the troops as they drilled, at the creaking carts from the outlying farms as they plied through the streets, at the driving to and fro from pasture of the horses and milch cows, or at the arrival of a vessel from Niagara or a brigade of fur-laden bateaux from the upper lakes.

In their paint and their cheap, dirty finery, these savages did not look very important; yet it was because of them that the British kept up their posts in these far-off forests, beside these great lonely waters; it was for their sakes that they tried to stem the inrush of the settlers of their own blood and tongue; for it was their presence alone which served to keep the wilderness as a game preserve for the fur merchants; it was their prowess in war which prevented French village and British garrison from being lapped up like drops of water before the fiery rush of the American advance. The British themselves, though fighting with and for them, loved them but little; like all frontiersmen, they soon grew to look down on their mean and trivial lives,—lives which nevertheless strongly attracted white men of evil and shiftless, but adventurous, natures, and to which white children, torn from their homes and brought up in the wigwams, became passionately attached. Yet back of the lazy and drunken squalor lay an element of the terrible, all the more terrible because it could not be reckoned with. Dangerous and treacherous allies, upon whom no real dependence could ever be placed, the Indians were nevertheless the most redoubtable of

The Indians.

all foes when the war was waged in their own
gloomy woodlands.

At such a post those standing high in authority
were partly civil officials, partly army officers. Of
the former, some represented the provincial The British
government, and others acted for the fur   Officers.
companies. They had much to do, both in govern-
ing the French townsfolk and countryfolk, in keeping the Indians friendly, and in furthering the
peculiar commerce on which the settlements sub-
sisted. But the important people were the army
officers. These were imperious, able, resolute men,
well drilled, and with a high military standard of
honor. They upheld with jealous pride the reputation of an army which in that century proved again
and again that on stricken fields no soldiery of continental Europe could stand against it. They wore
a uniform which for the last two hundred years has
been better known than any other wherever the
pioneers of civilization tread the world's waste
spaces or fight their way to the overlordship of barbarous empires; a uniform known to the southern
and the northern hemispheres, the eastern and the
western continents, and all the islands of the sea.
Subalterns wearing this uniform have fronted
dangers and responsibilities such as in most other
services only gray-headed generals are called upon
to face; and, at the head of handfuls of troops,
have won for the British crown realms as large, and
often as populous, as European kingdoms. The
scarlet-clad officers who serve the monarchy of Great
Britain have conquered many a barbarous people in

all the ends of the earth, and hold for their sovereign
the lands of Moslem and Hindoo, of Tartar and
Arab and Pathan, of Malay, Negro, and Polynesian.
In many a war they have overcome every European
rival against whom they have been pitted. Again
and again they have marched to victory against
Frenchman and Spaniard through the sweltering
heat of the tropics; and now, from the stupendous
mountain masses of mid Asia, they look northward
through the wintry air, ready to bar the advance of
the legions of the Czar. Hitherto they have never
gone back save once; they have failed only when
they sought to stop the westward march of a mighty
nation, a nation kin to theirs, a nation of their own
tongue and law, and mainly of their own blood.

The British officers and the American border
leaders found themselves face to face in the wilderness as rivals of one another. Sundered
by interest and ambition, by education and
habits of thought, trained to widely different ways of looking at life, and with the
memories of the hostile past fresh in their minds,
they were in no humor to do justice to one another.
Each side regarded the other with jealousy and dislike, and often with bitter hatred. Each often un-
wisely scorned the other. Each kept green in mind
the wrongs suffered at the other's hands, and remem-
bered every discreditable fact in the other's recent
history—every failure, every act of cruelty or stupid-
ity, every deed that could be held as the consequence
of the worst moral and mental shortcomings. Neither
could appreciate the other's many and real virtues.

*The Fron-
tiersmen
and the
British.*

The policies for which they warred were hostile and irreconcilable; the interests of the nations they represented were, as regards the northwestern wilderness, not only incompatible but diametrically opposed. The commanders of the British posts, and the men who served under them, were moved by a spirit of stern loyalty to the empire, the honor of whose flag they upheld, and endeavored faithfully to carry out the behests of those who shaped that empire's destinies; in obedience to the will of their leaders at home they warred to keep the Northwest a wilderness, tenanted only by the Indian hunter and the white fur trader. The American frontiersmen warred to make this wilderness the heart of the greatest of all Republics; they obeyed the will of no superior, they were not urged onward by any action of the supreme authorities of the land; they were moved only by the stirring ambition of a masterful people, who saw before them a continent which they claimed as their heritage. The Americans succeeded, the British failed; for the British fought against the stars in their courses, while the Americans battled on behalf of the destiny of the race.

Between the two sets of rivals lay leagues on leagues of forest, in which the active enemies of the Americans lived and hunted and marched to war. The British held the posts on the lakes; the frontiersmen held the land south of the Ohio. In the wilderness between dwelt the Shawnees, Wyandots, and Delawares, the Wabash Indians, the Miamis, and many others; and they had as allies all the fiercest and most adventurous of the tribes farther off, the Chippewas, the Winnebagos, the Sacs and Foxes. On the side of the whites the war was still urged by irregular levies of armed frontiersmen. The Federal garrisons on the Ohio were as yet too few and feeble to be of much account; and in the south, where the conflict was against Creek and Cherokee, there were no regular troops whatever.

The struggle was at first one of aggression on the part of the northwestern Indians. They were angered and Indian alarmed at the surveyors and the few reckless Inroads. would-be settlers, who had penetrated their country; but there was no serious encroachment on their lands, and Congress for some time forbade any expedition being carried on against them in their home. They themselves made no one formidable attack, sent no one overmastering force against the whites. But bands of young braves from all the tribes began to cross the Ohio, and ravage the settlements, from the Pennsylvania frontier to Kentucky. They stole horses, burned houses, and killed or carried into a dreadful captivity men, women, and children. The inroads were as usual marked by stealth, rapine, and horrible cruelty. It is hard for those accustomed only to treat of civilized warfare to realize the intolerable nature of these ravages, the fact that the loss and damage to the whites was out of all proportion to the strength of the Indian war parties, and the extreme difficulty in dealing an effective counter stroke.

The immense tangled forests increased beyond measure the difficulties of the problem. Under their shelter the Indians were able to attack at will and without warning, and though they would fight to the death against any odds when cornered, they invariably strove to make their attacks on the most helpless, on those who were powerless to resist. It was not the armed frontier levies, it was the immigrants coming in by pack train or by flatboat,—it was the unsuspecting settlers with their wives and little ones who had most to fear from an Indian fray; while, when once the blow was delivered, the savages vanished as smoke vanishes in the open. A small war party could thus work untold harm in a district precisely as a couple of man-eating jaguars may depopulate a forest village in tropical America; and many men and much time had to be spent before they could be beaten into submission, exactly as it needs a great hunting party to drive from their fastness and slay the big man-eating cats, though, if they came to bay in the open, they could readily be killed by a single skilful and resolute hunter.

Each settlement or group of settlements had to rely on the prowess of its own hunter-soldiers for safety. The real war, the war in which **Warfare of** by far the greatest loss was suffered by **the Settlers.** both sides, was that thus waged man against man. These innumerable and infinitely varied skirmishes, as petty as they were bloody, were not so decisive at the moment as the campaigns against the gathered tribes, but were often more important in their ultimate results. Under the incessant strain of the incessant warfare there arose here and there Indian fighters of special note, men who warred alone, or at the head of small parties of rangers, and who not only defended the settlements, but kept the Indian villages and the Indian war parties in constant dread by their vengeful retaliatory inroads. These men became the peculiar heroes of the frontier, and their names were household words in the log cabins of the children, and children's children, cf their contemporaries. They were warriors of the type of the rude champions who in the ages long past hunted the mammoth and the aurochs, and smote one another with stone-headed axes; their feats of ferocious personal prowess were of the kind that gave honor and glory to the mighty men of time primeval. Their deeds were not put into books while the men themselves lived ; they were handed down by tradition, and grew dim and vague in the recital. What one fierce partisan leader had done might dwindle or might grow in the telling or might finally be ascribed to some other; or else the same feat was twisted into such varying shapes that it became impossible to recognize which was nearest the truth, or what man had performed it.

Often in dealing with the adventures of one of these old-time border warriors—Kenton, Wetzel, Brady, Mansker, Castleman,--all we can say is that some given feat was commonly attributed to him, but may have been performed by somebody else, or indeed may only have been the kind of feat which might at any time have been performed by men of his stamp. Thus one set of traditions ascribe to Brady an adventure in which when bound to a stake, he escaped by suddenly

The Border Leaders.

throwing an Indian child into the fire, and dashing
off unhurt in the confusion; but other traditions
ascribe the feat not to Brady, but to some other
wild hunter of the day. Again one of the favorite
tales of Brady is his escape from a band of pursuing
Indians, by an extraordinary leap across a deep
ravine, at the bottom of which flowed a rapid
stream; but in some traditions this leap appears
as made by another frontier hero, or even by an
Indian whom Brady himself was pursuing. It is
therefore a satisfaction to come across, now and
then, some feat which is attested by contempora-
neous testimony. There is such contemporary record for one of Brady's deeds, which took place
towards the close of the Revolutionary war.

Brady had been on a raid in the Indian country
and was returning. His party had used all their
powder and had scattered, each man going
towards his own home, as they had nearly   **Brady's**
reached the settlements. Only three men   **Feats.**
were left with Brady, the four had but one charge
of powder apiece, and even this had been wet in
crossing a stream, though it had been carefully dried
afterwards. They had with them a squaw whom
they had captured. When not far from home they
ran into a party of seven Indians, likewise returning
from a raid, and carrying with them as prisoners a
woman and her child. Brady spied the Indians first
and instantly resolved to attack them, trusting that
they would be panic-struck and flee; though after a
single discharge of their rifles he and his men would
be left helpless. Slipping ahead he lay in ambush

until the Indians were close up. He then fired, killing the leader, whereat the others fled in terror,
leaving the woman and child. In the confusion,
however, the captive squaw also escaped and succeeded in joining the fleeing savages, to whom she
told the small number and woful plight of their
assailants; and they at once turned to pursue them.
Brady, however, had made good use of the time
gained, and was in full flight with his two rescued
prisoners; and before he was overtaken he encountered a party of whites who were themselves following the trail of the marauders. He at once turned
and in company with them hurried after the Indians;
but the latter were wary, and, seeing the danger,
scattered and vanished in the gloomy woodland.
The mother and child, thus rescued from a fearful
fate, reached home in safety. The letter containing
the account of this deed continues : "This young
officer, Captain Brady, has great merit as a partizan
in the woods. He has had the address to surprise
and beat the Indians three different times since I
came to the Department—he is brave, vigilant, and
successful."[1]

For a dozen years after the close of the Revolution
Brady continued to be a tower of strength to the
frontier settlers of Pennsylvania and Virginia. At
the head of his rangers he harassed the Indians
greatly, interfering with and assailing their war
parties, and raiding on their villages and home
camps. Like his foes he warred by ambush and

[1] Draper MSS. Alex. Fowler to Edward Hand, Pittsburgh, July 22,
1780.

surprise. Among the many daring backwoodsmen
who were his followers and companions the traditions pay particular heed to one Phouts, " a stout,
thick Dutchman of uncommon strength and
activity."

In spite of the counter strokes of the wild wood-
rangers, the Indian ravages speedily wrapped the
frontier in fire and blood. In such a war the small
parties were really the most dangerous, and in the
aggregate caused most damage. It is less of a para-
dox than it seems, to say that one reason why the
Indians were so formidable in warfare was because
they were so few in numbers. Had they been more
numerous they would perforce have been tillers of
the soil, and it would have been far easier for the
whites to get at them. They were able to wage a
war so protracted and murderous, only because of
their extreme elusiveness. There was little chance
to deliver a telling blow at enemies who had hardly
anything of value to destroy, who were so comparatively few in number that they could subsist year in
and year out on game, and whose mode of life rendered them as active, stealthy, cautious, and ferocious
as so many beasts of prey.

Though the frontiers of Pennsylvania and of Virginia proper suffered much, Kentucky suffered
more. The murderous inroads of the In- Ravages in
dians at about the close of the Revolution- Kentucky.
ary war caused a mortality such as could not be
paralleled save in a community struck down by some
awful pestilence; and though from thence on our
affairs mended, yet for many years the most com.

mon form of death was death at the hands of the Indians. A resident in Kentucky, writing to a friend, dwelt on the need of a system of vestries to take care of the orphans, who, as things were, were left solely to private charity; though, continues the writer, " of all countries I am acquainted with this abounds most with these unhappy objects."[1]

The roving war bands infested the two routes by which the immigrants came into the country; for Attacks on the companies of immigrants could usually Incoming be taken at a disadvantage, and yielded Settlers. valuable plunder. The parties who travelled the Wilderness Road were in danger of ambush by day and of onslaught by night. But there was often some protection for them, for whenever the savages became very bold, bodies of Kentucky militia were sent to patrol the trail, and these not only guarded the trains of incomers, but kept a sharp look-out for Indian signs, and, if any were found, always followed and, if possible, fought and scattered the marauders.

The Indians who watched the river-route down the Ohio had much less to fear in the way of pursuit by, or interference from, the frontier militia; although they too were now and then followed, overtaken, and vanquished. While in midstream the boats were generally safe, though occasionally the savages grew so bold that they manned flotillas of canoes and attacked the laden flat-boats in open day. But when any party landed, or wherever the current swept a boat inshore, within rifle range of

[1] Draper MSS., Clark MSS.   Darrell to Fleming, April 14, 1783.

the tangled forest on the banks, there was always danger. The white riflemen, huddled together with their women, children, and animals on the scows, were utterly unable to oppose successful resistance to foes who shot them down at leisure, while themselves crouching in the security of their hiding-places. The Indians practised all kinds of tricks and stratagems to lure their victims within reach. A favorite device was to force some miserable wretch whom they had already captured to appear alone on the bank when a boat came in sight, signal to it, and implore those on board to come to his rescue and take him off; the decoy inventing some tale of wreck or of escape from Indians to account for his presence. If the men in the boat suffered themselves to be overcome by compassion and drew inshore, they were sure to fall victims to their sympathy.

The boat once assailed and captured, the first action of the Indians was to butcher all the wounded. If there was any rum or whiskey on board they drank it, feasted on the provisions, and took whatever goods they could carry off. They then set off through the woods with their prisoners for distant Indian villages near the lakes. They travelled fast, and mercilessly tomahawked the old people, the young children, and the women with child, as soon as their strength failed under the strain of the toil and hardship and terror. When they had reached their villages they usually burned some of their captives and made slaves of the others, the women being treated as the concubines of their captors, and the children adopted by the families who wished them. Of the captives a few might fall into the hands of friendly traders, or of the British officers at Detroit; a few might escape, or be ransomed by their kinsfolk, or be surrendered in consequence of some treaty. The others succumbed to the perils of their new life, or gradually sank into a state of stolid savagery.

Naturally the ordinary Indian foray was directed against the settlements themselves; and of course

Forays on the Settlements. the settlements of the frontier, as it continually shifted westward, were those which bore the brunt of the attack and served as a shield for the more thickly peopled and peaceful region behind. Occasionally a big war party of a hundred warriors or over would come prepared for a stroke against some good-sized village or fort; but, as a rule, the Indians came in small bands, numbering from a couple to a dozen or score of individuals. Entirely unencumbered by baggage or by impediments of any kind, such a band lurked through the woods, leaving no trail, camping wherever night happened to overtake it, and travelling whithersoever it wished. The ravages committed by these skulking parties of murderous braves were monotonous in their horror. All along the frontier the people on the outlying farms were ever in danger, and there was risk for the small hamlets and block-houses. In their essentials the attacks were alike: the stealthy approach, the sudden rush, with its accompaniment of yelling war-whoops, the butchery of men, women, and children, and the hasty flight with whatever prisoners were for the moment spared, before the armed neighbors could gather for rescue and revenge.

In most cases there was no record of the outrage; it was not put into any book ; and, save among the survivors, all remembrance of it vanished as the logs of the forsaken cabin rotted and crumbled.

Yet tradition, or some chance written record kept alive the memory of some of these incidents, and a few such are worth reciting, if only to show what this warfare of savage and set- tler really was. Most of the tales deal merely with some piece of unavenged butchery.

Incidents of the War on the Frontier.

In 1785, on June 29th, the house of a settler named Scott, in Washington County, Virginia, was attacked. The Indians, thirteen in number, burst in the door just as the family were going to bed. Scott was shot; his wife was seized and held motionless, while all her four children were tomahawked, and their throats cut, the blood spouting over her clothes. The Indians loaded themselves with plunder, and, taking with them the wretched woman, moved off, and travelled all night. Next morning each man took his share and nine of the party went down to steal horses on the Clinch. The remaining four roamed off through the woods, and ten days later the woman succeeded in making her escape. For a month she wandered alone in the forest, living on the young cane and sassafras, until, spent and hag- gard with the horror and the hardship, she at last reached a small frontier settlement.

At about the same time three girls, sisters, walking together near Wheeling Creek, were pounced upon by a small party of Indians. After going a short distance the Indians halted, talked together for a few moments, and then without any warning a warrior turned and tomahawked one of the girls. The second instantly shared the same fate; the third jerked away from the Indian who held her, darted up a bank, and, extraordinary to relate, eluded her pursuer, and reached her home in safety. Another family named Doolin, suffered in the same year; and there was one singular circumstance connected with their fate. The Indians came to the door of the cabin in the early morning; as the man rose from bed the Indians fired through the door and shot him in the thigh. They then burst in, and tomahawked him and two children; yet for reasons unknown they did not harm the woman, nor the child in her arms.

No such mercy was shown by a band of six Indians who attacked the log houses of two settlers, brothers, named Edward and Thomas Cunningham. The two cabins stood side by side, the chinks between the logs allowing those in one to see what was happening in the other. One June evening, in 1785, both families were at supper. Thomas was away. His wife and four children were sitting at the table when a huge savage slipped in through the open door. Edward in the adjoining cabin, saw him enter, and seized his rifle. The Indian fired at him through a chink in the wall, but missed him, and, being afraid to retreat through the door, which would have brought him within range of Edward's rifle, he seized an axe and

began to chop out an opening in the rear wall. Another Indian made a dash for the door, but was shot
down by Edward; however, he managed to get over
the fence and out of range. Meanwhile the mother
and her four children remained paralyzed with fear
until the Indian inside the room had cut a hole
through the wall. He then turned, brained one of
the children with his tomahawk, threw the body out
into the yard through the opening, and motioned to
her to follow it. In mortal fear she obeyed, stepping out over the body of one of her children, with
two others screaming beside her, and her baby in
her arms. Once outside he scalped the murdered
boy, and set fire to the house, and then drove the
woman and the remaining children to a knoll where
the wounded Indian lay with the others around him.
The Indians hoped the flames would destroy both
cabins; but Edward Cunningham and his son went
into their loft, and threw off the boards of the roof,
as they kindled, escaping unharmed from the shots
fired at them; and so, though scorched by the flame
and choked by the smoke, they saved their house
and their lives. Seeing the failure of their efforts
the savages then left, first tomahawking and scalping
the two elder children. The shuddering mother,
with her baby, was taken along with them to a
cave, in which they hid her and the wounded Indian; and then with untold fatigue, hardship, and
suffering, for her brutal captors gave her for food
only a few papaw nuts and the head of a wild turkey, she was taken to the Indian towns. Some months
afterwards Simon Girty ransomed her and sent her

home. Edward Cunningham raised a body of men
and tried to follow the trail; but the crafty forest
warriors had concealed it with such care that no
effective pursuit could be made.

In none of the above-mentioned raids did the
Indians suffer any loss of life, and in none was there
Retaliation any successful pursuit. But in one in-
of the stance in this same year and same neigh-
Settlers. borhood the assailed settlers retaliated
with effect. It was near Wheeling. A lad
named John Wetzel, one of a noted border family
of coarse, powerful, illiterate Indian fighters, had
gone out from the fortified village in which his
kinsfolk were living to hunt horses. Another boy
went with him. There were several stray horses,
one being a mare which belonged to Wetzel's sister,
with a colt, and the girl had promised him the colt
if he would bring the mare back. The two boys
were vigorous young fellows, accustomed to life in
the forest, and they hunted high and low, and
finally heard the sound of horse-bells in a thicket.
Running joyfully forward they fell into the hands
of four Indians, who had caught the horses and tied
them in the thicket, so that by the tinkling of their
bells they might lure into the ambush any man
who came out to hunt them up. Young Wetzel
made a dash for liberty, but received a shot which
broke his arm, and then surrendered and cheerfully
accompanied his captors; while his companion, totally unnerved, hung back crying, and was promptly
tomahawked. Early next morning the party struck
the Ohio, at a point where there was a clearing.

The cabins on this clearing were deserted, the settlers having taken refuge in a fort because of the
Indian ravages; but the stock had been left running
in the woods. One of the Indians shot a hog and
tossed it into a canoe they had hidden under the
bank. The captive was told to enter the canoe and
lie down; three Indians then got in, while the fourth
started to swim the stolen horses across the river.

Fortunately for the captured boy three of the
settlers had chosen this day to return to the abandoned clearing and look after the loose stock. They
reached the place shortly after the Indians, and just
in time to hear the report of the rifle when the hog
was shot. The owner of the hogs, instead of sus-
pecting that there were Indians near by, jumped to
the conclusion that a Kentucky boat had landed,
and that the immigrants were shooting his hogs—
for the people who drifted down the Ohio in boats
were not, when hungry, over-scrupulous concerning
the right to stray live stock. Running forward, the
three men had almost reached the river, when they
heard the loud snorting of one of the horses as it
was forced into the water. As they came out on
the bank they saw the canoe, with three Indians in
it, and in the bottom four rifles, the dead hog, and
young Wetzel stretched at full length; the Indian
in the stern was just pushing off from the shore
with his paddle; the fourth Indian was swimming
the horses a few yards from shore. Immediately
the foremost white man threw up his rifle and shot
the paddler dead; and a second later one of his
companions coming up, killed in like fashion the

Indian in the bow of the canoe. The third Indian, stunned by the sudden onslaught, sat as if numb, never so much as lifting one of the rifles that lay at his feet, and in a minute he too was shot and fell over the side of the canoe, but grasped the gunwale with one hand, keeping himself afloat. Young Wetzel, in the bottom of the canoe, would have shared the same fate, had he not cried out that he was white and a prisoner; whereupon they bade him knock loose the Indian's hand from the side of the canoe. This he did, and the Indian sank. The current carried the canoe on a rocky spit of land, and Wetzel jumped out and waded ashore, while the little craft spun off and again drifted towards midstream. One of the men on shore now fired at the only remaining Indian, who was still swimming his horse for the opposite bank. The bullet splashed the water on his naked skin, whereat he slipped off his horse, swam to the empty canoe, and got into it. Unhurt he reached the farther shore, where he leaped out and caught the horse as it swam to land, mounted it, rifle in hand, turned to yell defiance at his foes, and then vanished in the forest-shrouded wilderness. He left behind him the dead bodies of his three friends, to be washed on the shallows by the turbid flood of the great river.[1]

These are merely some of the recorded incidents

[1] De Haas, pp. 283–292. De Haas gathered the facts of these and numerous similar incidents from the pioneers themselves in their old age; doubtless they are often inaccurate in detail, but on the whole De Haas has more judgment and may be better trusted than the other compilers. In the Draper MSS. are volumes of such traditional stories, gathered with no discrimination whatever.

which occurred in the single year 1785, in one comparatively small portion of the vast stretch Monotonous of territory which then formed the Indian Horror of the frontier. Many such occurred on all Ravages. parts of this frontier in each of the terrible years of Indian warfare. They varied infinitely in detail, but they were monotonously alike in their characteristics of stealthy approach, of sudden onfall, and of butcherly cruelty ; and there was also a terrible sameness in the brutality and ruthlessness with which the whites, as occasion offered, wreaked their revenge. Generally the Indian war parties were successful, and suffered comparatively little, making their attacks by surprise, and by preference on unarmed men cumbered with women and children. Occasionally they were beaten back ; occasionally parties of settlers or hunters stumbled across and scattered the prowling bands ; occasionally the Indian villages suffered from retaliatory inroads.

One attack, simple enough in its incidents, deserves notice for other reasons. In 1784 a family of " poor white " immigrants who had just Attack on settled in Kentucky were attacked in the the Lincoln daytime, while in the immediate neighbor- Family. hood of their squalid cabin. The father was shot, and one Indian was in the act of tomahawking the six-year-old son, when an elder brother, from the doorway of the cabin, shot the savage. The Indians then fled. The boy thus rescued grew up to become the father of Abraham Lincoln.[1]

Now and then the monstrous uniformity of horror

[1] Hay and Nicolay.

in assault and reprisal was broken by some deed
out of the common ; some instance where despair nerved the frame of woman or of half-grown
boy; some strange incident in the career of a
backwoods hunter, whose profession perpetually
exposed him to Indian attack, but also trained him
as naught else could to evade and repel it. The
wild turkey was always much hunted by the
settlers; and one of the common Indian tricks was
to imitate the turkey call and shoot the hunter when
thus tolled to his foe's ambush; but it was only less
common for a skilled Indian fighter to detect the
ruse and himself creep up and slay the would-be
slayer.   More than once, when a cabin was attacked
in the absence or after the death of the men, some
brawny frontierswoman, accustomed to danger and
violent physical exertion, and favored by peculiar
circumstances, herself beat off the assailants.

In one such case, two or three families were living
together in a block-house. One spring day, when
Prowess of there were in the house but two men and
Frontier one woman, a Mrs. Bozarth, the children
Women. who had been playing in the yard suddenly screamed that Indians were coming. One of
the men sprang to the door only to fall back with a
bullet in his breast, and in another moment an
Indian leaped over the threshold and attacked the
remaining man before he could grasp a weapon.
Holding his antagonist the latter called out to Mrs.
Bozarth to hand him a knife; but instead she
snatched up an axe and killed the savage on the
spot.   But that instant another leaped into the

doorway, and firing, killed the white man who had been struggling with his companion ; but the woman instantly turned on him, as he stood with his smoking gun, and ripped open his body with a stroke of her axe.   Yelling for help he sank on the threshold, and his comrades rushed to his rescue ; the woman, with her bloody weapon, cleft open the skull of the first, and the others fell back, so that she was able to shut and bar the door.   Then the savages moved off, but they had already killed the children in the yard.

A similar incident took place in Kentucky, where the cabin of a man named John Merrill was attacked at night.   He was shot in several places, and one arm and one thigh broken, as he stood by the open door, and fell calling out to his wife to close it. This she did; but the Indians chopped a hole in the stout planks with their tomahawks, and tried to crawl through.   The woman, however, stood to one side and struck at the head of each as it appeared, maiming or killing the first two or three.   Enraged at being thus baffled by a woman, two of the Indians clambered on the roof of the cabin, and prepared to drop down the wide chimney; for at night the fire in such a cabin was allowed to smoulder, the coals being kept alive in the ashes.   But Mrs. Merrill seized a feather-bed and, tearing it open, threw it on the embers; the flame and stifling smoke leaped up the chimney, and in a moment both Indians came down, blinded and half smothered, and were killed by the big resolute woman before they could recover themselves.   No further attempt was made to molest the cabin or its inmates.

One of the incidents which became most widely noised along the borders was the escape of the two Johnson boys, in the fall of 1788.   Their father was one of the restless pioneers along the upper Ohio, who were always striving to take up claims across the river, heedless of the Indian treaties.   The two boys, John and Henry, were at the time thirteen and eleven years old respectively.   One Sunday, about noon, they went to find a hat which they had lost the day before at the spot where they had been working, three quarters of a mile from the house.   Having found the hat they sat down by the roadside to crack nuts, and were surprised by two Indians; they were not harmed, but were forced to go with their captors, who kept travelling slowly through the woods on the outskirts of the settlements, looking for horses.   The elder boy soon made friends with the Indians, telling them that he and his brother were ill-treated at home, and would be glad to get a chance to try Indian life. By degrees they grew to believe he was in earnest, and plied him with all kinds of questions concerning the neighbors, their live stock, their guns, the number of men in the different families, to all of which he replied with seeming eagerness and frankness. At night they stopped to camp, one Indian scouting through the woods, while the other kindled a fire by flashing powder in the pan of his rifle.   For supper they had parched corn and pork roasted over the coals; there was then some further talk, and the Indians lay down to sleep, one on each side of the boys. After a while, supposing that their captives were

Story of Two Boys.

asleep, and anticipating no trouble from two un-armed boys, one Indian got up and lay down on the other side of the fire, where he was soon snoring heavily. Then the lads, who had been wide awake, biding their time, whispered to one another, and noiselessly rose. The elder took one of the guns, silently cocked it, and, pointing it at the head of one Indian, directed the younger boy to take it and pull trigger, while he himself stood over the head of the other Indian with drawn tomahawk. The one boy then fired, his Indian never moving after receiving the shot, while the other boy struck at the same moment; but the tomahawk went too far back on the neck, and the savage tried to spring to his feet, yell-ing loudly. However the boy struck him again and again as he strove to rise, and he fell back and was soon dead. Then the two boys hurried off through the darkness, fearing lest other Indians might be in the neighborhood. Not very far away they struck a path which they recognized, and the elder hung up his hat, that they might find the scene of their feat when they came back. Continuing their course they reached a block-house shortly before daybreak. On the following day a party of men went out with the elder boy and found the two dead Indians.[1]

After any Indian stroke the men of the neighbor-hood would gather under their local militia officers, and, unless the Indians had too long a start, would endeavor to overtake them, and either avenge the slain or rescue the prisoners. In the more exposed settlements bands of rangers were kept continually

[1] De Haas.

patrolling the woods. Every man of note in the Cumberland country took part in this duty. In Kentucky the county lieutenants and their subordinates were always on the lookout. Logan paid especial heed to the protection of the immigrants who came in over the Wilderness Road. Kenton's spy company watched the Ohio, and continually crossed it on the track of marauding parties, and, though very often baffled, yet Kenton and his men succeeded again and again in rescuing hapless women and children, or in scattering—although usually with small loss—war parties bound against the settlements.

One of the best known Indian fighters in Kentucky was William Whitley, who lived at Walnut Flat, some five miles from Crab Orchard. **Feats of an Indian Fighter.** He had come to Kentucky soon after its settlement, and by his energy and ability had acquired property and leadership, though of unknown ancestry and without education. He was a stalwart man, skilled in the use of arms, jovial and fearless; the backwoods fighters followed him readily, and he loved battle; he took part in innumerable Indian expeditions, and in his old age was killed fighting against Tecumseh at the battle of the Thames. In 1786 or '87 he built the first brick house ever built in Kentucky. It was a very handsome house for those days, every step in the hall stairway having carved upon it the head of an eagle bearing in its beak an olive branch. Each story was high, and the windows were placed very high from the ground, to prevent the Indians from shooting through them at the occupants. The glass was brought from Virginia by pack train. He feasted royally the hands who put up the house; and to pay for the whiskey they drank he had to sell one of his farms.

In 1785 (the year of the above recited ravages on the upper Ohio in the neighborhood of Wheeling), Colonel Whitley led his rangers, once and again, against marauding Indians. In January he followed a war party, rescued a captive white man, and took prisoner an Indian who was afterwards killed by one of the militia—"a cowardly fellow," says Whitley. In October a party of immigrants, led by a man named McClure, who had just come over the Wilderness trace, were set upon at dawn by Indians, not far from Whitley's house; two of the men were killed. Mrs. McClure got away at first, and ran two hundred yards, taking her four children with her; in the gloom they would all have escaped had not the smallest child kept crying. This led the Indians to them. Three of the children were tomahawked at once; next morning the fourth shared the same fate. The mother was forced to cook breakfast for her captors at the fire before which the scalps were drying. She was then placed on a half-broken horse and led off with them. When word of the disaster was brought to Whitley's, he was not at home, but his wife, a worthy helpmeet, immediately sent for him, and meanwhile sent word to his company. On his return he was able to take the trail at once with twenty-one riflemen, as true as steel. Following hard, but with stealth equal to their own, he overtook the Indians at sundown on the second day, and fell on them in their camp. Most of them escaped through the thick forest, but he killed two, rescued six prisoners, and captured sixteen horses and much plunder.

Ten days after this another party of immigrants, led by a man named Moore, were attacked on the Wilderness Road and nine persons killed. Whitley raised thirty of his horse-riflemen, and, guessing from the movements of the Indians that they were following the war trace northward, he marched with all speed to reach it at some point ahead of them, and succeeded. Finding they had not passed he turned and went south, and in a thick canebrake met his foes face to face. The whites were spread out in line, while the Indians, twenty in number, came on in single file, all on horseback. The cane was so dense that the two parties were not ten steps apart when they saw one another. At the first fire the Indians, taken utterly unaware, broke and fled, leaving eight of their number dead ; and the victors also took twenty-eight horses. [1]

In the following spring another noted Indian fighter, less lucky than Whitley, was killed while

Death of Black Wolf and Col. Christian.

leading one of these scouting parties. Early in 1786, the Indians began to commit numerous depredations in Kentucky, and the alarm and anger of the inhabitants became great.[2] In April, a large party of savages under a

[1] Draper MSS. Whitley's MSS. Narrative, apparently dictated some time after the events described. It differs somewhat from the printed account in Collins.

[2] Draper MSS. Clark Papers, *passim* for 1786. Wm. Finney to G. R. Clark, March 24 and 26, 1786. Also Wm. Croghan to G. R. Clark, Nov. 3, and Nov. 16, 1785.

chief named Black Wolf, made a raid along Beargrass.
Col. William Christian, a very gallant and honorable
man, was in command of the neighboring militia.   At
once, as was his wont, he raised a band of twenty
men, and followed the plunderers across the Ohio.
Riding well in advance of his followers, with but
three men in company with him, he overtook the
three rearmost Indians, among whom was Black
Wolf.   The struggle was momentary but bloody.
All three Indians were killed, but Colonel Christian and one of his captains were also slain.[1]

The Kentuckians were by this time thoroughly
roused, and were bent on making a retaliatory expedition in force.   They felt that the efforts   Anger
made by Congress to preserve peace by of the Ken-
treaties, at which the Indians were loaded   tuckians.
with presents, merely resulted in making them think
that the whites were afraid of them, and that if they
wished gifts all they had to do was to go to war.[2]
The only effective way to deal with the Indians was
to strike them in their own country, not to try to
parry the strokes they themselves dealt.   Clark, who
knew the savages well, scoffed at the idea that a vigorous blow, driven well home, would rouse them to
desperation ; he realized that, formidable though
they were in actual battle, and still more in plundering raid, they were not of the temper to hazard all
on the fate of war, or to stand heavy punishment,

[1] State Department MSS. Papers Continental Congress. Sam McDowell
to Governor of Virginia, April 18, 1786.   John May to *Do.*, April 19, 1786.
Clark MSS. Bradford's Notes on Kentucky. John Clark to Johnathan
Clark, April 21, 1786.

[2] Draper MSS. Jon. Clark Papers. John Clark to Johnathan Clark,
March 29, 1786.   Also, G. R. Clark to J. Clark, April 20, 1788.

and that they would yield very quickly, when once they were convinced that unless they did so they and their families would perish by famine or the sword.[1] At this time he estimated that some fifteen hundred warriors were on the war-path and that they were likely to be joined by many others.

The condition of affairs at the French towns of the Illinois and Wabash afforded another strong reason for war, or at least for decided measures of some kind. Almost absolute anarchy reigned in these towns. The French inhabitants had become profoundly discontented with the United States Government. This was natural, for they were neither kept in order nor protected, in spite of their petitions to Congress that some stable government might be established.[2] The quarrels between the French and the intruding American settlers had very nearly reached the point of a race war; and the Americans were further menaced by the Indians. These latter were on fairly good terms with the French, many of whom had intermarried with them, and lived as they did; although the French families of the better class were numerous, and had attained to what was for the frontier a high standard of comfort and refinement.

Anarchy on the Wabash.

The French complained with reason of the lawless and violent character of many of the American new-comers, and also of the fact that already speculators were trying by fraud and foul means to purchase large

Quarrels between French and Americans.

---

[1] State Department MSS., No. 56, p. 282.   G. R. Clark to R. H. Lee.

[2] State Department MSS., No. 30, p. 453, Dec. 8, 1784.   Also p. 443, Nov. 10, 1784.   Draper MSS. J. Edgar to G. R. Clark, Oct. 23, 1786.

tracts of land, not for settlement, but to hold until it should rise in value. On the other hand, the Americans complained no less bitterly of the French, as a fickle, treacherous, undisciplined race, in close alliance with the Indians, and needing to be ruled with a rod of iron.[1] It is impossible to reconcile the accounts the two parties gave of one another's deeds; doubtless neither side was guiltless of grave wrongdoing. So great was Clark's reputation for probity and leadership that both sides wrote him urgently, requesting that he would come to them and relieve their distress.[2] One of the most fruitful sources of broils and quarrels was the liquor trade with the Indians. The rougher among the newcomers embarked eagerly in this harmful and disreputable business, and the low-class French followed their example. The commandant, Monsieur J. M. P. Legrace, and the Creole court forbade this trade; a decision which was just and righteous, but excited much indignation, as the other inhabitants believed that the members of the court themselves followed it in secret.[3]

In 1786 the ravages of the Indians grew so serious, and the losses of the Americans near Vincennes became so great, that they abandoned their outlying farms, and came into the town.[4] Vincennes then consisted of upwards of three hundred houses. The Americans numbered some sixty families, and had

[1] State Dept. MSS., No. 56. J. Edgar to G. R. Clark, Nov. 7, 1785. Draper MSS. Petition of Americans of Vincennes to Congress, June 1, 1786.

[2] Draper MSS. Petition to G. R. Clark from Inhabitants of Vincennes, March 16, 1786.

[3] *Do.*, John Filson ; MS. Journey of Two Voyages, etc.

[4] *Do.*, Moses Henry to G. R. Clark, June 7, 1786.

built an American quarter, with a strong block-house. They only ventured out to till their corn-fields in bodies of armed men, while the French worked their lands singly and unarmed.

The Indians came freely into the French quarter of the town, and even sold to the inhabitants plun-

Indians Attack Americans. der taken from the Americans; and when complaint of this was made to the Creole magistrates, they paid no heed. One of the men who suffered at the hands of the savages was a wandering schoolmaster, named John Filson,[1] the first historian of Kentucky, and the man who took down, and put into his own quaint and absurdly stilted English, Boone's so-called "autobiography." Filson, having drifted west, had travelled up and down the Ohio and Wabash by canoe and boat. He was much struck with the abundance of game of all kinds which he saw on the northwestern side of the Ohio, and especially by the herds of buffaloes which lay on the sand-bars; his party lived on the flesh of bears, deer, wild turkeys, coons, and water-turtles. In 1785 the Indians whom he met seemed friendly; but on June 2, 1786, while on the Wabash, his canoe was attacked by the savages, and two of his men were slain. He himself escaped with dif-ficulty, and reached Vincennes after an exhausting journey, but having kept possession of his "two small trunks."[2]

Two or three weeks after this misadventure of the unlucky historian, a party of twenty-five Americans,

[1] *Do.*, John Small to G. R. Clark, June 23, 1786.
[2] *Do.*, Filson's Journal.

under a captain named Daniel Sullivan,[1] were attacked while working in their cornfields at Vincennes.[2] They rallied and drove back the Indians,
but two of their number were wounded. One of the
wounded fell for a moment into the hands of the
Indians and was scalped; and though he afterwards
recovered, his companions at the time expected him
to die. They marched back to Vincennes in furious
anger, and finding an Indian in the house of a
Frenchman, they seized and dragged him to their
block-house, where the wife of the scalped man,
whose name was Donelly, shot and scalped him.

This greatly exasperated the French, who kept a
guard over the other Indians who were in town, and
next day sent them to the woods. Then
their head men, magistrates, and officers of
the militia, summoned the Americans before a council, and ordered all who had not regular
passports from the local court to leave at once,
"bag and baggage." This created the utmost con-
sternation among the Americans, whom the French
outnumbered five to one, while the savages certainly
would have destroyed them had they tried to go
back to Kentucky. Their leaders again wrote
urgent appeals for help to Clark, asking that a
general guard might be sent them if only to take
them out of the country. Filson had already gone
overland to Louisville and told the authorities of

French
Threaten
Americans.

---

[1] *Do.*, Daniel Sullivan to G. R. Clark, June 23, 1786. Small's letter says
June 21st.

[2] State Dept. MSS. Papers Continental Congress, No. 150, vol. ii., Letter of J. M. P. Legrace, "Au Général George Rogé Clarck—a la Chûte"
(at the Falls—Louisville), July 22, 1786.

the straits of their brethren at Vincennes, and immediately an expedition was sent to their relief under Captains Hardin and Patton.

Meanwhile, on July 15th, a large band of several hundred Indians, bearing red and white flags, came down the river in forty-seven canoes to attack the Americans at Vincennes, sending word to the French that if they remained neutral they would not be molested. The French sent envoys to dissuade them from their purpose, but the war chiefs and sachems answered that the red people were at last united in opposition to "the men wearing hats," and gave a belt of black wampum to the wavering Piankeshaws, warning them that all Indians who refused to join against the whites would thenceforth be treated as foes. However, their deeds by no means corresponded with their threats. Next day they assailed the American block-house or stockaded fort, but found they could make no impression and drew off. They burned a few outlying cabins and slaughtered many head of cattle, belonging both to the Americans and the French; and then, seeing the French under arms, held further parley with them, and retreated, to the relief of all the inhabitants.

At the same time the Kentuckians, under Hardin and Patton, stumbled by accident on a party of Indians, some of whom were friendly Piankeshaws and some hostile Miamis. They attacked them without making any discrimination between friend and foe, killed six, wounded seven, and drove off the remainder. But

they themselves lost one man killed and four
wounded, including Hardin, and fell back to Louisville without doing anything more.[1]

These troubles on the Wabash merely hardened
the determination of the Kentuckians no longer to
wait until the Federal Government acted.   Clark's
With the approval of Governor Patrick Expedition.
Henry, they took the initiative themselves.   Early
in August the field officers of the district of Kentucky met at Harrodsburg, Benjamin Logan presiding, and resolved on an expedition, to be commanded
by Clark, against the hostile Indians on the Wabash.
Half of the militia of the district were to go; the
men were to assemble, on foot or on horseback, as
they pleased, at Clarksville on September 10th.[2]
Besides pack-horses, salt, flour, powder, and lead
were impressed,[3] not always in strict compliance
with law, for some of the officers impressed quantities of spirituous liquors also.[4] The troops themselves however came in slowly.[5] Late in September

[1] Letter of Legrace and Filson's Journal. The two contradict one another as to which side was to blame. Legrace blames the Americans
heavily for wronging both the French and the Indians ; and condemns
in the strongest terms, and probably with justice, many of their number,
and especially Sullivan. He speaks, however, in high terms of Henry and
Small ; and both of these, in their letters referred to above, paint the conduct of the French and Indians in very dark colors, throwing the blame on
them. Legrace is certainly disingenuous in suppressing all mention of the
wrongs done to the Americans. For Filson's career and death in the woods,
see the excellent Life of Filson, by Durrett, in the Filson club publications.

[2] Draper MSS. Minutes of meetings of the officers of the district of
Kentucky, Aug. 2, 1786. State Dept. MSS., No. 150, vol. ii. Letter of
P. Henry, May 16, 1786.

[3] Draper MSS. J. Cox to George Rogers Clark, Aug. 8, 1786.

[4] State Dept. MSS., Madison papers. Letter of Caleb Wallace Nov. 20, 1786.

[5] State Dept. MSS., Papers Continental Congress. No. 150, vol. ii.
Letter of Major Wm. North, Sept. 15, 1786.

when twelve hundred men had been gathered, Clark moved forward. But he was no longer the man he had been. He failed to get any hold on his army. His followers, on their side, displayed all that unruly fickleness which made the militia of the Revolutionary period a weapon which might at times be put to good use in the absence of any other, but which was really trusted only by men whose military judgment was as fatuous as Jefferson's.

After reaching Vincennes the troops became mutinous, and at last flatly refused longer to obey Clark's orders, and marched home as a disorderly Failure. mob, to the disgrace of themselves and their leader. Nevertheless the expedition had really accomplished something, for it overawed the Wabash and Illinois Indians, and effectively put a stop to any active expressions of disloyalty or disaffection on the part of the French. Clark sent officers to the Illinois towns, and established a garrison of one hundred and fifty men at Vincennes,[1] besides seizing the goods of a Spanish merchant in retaliation for wrongs committed on American merchants by the Spaniards.

This failure was in small part offset by a successful expedition led by Logan at the same time against the Shawnee towns.[2] On October 5th, he attacked them with seven hundred and ninety men. Logan's There was little or no resistance, most of Expedition. the warriors having gone to oppose Clark. Logan took ten scalps and thirty-two prisoners,

[1] *Do.* Virginia State Papers. G. R. Clark to Patrick Henry. Draper MSS., Proceedings of Committee of Kentucky Convention, Dec. 19, 1786.

[2] State Department MSS., Virginia State Papers, Logan to Patrick Henry, December 17, 1786.

burned two hundred cabins and quantities of corn, and returned in triumph after a fortnight's absence. One deed of infamy sullied his success. Among his colonels was the scoundrel McGarry, who, in cold blood, murdered the old Shawnee chief, Molunthee, several hours after he had been captured; the shame of the barbarous deed being aggravated by the fact that the old chief had always been friendly to the Americans.[1] Other murders would probably have followed, had it not been for the prompt and honorable action of Colonels Robert Patterson and Robert Trotter, who ordered their men to shoot down any one who molested another prisoner. McGarry then threatened them, and they in return demanded that he be court-martialled for murder.[2] Logan, to his discredit, refused the court-martial, for fear of creating further trouble. The bane of the frontier military organization was the helplessness of the elected commanders, their dependence on their followers, and the inability of the decent men to punish the atrocious misdeeds of their associates.

These expeditions were followed by others on a smaller scale, but of like character. They did enough damage to provoke, but not to overawe, the Indians. With the spring of 1787, the ravages began on an enlarged scale, with all their dreadful accompaniments of rapine, murder, and torture. All along the Ohio frontier, from Pennsylvania to Kentucky, the settlers were harried; and in some places they abandoned their clearings and hamlets, so that the frontier

[1] Draper MSS., Caleb Wallace to Wm. Fleming, October 23, 1786. State Department MSS., No. 150, vol. ii., Harmar's Letter, November 15, 1786.

[2] Virginia State Papers, vol. iv., p. 212.

shrank back.[1] Logan, Kenton, and many other leaders headed counter expeditions, and now and then broke up a war party or destroyed an Indian town;[2] but nothing decisive was accomplished, and Virginia paralyzed the efforts of the Kentuckians and waked them to anger, by forbidding them to follow the Indian parties beyond the frontier.[3]

The most important stroke given to the hostile Indians in 1787 was dealt by the Cumberland people. During the preceding three or four years, some scores of the settlers on the Cumberland had been slain by small predatory parties of Indians, mostly Cherokees and Creeks. No large war band attacked the settlements; but no hunter, surveyor, or traveller, no wood-chopper or farmer, no woman alone in the cabin with her children, could ever feel safe from attack. Now and then a savage was killed in such an attack, or in a skirmish with some body of scouts; but nothing effectual could be thus accomplished.

The most dangerous marauders were some Creek and Cherokee warriors who had built a town on the Coldwater, a tributary of the Tennessee near the **Ravages in** Muscle Shoals, within easy striking dis-**Cumberland** tance of the Cumberland settlements. **Country.** This town was a favorite resort of French traders from the Illinois and Wabash, who came up the Tennessee in bateaux. They provided the Indians with guns and ammunition, and in return often

<hr />

[1] Durret MSS., Daniel Dawson to John Campbell, Pittsburg, June 17, 1787. Virginia State Papers, vol. iv., p. 419.

[2] Draper, MSS., T. Brown to T. Preston, Danville, June 13, 1787. Virginia State Papers, vol. iv., pp. 254, 287, etc.

[3] Virginia State Papers, vol. iv., p. 344.

received goods plundered from the Americans; and they at least indirectly and in some cases directly encouraged the savages in their warfare against the settlers.[1]

Early in June, Robertson gathered one hundred and thirty men and marched against the Coldwater town, with two Chickasaws as guides. Another small party started at the same time by water, but fell into an ambush, and then came back. Robertson and his force followed the trail of a marauding party which had just visited the settlements. They marched through the woods towards the Tennessee until they heard the voice of the great river as it roared over the shoals. For a day they lurked in the cane on the north side, waiting until they were certain no spies were watching them. In the night some of the men swam over and stole a big canoe, with which they returned. At daylight the troops crossed, a few in this canoe, the others swimming with their horses. After landing, they marched seven miles and fell on the town, which was in a ravine, with cornfields round about. Taken by surprise, the warriors, with no effective resistance, fled to their canoes. The white riflemen thronged after them. Most of the warriors escaped, but over twenty were slain; as were also four or five French traders, while half a dozen Frenchmen and one Indian squaw were captured. All the cabins were destroyed, the

Robertson's Expedition against the Coldwater Town.

[1] Robertson MSS., Robertson to some French man of note in Illinois, June, 1787. This is apparently a copy, probably by Robertson's wife, of the original letter. In Robertson's own original letters, the spelling and handwriting are as rough as they are vigorous.

live stock was slain, and much plunder taken. The prisoners were well treated and released ; but on the way home another party of French traders were encountered, and their goods were taken from them. The two Chickasaws were given their full share of all the plunder.

This blow gave a breathing spell to the Cumberland settlements. Robertson at once wrote to the French in the Illinois country, and also to some Delawares, who had recently come to the neighborhood, and were preserving a dubious neutrality. He explained the necessity of their expedition, and remarked that if any innocent people, whether Frenchmen or Indians, had suffered in the attack, they had to blame themselves; they were in evil company, and the assailants could not tell the good from the bad. If any Americans had been there, they would have suffered just the same. In conclusion he warned the French that if their traders continued to furnish the hostile Indians with powder and lead, they would "render themselves very insecure"; and to the Indians he wrote that, in the event of a war, "you will compell ous to retaliate, which will be a grate pridgedes to your nation." [1] He did not spell well; but his meaning was plain, and his hand was known to be heavy.

[1] Robertson MSS. His letter above referred to, and another, in his own hand, to the Delawares, of about the same date.

CHAPTER III.

THE NAVIGATION OF THE MISSISSIPPI ; SEPA-
RATIST MOVEMENTS AND SPANISH
INTRIGUES, 1784–1788.

It was important for the frontiersmen to take the
Lake Posts from the British ; but it was even more
important to wrest from the Spaniards the free navigation of the Mississippi. While the Lake Posts
were held by the garrisons of a foreign power, the
work of settling the northwestern territory was
bound to go forward slowly and painfully ; but
while the navigation of the Mississippi was barred,
even the settlements already founded could not attain to their proper prosperity and importance.

The lusty young commonwealths which were
springing into life on the Ohio and its tributaries
knew that commerce with the outside world
was essential to their full and proper
growth. The high, forest-clad ranges of
the Appalachians restricted and hampered
their mercantile relations with the older States, and
therefore with the Europe which lay beyond ; while
the giant river offered itself as a huge trade artery to
bring them close to all the outer world, if only they
were allowed its free use.

Need of Free Navi-gation of the Mississippi.

Navigable rivers are of great importance to a country's trade now; but a hundred years ago their importance was relatively far greater. Steam, railroads, electricity, have worked a revolution so stupendous, that we find it difficult to realize the facts of the life which our forefathers lived. The conditions of commerce have changed much more in the last hundred years than in the preceding two thousand. The Kentuckians and Tennesseans knew only the pack train, the wagon train, the river craft and the deep-sea ship; that is, they knew only such means of carrying on commerce as were known to Greek and Carthaginian, Roman and Persian, and the nations of mediæval Europe. Beasts of draught and of burden, and oars and sails,—these, and these only,—were at the service of their merchants, as they had been at the service of all merchants from time immemorial. Where trade was thus limited the advantages conferred by water carriage, compared to land carriage, were incalculable. The Westerners were right in regarding as indispensable the free navigation of the Mississippi. They were right also in their determination ultimately to acquire the control of the whole river, from the source to the mouth.

However, the Westerners wished more than the privilege of sending down stream the products of their woods and pastures and tilled farms.
Desire to Seize the Spanish Lands. They had already begun to cast longing eyes on the fair Spanish possessions. Spain was still the greatest of colonial powers. In wealth, in extent, and in population—both native

and European—her colonies surpassed even those of England ; and by far the most important of her possessions were in the New World.   For two centuries her European rivals, English, French, and Dutch, had warred against her in America, with the net result of taking from her a few islands in the West Indies. On the American mainland her possessions were even larger than they had been in the age of the great Conquisadores ; the age of Cortes, Pizarro, De Soto, and Coronado.   Yet it was evident that her grasp had grown feeble.   Every bold, lawless, ambitious leader among the frontier folk dreamed of wresting from the Spaniard some portion of his rich and ill-guarded domain.

It was not alone the attitude of the frontiersmen towards Spain that was novel, and based upon a situation for which there was little prece- Relations of dent.   Their relations with one another, the Frontiersmen to with their brethren of the seaboard, and the Central with the Federal Government, likewise Government. had to be adjusted without much chance of profiting by antecedent experience.   Many phases of these relations between the people who stayed at home, and those who wandered off to make homes, between the frontiersmen as they formed young States, and the Central Government representing the old States, were entirely new, and were ill-understood by both parties.   Truths which all citizens have now grown to accept as axiomatic were then seen clearly only by the very greatest men, and by most others were seen dimly, if at all. What is now regarded as inevitable and proper was then held as something abnormal, unnatural, and greatly to be dreaded. The men engaged in building new commonwealths did not, as yet, understand that they owed the Union as much as did the dwellers in the old States. They were apt to let liberty become mere anarchy and license, to talk extravagantly about their rights while ignoring their duties, and to rail at the weakness of the Central Government while at the same time opposing with foolish violence every effort to make it stronger. On the other hand, the people of the long-settled country found difficulty in heartily accepting the idea that the new communities, as they sprang up in the forest, were entitled to stand exactly on a level with the old, not only as regards their own rights, but as regards the right to shape the destiny of the Union itself.

The Union was as yet imperfect. The jangling colonies had been welded together, after a fashion, in **The Union still Inchoate.** the slow fire of the Revolutionary war; but the old lines of cleavage were still distinctly marked. The great struggle had been of incalculable benefit to all Americans. Under its stress they had begun to develop a national type of thought and character. Americans now held in common memories which they shared with no one else; for they held ever in mind the feats of a dozen crowded years. Theirs was the history of all that had been done by the Continental Congress and the Continental armies; theirs the memory of the toil and the suffering and the splendid ultimate triumph. They cherished in common the winged words of their statesmen, the edged deeds of their soldiers; they yielded to the spell of mighty names which sounded alien to all men save themselves. But though the successful struggle had laid deep the foundations of a new nation, it had also of necessity stirred and developed many of the traits most hostile to assured national life. All civil wars loosen the bands of orderly liberty, and leave in their train disorder and evil. Hence those who cause them must rightly be held guilty of the gravest wrong-doing unless they are not only pure of purpose, but sound of judgment, and unless the result shows their wisdom. The Revolution had left behind it among many men love of liberty, mingled with lofty national feeling and broad patriotism; but to other men it seemed that the chief lessons taught had been successful resistance to authority, jealousy of the central Government, and intolerance of all restraint. According as one or the other of these mutually hostile sets of sentiments prevailed, the acts of the Revolutionary leaders were to stand justified or condemned in the light of the coming years. As yet the success had only been in tearing down; there remained the harder and all-important task of building up.

This task of building up was accomplished, and the acts of the men of the Revolution were thus justified. It was the after result of the Revolution, not the Revolution itself, which gave to the governmental experiment inaugurated by the Second Continental Congress its unique and lasting value. It was this

Task of the Nation-Builders.

result which marks most clearly the difference between the careers of the English-speaking and
Spanish-speaking peoples on this continent. The
wise statesmanship typified by such men as Washington and Marshall, Hamilton, Jay, John Adams,
and Charles Cotesworth Pinckney, prevailed over
the spirit of separatism and anarchy. Seven years
after the war ended, the Constitution went into
effect, and the United States became in truth a nation. Had we not thus become a nation, had the
separatists won the day, and our country become
the seat of various antagonistic States and confederacies, then the Revolution by which we won liberty and independence would have been scarcely
more memorable or noteworthy than the wars which
culminated in the separation of the Spanish-American colonies from Spain; for we would thereby
have proved that we did not deserve either liberty
or independence.

The Revolutionary war itself had certain points
of similarity with the struggles of which men like
Over-Mas- Bolivar were the heroes; where the parallel
tering Im- totally fails is in what followed. There
portance of
the Union. were features in which the campaigns of
the Mexican and South American insurgent leaders
resembled at least the partisan warfare so often
waged by American Revolutionary generals; but
with the deeds of the great constructive statesman
of the United States there is nothing in the career
of any Spanish-American community to compare. It
was the power to build a solid and permanent Union,
the power to construct a mighty nation out of the

wreck of a crumbling confederacy, which drew a
sharp line between the Americans of the north and
the Spanish-speaking races of the south.

In their purposes and in the popular sentiment
to which they have appealed, our separatist leaders
of every generation have borne an ominous likeness
to the horde of dictators and half-military, half-
political adventurers who for three quarters of a
century have wrought such harm in the lands between the Argentine and Mexico; but the men who
brought into being and preserved the Union have
had no compeers in Southern America. The North
American colonies wrested their independence from
Great Britain as the colonies of South America
wrested theirs from Spain; but whereas the United
States grew with giant strides into a strong and
orderly nation, Spanish America has remained split
into a dozen turbulent states, and has become a by-
word for anarchy and weakness.

The separatist feeling has at times been strong in
almost every section of the Union, although in some
regions it has been much stronger than in
others. Calhoun and Pickering, Jefferson
and Gouverneur Morris, Wendell Phillips
and William Taney, Aaron Burr and Jefferson
Davis—these and many other leaders of thought and
action, east and west, north and south, at different
periods of the nation's growth, and at different stages
of their own careers, have, for various reasons, and
with widely varying purity of motive, headed or
joined in separatist movements. Many of these men
were actuated by high-minded, though narrow, pa-

triotism; and those who, in the culminating catastrophe of all the separatist agitations, appealed to the sword, proved the sincerity of their convictions by their resolute courage and self-sacrifice. Nevertheless they warred against the right, and strove mightily to bring about the downfall and undoing of the nation.

The men who brought on and took part in the disunion movements were moved sometimes by good and sometimes by bad motives; but even when their motives were disinterested and their purposes pure, and even when they had received much provocation, they must be adjudged as lacking the wisdom, the foresight, and the broad devotion to all the land over which the flag floats, without which no statesman can rank as really great. The enemies of the Union were the enemies of America and of mankind, whose success would have plunged their country into an abyss of shame and misery, and would have arrested for generations the upward movement of their race.

Evils of the Disunion Movements.

Yet, evil though the separatist movements were, they were at times imperfectly justified by the spirit of sectional distrust and bitterness rife in portions of the country which at the moment were themselves loyal to the Union. This was especially true of the early separatist movements in the West. Unfortunately the attitude towards the Westerners of certain portions of the population in the older States, and especially in the northeastern States, was one of unreasoning jealousy and suspicion; and though this

Eastern Jealousy of the Young West.

mental attitude rarely crystallized into hostile deeds,
its very existence, and the knowledge that it did
exist, embittered the men of the West. Moreover
the people among whom these feelings were strongest were, unfortunately, precisely those who on the
questions of the Union and the Constitution showed
the broadest and most far-seeing statesmanship.
New England, the towns of the middle States and
Maryland, the tidewater region of South Carolina,
and certain parts of Virginia were the seats of the
soundest political thought of the day. The men
who did this sane, wholesome political thinking were
quite right in scorning and condemning the crude
unreason, often silly, often vicious, which characterized so much of the political thought of their opponents. The strength of these opponents was largely
derived from the ignorance and suspicion of the raw
country districts, and from the sour jealousy with
which the backwoodsmen regarded the settled
regions of the seaboard.

But when these sound political thinkers permitted
their distrust of certain sections of the country to
lead them into doing injustice to those sections, they
in their turn deserved the same condemnation which
should be meted to so many of their political foes.
When they allowed their judgment to become so
warped by their dissatisfaction with the traits in-
evitably characteristic of the earlier stages of frontier development that they became opposed to all
extension of the frontier ; when they allowed their
liking for the well-ordered society of their own districts to degenerate into indifference to or dislike of

the growth of the United States towards continental greatness; then they themselves sank into the position of men who in cold selfishness sought to mar the magnificent destiny of their own people.

In the northeastern States, and in New England especially, this feeling showed itself for two genera-

Blindness of the New Englanders as Regards the West. tions after the close of the Revolutionary War. On the whole the New Englanders have exerted a more profound and wholesome influence upon the development of our common country than has ever been exerted by any other equally numerous body of our people. They have led the nation in the path of civil liberty and sound governmental administration. But too often they have viewed the nation's growth and greatness from a narrow and provincial standpoint, and have grudgingly acquiesced in, rather than led the march towards, continental supremacy. In shaping the nation's policy for the future their sense of historic perspective seemed imperfect. They could not see the all-importance of the valley of the Ohio, or of the valley of the Columbia, to the Republic of the years to come. The value of a county in Maine offset in their eyes the value of these vast, empty regions. Indeed, in the days immediately succeeding the Revolution, their attitude towards the growing West was worse than one of mere indifference; it was one of alarm and dislike. They for the moment adopted towards the West a position not wholly unlike that which England had held towards the American colonies as a whole. They came dangerously near repeating, in their feeling towards their younger brethren on the Ohio, the very blunder committed in reference to themselves by their elder brethren in Britain. For some time they seemed, like the British, unable to grasp the grandeur of their race's imperial destiny. They hesitated to throw themselves with hearty enthusiasm into the task of building a nation with a continent as its base. They rather shrank from the idea as implying a lesser weight of their own section in the nation; not yet understanding that to an American the essential thing was the growth and well-being of America, while the relative importance of the locality where he dwelt was a matter of small moment.

The extreme representatives of this northeastern sectionalism not only objected to the growth of the West at the time now under consideration, but even avowed a desire to work it harm, by shutting the Mississippi, so as to benefit the commerce of the Atlantic States—a manifestation of cynical and selfish disregard of the rights of their fellow-countrymen quite as flagrant as any piece of tyranny committed or proposed by King George's ministers in reference to America. These intolerant extremists not only opposed the admission of the young western States into the Union, but at a later date actually announced that the annexation by the United States of vast territories beyond the Mississippi offered just cause for the secession of the northeastern States. Even those who did not take such an advanced ground felt an unreasonable dread lest the

Eastern Efforts to Shear the West's Strength.

West might grow to overtop the East in power. In their desire to prevent this (which has long since happened without a particle of damage resulting to the East), they proposed to establish in the Constitution that the representatives from the West should never exceed in number those from the East,—a proviso which would not have been merely futile, for it would quite properly have been regarded by the West as unforgivable.

A curious feature of the way many honest men looked at the West was their inability to see how essentially transient were some of the characteristics to which they objected. Thus they were alarmed at the turbulence and the lawless shortcomings of various kinds which grew out of the conditions of frontier settlement and sparse population. They looked with anxious foreboding to the time when the turbulent and lawless people would be very numerous, and would form a dense and powerful population; failing to see that in exact proportion as the population became dense, the conditions which caused the qualities to which they objected would disappear. Even the men who had too much good sense to share these fears, even men as broadly patriotic as Jay, could not realize the extreme rapidity of western growth. Kentucky and Tennessee grew much faster than any of the old frontier colonies had ever grown; and from sheer lack of experience, eastern statesmen could not realize that this rapidity of growth made the navigation of the Mississippi a matter of immediate and not of future interest to the West.

In short, these good people were learning with reluctance and difficulty to accept as necessary certain facts which we regard as part of the order of our political nature. We look at territorial expansion, and the admission of new States, as part of a process as natural as it is desirable. To our forefathers the process was novel, and, in some of its features, repugnant. Many of them could not divest themselves of the feeling that the old States ought to receive more consideration than the new; whereas nowadays it would never occur to anyone that Pennsylvania and Georgia ought to stand either above or below California and Montana. It is an inestimable boon to all four States to be in the Union, but this is because the citizens of all of them are on a common footing. If the new commonwealths in the Rocky Mountains and on the Pacific slope were not cordially accepted by the original Thirteen States as having exactly the same rights and privileges of every kind, it would be better for them to stand alone. As a matter of fact, we have become so accustomed to the idea of the equality of the different States, that it never enters our heads to conceive of the possibility of its being otherwise. The feeling in its favor is so genuine and universal that we are not even conscious that it exists. Nobody dreams of treating the fact that the new commonwealths are offshoots of the old as furnishing grounds for any discrimination in reference to them, one way or the other. There still exist dying jealousies between different States and sections, but this

Failure to Perceive Truths Now Regarded as Self-Evident.

particular feeling does not enter into them in any way whatsoever.

At the time when Kentucky was struggling for statehood, this feeling, though it had been given its death-blow by the success of the Revolution, still lingered here and there on the Atlantic coast. It was manifest in the attitude of many prominent people—the leaders in their communities—towards the new commonwealths growing up beyond the Alleghanies. Had this intolerant sectional feeling ever prevailed and been adopted as the policy of the Atlantic States, the West would have revolted, and would have been right in revolting. But the manifestations of this sectionalism proved abortive; the broad patriotism of leaders like Washington prevailed. In the actual event the East did full and free justice to the West. In consequence we are now one nation.

The East Distrusts the Trans-Alleghany People.

While many of the people on the eastern seaboard thus took an indefensible position in reference to the trans-Alleghany settlements, in the period immediately succeeding the Revolution, there were large bodies of the population of these same settlements, including very many of their popular leaders, whose own attitude towards the Union was, if anything, even more blameworthy. They were clamorous about their rights, and were not unready to use veiled threats of disunion when they deemed these rights infringed; but they showed little appreciation of their own duties to the Union. For certain of the

Separatist and Disunion Feeling in the West.

positions which they assumed no excuse can be offered. They harped continually on the feebleness of the Federal authorities, and the inability of these authorities to do them justice or offer them adequate protection against the Indian and the Spaniard; yet they bitterly opposed the adoption of the very Constitution which provided a strong and stable Federal Government, and turned the weak confederacy, despised at home and abroad, into one of the great nations of the earth. They showed little self-control, little willingness to wait with patience until it was possible to remedy any of the real or fancied wrongs of which they complained. They made no allowance for the difficulties so plentifully strewn in the path of the Federal authorities. They clamored for prompt and effective action, and yet clamored just as loudly against the men who sought to create a national executive with power to take this prompt and effective action. They demanded that the United States wrest from the British the Lake Posts, and from the Spaniards the navigation of the Mississippi. Yet they seemed incapable of understanding that if they separated from the Union they would thereby forfeit all chance of achieving the very purposes they had in view, because they would then certainly be at the mercy of Britain, and probably, at least for some time, at the mercy of Spain also. They opposed giving the United States the necessary civil and military power, although it was only by the possession and exercise of such power that it would be possible to secure for the westerners what they wished. In all human probability, the whole country round the Great Lakes would still be British territory, and the mouth of the Mississippi still in the hands of some European power, had the folly of the separatists won the day and had the West been broken up into independent States.

These shortcomings were not special or peculiar to the frontiersmen of the Ohio valley at the close

Shortcomings of the Frontiersmen.

of the eighteenth century. All our frontiersmen have betrayed a tendency towards them at times, though the exhibitions of this tendency have grown steadily less and less decided. In Vermont, during the years between the close of the Revolution and the adoption of the Constitution, the state of affairs was very much what it was in Kentucky at the same time.[1] In each territory there was acute friction with a neighboring State. In each there was a small knot of men who wished the community to keep out of the new American nation, and to enter into some sort of alliance with a European nation, England in one case, Spain in the other. In each there was a considerable but fluctuating separatist party, desirous that the territory should become an independent nation on its own account. In each case the separatist movements failed, and the final triumph lay with the men of broadly national ideas, so that both Kentucky and Vermont became States of one indissoluble Union.

This final triumph of the Union party in these first-formed frontier States was fraught with im-

---

[1] *Pennsylvania Magazine of History and Biography*, xi., No. 2, pp. 160-165, Letters of Levi Allen, Ethan Allen, and others, from 1787 to 1790.

measurable good for them and for the whole nation of which they became parts. It established a precedent for the action of all the other States that sprang into being as the frontier rolled westward. It decided that the interior of North America should form part of one great Republic, and should not be parcelled out among a crowd of English-speaking Uruguays and Ecquadors, powerful only to damage one another, and helpless to exact respect from alien foes or to keep order in their own households. It vastly increased the significance of the outcome of the Revolution, for it decided that its after-effects should be felt throughout the entire continent, not merely in the way of example, but by direct impress. The creation of a nation stretching along the Atlantic seaboard was of importance in itself, but the importance was immensely increased when once it was decided that the nation should cover a region larger than all Europe.

Final Triumph of the Union Party.

While giving unlimited praise to the men so clear-sighted, and of such high thought, that from the beginning they foresaw the importance of the Union, and strove to include all the West therein, we must beware of blaming overmuch those whose vision was less acute. The experiment of the Union was as yet inchoate; its benefits were prospective; and loyalty to it was loyalty to a splendid idea the realization of which lay in the future rather than in the present. All honor must be awarded to the men who under such conditions could be loyal to so high an ideal;

Excuses for Some of the Separatists.

but we must not refuse to see the many strong and
admirable qualities in some of the men who looked
less keenly into the future. It would be mere folly[1]
to judge a man who in 1787 was lukewarm or even
hostile to the Union by the same standard we
should use in testing his son's grandson a century
later. Finally, where a man's general course was
one of devotion to the Union, it is easy to forgive
him some momentary lapse, due to a misconception
on his part of the real needs of the hour, or to
passing but intense irritation at some display of
narrow indifference to the rights of his section by
the people of some other section. Patrick Henry
himself made one slip when he opposed the adoption of the Federal Constitution; but this does not
at all offset the services he rendered our common
country both before and afterwards. Every statesman makes occasional errors; and the leniency of
judgment needed by Patrick Henry, and needed far
more by Ethan Allen, Samuel Adams, and George
Clinton, must be extended to frontier leaders for
whose temporary coldness to the Union there was
much greater excuse.

When we deal, not with the leading statesmen of
the frontier communities, but with the ordinary
frontier folk themselves, there is need to
apply the same tests used in dealing with
the rude, strong peoples of by-gone ages.
The standard by which international, and
even domestic, morality is judged, must vary for different countries under widely different conditions,

Character-
istics of the
Frontiers-
men.

---

[1] R. T. Durrett, "Centenary of Kentucky," 64.

for exactly the same reasons that it must vary for
different periods of the world's history. We cannot
expect the refined virtues of a highly artificial civilization from frontiersmen who for generations have
been roughened and hardened by the same kind of
ferocious wilderness toil that once fell to the lot of
their remote barbarian ancestors.

The Kentuckian, from his clearing in the great
forest, looked with bold and greedy eyes at the
Spanish possessions, much as Markman, Goth, and
Frank had once peered through their marshy woods
at the Roman dominions. He possessed the virtues
proper to a young and vigorous race; he was tram-
melled by few misgivings as to the rights of the men
whose lands he coveted; he felt that the future was
for the stout-hearted, and not for the weakling. He
was continually hampered by the advancing civilization of which he was the vanguard, and of which his
own sons were destined to form an important part.
He rebelled against the restraints imposed by his
own people behind him exactly as he felt impelled
to attack the alien peoples in front of him. He did
not care very much what form the attack took. On
the whole he preferred that it should be avowed war,
whether waged under the stars and stripes or under
some flag new-raised by himself and his fellow-
adventurers of the border. In default of such a
struggle, he was ready to serve under alien banners,
either those of some nation at the moment hostile to
Spain, or else those of some insurgent Spanish leader.
But he was also perfectly willing to obtain by diplomacy what was denied by force of arms; and if the

United States could not or would not gain his ends for him in this manner, then he wished to make use of his own power. He was eager to enter in and take the land, even at the cost of becoming for the time being a more or less nominal vassal of Spain ; and he was ready to promise, in return for this privilege of settlement, to form a barrier state against the further encroachment of his fellows. When fettered by the checks imposed by the Central Government, he not only threatened to revolt and establish an independent government of his own, but even now and then darkly hinted that he would put this government under the protection of the very Spanish power at whose cost he always firmly intended to take his own strides towards greatness. As a matter of fact, whether he first established himself in the Spanish possessions as an outright enemy, or as a nominal friend and subject, the result was sure to be the same in the end. The only difference was that it took place sooner in one event than in the other. In both cases alike the province thus acquired was certain finally to be wrested from Spain.

The Spaniards speedily recognized in the Americans the real menace to their power in Florida, Louisiana, and Mexico. They did not, however, despair of keeping them at bay. The victories won by Galvez over both the British regulars and the Tory American settlers were fresh in their minds ; and they felt they had a chance of success even in a contest of arms. But the weapons upon which they relied most were craft and intrigue. If the Union could be broken up,

Spanish Dread of the Westerners.

or the jealousies between the States and sections
fanned into flame, there would be little chance of a
successful aggressive movement by the Americans of
any one commonwealth. The Spanish authorities
sought to achieve these ends by every species of
bribery and corrupt diplomacy. They placed even
more reliance upon the war-like confederacies of the
Creeks, Cherokees, Choctaws, and Chickasaws, thrust
in between themselves and the frontier settlements;
and while protesting to the Americans with smooth
treachery that they were striving to keep the Indians
at peace, they secretly incited them to hostilities,
and furnished them with arms and munitions of war.
The British held the Lake Posts by open exhibition of
strength, though they too were not above conniving
at treachery and allowing their agents covertly to
urge the red tribes to resist the American advance;
but the Spaniards, by preference, trusted to fraud
rather than to force.

In the last resort the question of the navigation
of the Mississippi had to be decided between the
Governments of Spain and the United
States; and it was chiefly through the   Negotia-
latter that the westerners could, indi-   tions be-
                                             tween Spain
rectly, but most powerfully, make their   and the
influence felt. In the long and intricate   United
                                             States Con-
negotiations carried on towards the close   cerning the
of the Revolutionary War between the   Free Navi-
                                             gation of
representatives of Spain, France, and the   the Missis-
United States, Spain had taken high   sippi.
ground in reference to this and to all other western
questions, and France had supported her in her de-

sire to exclude the Americans from all rights in the vast regions beyond the Alleghanies. At that time the delegates from the southern, no less than from the northern, States, in the Continental Congress, showed much weakness in yielding to this attitude of France and Spain. On the motion of those from Virginia all the delegates with the exception of those from North Carolina voted to instruct Jay, then Minister to Spain, to surrender outright the free navigation of the Mississippi. Later, when he was one of the Commissioners to treat for peace, they practically repeated the blunder by instructing Jay and his colleagues to assent to whatever France proposed. With rare wisdom and courage Jay repudiated these instructions. The chief credit for the resulting diplomatic triumph, almost as essential as the victory at Yorktown itself to our national well-being, belongs to him, and by his conduct he laid the men of the West under an obligation which they never acknowledged during his lifetime.[1]

Shortly after his return to America he was made Secretary of Foreign Affairs, and was serving as **Jay and** such when, in the spring of 1785, Don **Gardoqui.** Diego Gardoqui arrived in Philadelphia, bearing a commission from his Catholic Majesty to Congress. At this time the brilliant and restless soldier Galvez had left Louisiana and become Viceroy of Mexico, thus removing from Louisiana the one Spaniard whose energy and military capacity would have rendered him formidable to the Ameri-

[1] It is not the least of Mann Butler's good points that in his " History " he does full justice to Jay. Another Kentuckian, Mr. Thomas Marshall Green, has recently done the same in his " Spanish Conspiracy."

cans in the event of war. He was succeeded in the government of the creole province by Don Estevan Miro, already colonel of the Louisiana regiment.

Gardoqui was not an able man, although with some capacity for a certain kind of intrigue. He was a fit representative of the Spanish court, with its fundamental weakness and its impossible pretensions. He entirely misunderstood the people with whom he had to deal, and whether he was or was not himself personally honest, he based his chief hopes of success in dealing with others upon their supposed susceptibility to the influence of corruption and dishonorable intrigue. He and Jay could come to no agreement, and the negotiations were finally broken off. Before this happened, in the fall of 1786, Jay in entire good faith had taken a step which aroused furious anger in the West.[1] Like so many other statesmen of the day, he did not realize how fast Kentucky had grown, and deemed the navigation question one which would not be of real importance to the West for two decades to come. He absolutely refused to surrender our right to navigate the Mississippi; but, not regarding it as of immediate consequence, he proposed both to Congress and Gardoqui that in consideration of certain concessions by Spain we should agree to forbear to exercise this right for twenty or twenty-five years. The delegates from the northern States assented to Jay's views; those from the southern States strongly opposed them. In 1787, after a series of conferences

[1] State Dep. MSS., No. 81, vol. ii., pp. 193, 241, 285, etc. ; Reports of Sec'y John Jay.

between Jay and Gardoqui, which came to naught, the Spaniard definitely refused to entertain Jay's proposition. Even had he not refused nothing could have been done, for under the confederation a treaty had to be ratified by the votes of nine States, and there were but seven which supported the policy of Jay.

Unquestionably Jay showed less than his usual far-sightedness in this matter, but it is only fair to remember that his views were shared by **Washington and Lee** some of the greatest of American states- **agree with** men, even from Virginia. "Lighthorse **Jay.** Harry" Lee substantially agreed with them. Washington, with his customary broad vision and keen insight, realized the danger of exciting the turbulent Westerners by any actual treaty which might seem to cut off their hope of traffic down the Mississippi; but he advocated pursuing what was, except for defining the time limit, substantially the same policy under a different name, recommending that the United States should await events and for the moment neither relinquish nor push their claim to free navigation of the great river.[1] Even in Kentucky itself a few of the leading men were of the opinion that the right of free navigation would be of little real benefit during the lifetime of the existing generation.[2] It was no discredit to Jay to hold the views he did when they were shared by intelligent men of affairs who were actually in the district most

---

[1] "The Spanish Conspiracy," Thos. Marshall Green, p. 31.
[2] State Dept. MSS., Madison Papers, Caleb Wallace to Madison, Nov. 21, 1787. Wallace himself shared this view.

concerned.   He was merely somewhat slow in abandoning opinions which half a dozen years before were
held generally throughout the Union.   Nevertheless it was fortunate for the country that the southern States, headed by Virginia, were so resolute in
their opposition, and that Gardoqui, a fit representative of his government, declined to agree to a treaty
which if ratified would have benefited Spain, and
would have brought undreamed of evil upon the
United States.   Jefferson, to his credit, was very
hostile to the proposition.   As a statesman Jefferson stood for many ideas which in their actual working have proved pernicious to our country, but he
deserves well of all Americans, in the first place because of his services to science, and in the next place,
what was of far more importance, because of his
steadfast friendship for the great West, and his appreciation of its magnificent future.

As soon as the Revolutionary War came to an end
adventurers in Kentucky began to trade down the
Mississippi.   Often these men were merchants by profession, but this was not **Methods of
the River
Trade.**
necessary, for on the frontier men shifted
from one business to another very readily.
A farmer of bold heart and money-making temper
might, after selling his crop, build a flatboat, load it
with flour, bacon, salt, beef, and tobacco, and start
for New Orleans.[1]   He faced dangers from the
waters, from the Indians, from lawless whites of his
own race, and from the Spaniards themselves.   The
New Orleans customs officials were corrupt,[2] and the

[1] McAfee MSS.   [2] Do.

regulations very absurd and oppressive. The policy of the Spanish home government in reference to the trade was unsettled and wavering, and the attitude towards it of the Governors of Louisiana changed with their varying interests, beliefs, caprices, and apprehensions. In consequence the conditions of the trade were so uncertain that to follow it was like indulging in a lottery venture. Special privileges were allowed certain individuals who had made private treaties with, or had bribed, the Spanish officials; and others were enabled to smuggle their goods in under various pretences, and by various devices; while the traders who were without such corrupt influence or knowledge found this river commerce hazardous in the extreme. It was small wonder that the Kentuckians should chafe under such arbitrary and unequal restraints, and should threaten to break through them by force.[1]

The most successful traders were of course those who contrived to establish relations with some one in New Orleans, or perhaps in Natchez, who would act as their agent or correspondent. The profits from a successful trip made amends for much disaster, and enabled the trader to repeat his adventure on a larger scale. Thus, among the papers of George Rogers Clark there is a letter from one of his friends who was living in Kaskaskia in 1784, and was engaged in the river trade.[2] The letter was evidently to the writer's father, beginning "My dear daddy." It describes how he had started on one trip to New

[1] Va. State Papers, iv., 630.
[2] Draper MSS. Letter of John Williams, June 20, 1784.

Orleans, but had been wrecked; how, nothing daunted, he had tried again with a cargo of forty-two beeves, which he sold in New Orleans for what he deemed the good sum of $738; and how he was about to try his luck once more, buying a bateau and thirty bushels of salt, enough to pickle two hundred beeves.

The traders never could be certain when their boats would be seized and their goods confiscated by some Spanish officer; nor when they started could they tell whether they would or would not find when they reached New Orleans that the Spanish authorities had declared the navigation closed. In 1783 and the early part of 1784 traders were descending the Mississippi without overt resistance from the Spaniards, and were selling their goods at a profit in New Orleans. In midsummer of 1784 the navigation of the river was suddenly and rigorously closed. In 1785 it was again partially opened; so that we find traders purchasing flour in Louisville at twenty-four shillings a hundred-weight, and carrying it down stream to sell in New Orleans at thirty dollars a barrel. By summer of the same year the Spaniards were again shutting off traffic, being in great panic over a rumored piratical advance by the frontiersmen, to oppose which they were mustering their troops and making ready their artillery.[1]

Among the articles the frontier traders received for their goods horses held a high place.[2] The

---

[1] Draper MSS.   J. Girault to William Clark, July 22, 1784 ; May 23, 1785 ; July 2, 1785 ; certificate of French merchants testified to by Miro in 1785,   [2] *Do.*   Girault to Clark July 9, 1784.

horse trade was risky, as in driving them up to Kentucky many were drowned, or played out, or were stolen by the Indians; but as picked horses and mares cost but twenty dollars a head in Louisiana and were sold at a hundred dollars a head in the United States, the losses had to be very large to eat up the profits.

The French Creoles, who carried on much of the river trade and who lived some under the American Creole and some under the Spanish flag, of course Traders. suffered as much as either Americans or Spaniards. Often these Creoles loaded their canoes with a view to trading with the Indians, rather than at New Orleans. Whether this was so or not, those officially in the service of the two powers soon grew as zealous in oppressing one another as in oppressing men of different nationalities. Thus in 1787 a Vincennes Creole, having loaded his pirogue with goods to the value of two thousand dollars, sent it down to trade with the Indians near the Chickasaw Bluffs. Here it was seized by the Creole commandant of the Spanish post at the Arkansas. The goods were confiscated and the men imprisoned. The owner appealed in vain to the commandant, who told him that he was ordered by the Spanish authorities to seize all persons who trafficked on the Mississippi below the mouth of the Ohio, inasmuch as Spain claimed both banks of the river; and when he made his way to New Orleans and appealed to Miro he was summarily dismissed with a warning that a repetition of the offence would ensure his being sent to the mines of Brazil.[1]

[1] State Dept. MSS., No. 150 vol. iii., p. 519. Letter of Joseph St. Mary, Vincennes, August 23, 1788.

Outrages of this kind, continually happening alike
to Americans and to Creoles under American protection, could not have been tamely borne by
any self-respecting people.   The fierce
and hardy frontiersmen were goaded to
anger by them, and were ready to take

Retaliation
of the
Frontiers-
men.

part in, or at least to connive at, any piece of lawless
retaliation.   Such an act of revenge was committed
by Clark at Vincennes, as one result of his ill-starred
expedition against the Wabash Indians in 1786.
As already said, when his men mutinied and refused
to march against the Indians, most of them returned
home ; but he kept enough to garrison the Vincennes
fort.   Unpaid, and under no regular authority,
these men plundered the French inhabitants and
were a terror to the peaceable, as well as to the lawless, Indians.   Doubtless Clark desired to hold them
in readiness as much for a raid on the Spanish possessions as for a defence against the Indians.   Nevertheless they did some service in preventing any
actual assault on the place by the latter, while they
prevented any possible uprising by the French,
though the harassed Creoles, under this added burden of military lawlessness, in many instances
accepted the offers made them by the Spaniards
and passed over to the French villages on the
west side of the Mississippi.

Before Clark left Vincennes, he summoned a
court of his militia officers, and got them to sanction the seizure of a boat loaded with
valuable goods, the property of a Creole
trader from the Spanish possessions.[1]   The
avowed reason for this act was revenge for the

Clark
Seizes a
Spanish
Boat.

wrongs perpetrated in like manner by the Spaniards on the American traders ; and this doubtless was the controlling motive in Clark's mind ; but it was also true that the goods thus confiscated were of great service to Clark in paying his mutinous and irregularly employed troops, and that this fact, too, had influence with him.

The more violent and lawless among the backwoodsmen of Kentucky were loud in exultation

The Backwoodsmen Approve Clark's Deed.

over this deed. They openly declared that it was not merely an act of retaliation on the Spaniards, but also a warning that, if they did not let the Americans trade down the river, they would not be allowed to trade up it; and that the troops who garrisoned Vincennes offered an earnest of what the frontiersmen would do in the way of raising an army of conquest if the Spaniards continued to wrong them.[1] They defied the Continental Congress and the seaboard States to interfere with them. They threatened to form an independent government, if the United States did not succor and countenance them. They taunted the eastern men with knowing as little of the West as Great Britain knew of America. They even threatened that they would, if necessary, re-join the British dominions, and boasted that, if united to Canada, they would some day be able themselves to conquer the Atlantic Commonwealths.[2]

Both the Federal and the Virginia authorities were

[1] Draper MSS. Minutes of Court-Martial, Summoned by George Rogers Clark, at Vincennes, October 18, 1786,

[2] State Dept. MSS. Reports of John Jay, No. 124, vol. iii., pp. 31, 37, 44, 48, 53, 56, etc.

much alarmed and angered, less at the insult to Spain than at the threat of establishing a separate government in the West.

The Government Authorities Disapprove.

From the close of the revolution the Virginian government had been worried by the separatist movements in Kentucky. In 1784 two " stirrers-up of sedition " had been fined and imprisoned, and an adherent of the Virginian government, writing from Kentucky, mentioned that one of the worst effects of the Indian inroads was to confine the settlers to the stations, which were hot-beds of sedition and discord, besides excuses for indolence and rags.[1] The people who distrusted the frontiersmen complained that among them were many knaves and outlaws from every State in the Union, who flew to the frontier as to a refuge ; while even those who did not share this distrust admitted that the fact that the people in Kentucky came from many different States helped to make them discontented with Virginia.[2]

In Georgia the conditions were much as they were on the Ohio. Georgia was a frontier State, with the ambitions and the lawlessness of the frontier; and the backwoodsmen felt towards her as they did towards no other member of the old Thirteen. Soon after Clark

Georgia and the Frontiersmen.

established his garrison in Vincennes, various inflammatory letters were circulated in the western country, calling for action against both the Central Govern-

---

[1] Va. State Papers, III., pp. 585, 589.
[2] Draper MSS. Clark Papers, Walter Darrell to William Fleming, April 14, 1783.

ment and the Spaniards, and appealing for sympathy and aid both to the Georgians and to Sevier's insurrectionary State of Franklin. Among others, a Kentuckian wrote from Louisville to Georgia, bitterly complaining about the failure of the United States to open the Mississippi; denouncing the Federal Government in extravagant language, and threatening hostilities against the Spaniards, and a revolt against the Continental Congress.[1] This letter was intercepted, and, of course, increased still more the suspicion felt about Clark's motives, for though Clark denied that he had actually seen the letter, he was certainly cognizant of its purport, and approved the movement which lay behind it.[2] One of his fellow Kentuckians, writing about him at this time, remarks: " Clark is playing hell . . . eternally drunk and yet full of design. I told him he would be hanged. He laughed, and said he would take refuge among the Indians."[3]

The Governor of Virginia issued a proclamation disavowing all Clark's acts.[4] A committee of the Kentucky Convention, which included the leaders of Kentucky's political thought and life, examined into the matter,[5] and gave Clark's version of the facts, but reprobated and disowned his course. Some of the members of this Convention were afterwards identified with various separatist movements, and skirted

Public disavowal of Clark's Actions.

[1] *Do.*, Letter of Thomas Green to the Governor of Georgia, December 23, 1786.

[2] Green's " Spanish Conspiracy," p. 74.

[3] Va. State Papers, IV., 202, condensed.

[4] Draper MSS. Proclamation of Edmund Randolph, March 4, 1787.

[5] State Dept. MSS., No. 71, vol. ii., p. 503. Report of Dec. 19, 1786.

the field of perilous intrigue with a foreign power; but they recognized the impossibility of countenancing such mere buccaneering lawlessness as Clark's; and not only joined with their colleagues in denouncing it to the Virginia Government, but warned the latter that Clark's habits were such as to render him unfit longer to be trusted with work of importance.[1]

The rougher spirits, all along the border of course sympathized with Clark. In this same year 1786, the goods and boats of a trader from the Cumberland district were seized and confiscated by the Spanish commandant at Natchez.[2] At first the Cumberland Indian-fighters determined to retaliate in kind, at no matter what cost; but the wiser among their leaders finally "persuaded them not to imitate their friends of Kentucky, and to wait patiently until some advice could be received from Congress." One of these wise leaders, a representative from the Cumberland district in the North Carolina legislature, in writing to the North Carolina delegates to the Continental Congress, after dwelling on the necessity of acquiring the right to the navigation of the Mississippi, added with sound common-sense : "You may depend on our exertions to keep all things quiet, and we agree entirely with you that if our people are once let loose there will be no stopping them, and that acts of retaliation poison the mind and give a licen-

Experience of a Cumberland Trader.

---

[1] Green, p. 78.

[2] State Dept. MSS., No. 124, vol. iii. Papers transmitted by Blount, Hawkins, and Ashe, March 29, 1787, including deposition of Thomas Amis, Nov. 13, 1786. Letter from Fayettsville, Dec. 29, 1786, etc.

tiousness to manners that can with great difficulty be restrained." Washington was right in his belief that in this business there was as much to be feared from the impetuous turbulence of the backwoodsmen as from the hostility of the Spaniards.

The news of Jay's attempted negotiations with Gardoqui, distorted and twisted, arrived right on top **Wrath over** of these troubles, and threw the already **Jay's Nego-** excited backwoods men into a frenzy. **tiations.** There was never any real danger that Jay's proposition would be adopted; but the Westerners did not know this. In all the considerable settlements on the western waters, committees of correspondence were elected to remonstrate and petition Congress against any agreement to close the Mississippi.[1] Even those who had no sympathy with the separatist movement warned Congress that if any such agreement were entered into it would probably entail the loss of the western country.[2]

There was justification for the original excitement; there was none whatever for its continuance after **Inconsisten-** Jay's final report to Congress, in April, **cies of the** 1787,[3] and after the publication by Con- **Frontiers-** gress of its resolve never to abandon its **men.** claim to the Mississippi. Jay in this report took what was unquestionably the rational position. He urged that the United States was undoubtedly in the right; and that it should either insist upon a treaty

[1] Madison MSS. Letter of Caleb Wallace, Nov. 12, 1787.

[2] State Dept. MSS., No. 56. Symmes to the President of Congress, May 3, 1787.

[3] W. H. Trescott, " Diplomatic History of the Administrations of Washington and Adams," p. 46.

with Spain, by which all conflicting claims would be reconciled, or else simply claim the right, and if Spain refused to grant it promptly declare war.

So far he was emphatically right. His cool and steadfast insistence on our rights, and his clearsighted recognition of the proper way to obtain them, contrasted well with the mixed turbulence and foolishness of the Westerners who denounced him. They refused to give up the Mississippi; and yet they also refused to support the party to which Jay belonged, and therefore refused to establish a government strong enough to obtain their rights by open force.

But Jay erred when he added, as he did, that there was no middle course possible; that we must either treat or make war. It was undoubtedly to our discredit, and to our temporary harm, that we refused to follow either course; it showed the existence of very undesirable national qualities, for it showed that we were loud in claiming rights which we lacked the resolution and foresight to enforce. Nevertheless, as these undesirable qualities existed, it was the part of a wise statesman to recognize their existence and do the best he could in spite of them. The best course to follow under such circumstances was to do nothing until the national fibre hardened, and this was the course which Washington advocated.

In this summer of 1787 there rose to public prominence in the western country a man whose influence upon it was destined to be malign in intention rather than in actual fact. James Wilkinson, by birth a Marylander, came to Kentucky in 1784. He had done his duty respecta- Wilkinson Rises to Prominence.

bly as a soldier in the Revolutionary War, for he possessed sufficient courage and capacity to render average service in subordinate positions, though at a later date he showed abject inefficiency as commander of an army. He was a good-looking, plausible, energetic man, gifted with a taste for adventure, with much proficiency in low intrigue, and with a certain address in influencing and managing bodies of men. He also spoke and wrote well, according to the rather florid canons of the day. In character he can only be compared to Benedict Arnold, though he entirely lacked Arnold's ability and brilliant courage. He had no conscience and no scruples; he had not the slightest idea of the meaning of the word honor; he betrayed his trust from the basest motives, and he was too inefficient to make his betrayal effective. He was treacherous to the Union while it was being formed and after it had been formed; and his crime was aggravated by the sordid meanness of his motives, for he eagerly sought opportunities to barter his own infamy for money. In all our history there is no more despicable character.

Wilkinson was a man of broken fortune when he came to the West. In three years he made a good **He Trades** position for himself, in matters commercial **to New** and political, and his restless, adventurous **Orleans.** nature, and thirst for excitement and intrigue, prompted him to try the river trade, with its hazards and its chances of great gain. In June, 1787, he went down the Mississippi to New Orleans with a loaded flat-boat, and sold his cargo at a high profit, thanks to the understanding he immediately established with Miro.[1] Doubtless he started with the full intention of entering into some kind of corrupt arrangement with the Louisiana authorities, leaving the precise nature of the arrangement to be decided by events.

The relations that he so promptly established with the Spaniards were both corrupt and treacherous; that is, he undoubtedly gave and took bribes, and promised to intrigue against his own country for pecuniary reward; but exactly what the different agreements were, and exactly how far he tried or intended to fulfil them, is, and must always remain, uncertain. He was so ingrainedly venal, treacherous, and mendacious that nothing he said or wrote can be accepted as true, and no sentiments which he at any time professed can be accepted as those he really felt. He and the leading Louisiana Spaniards had close mercantile relations, in which the governments of neither were interested, and by which the governments of both were in all probability defrauded. He persuaded the Spaniards to give him money for using his influence to separate the West from the Union, which was one of the chief objects of Spanish diplomacy.[2] He was obliged to try to earn the money by leading the separatist intrigues in Kentucky, but it is doubtful if he ever had enough straightforwardness in him to be a thoroughgoing villain. All he cared for was the money; if he could not get it otherwise, he was quite willing to do any damage he could to his country, even when

[1] *Wilkinson's Memoirs*, ii., 112.
[2] *History of Louisiana*, Charles Gayarré, iii., 198.

he was serving it in a high military position. But if it was easier, he was perfectly willing to betray the people who had bribed him.

However he was an adept in low intrigue; and though he speedily became suspected by all honest men, he covered his tracks so well that it was not until after his death, and after the Spanish archives had been explored, that his guilt was established.

His Corrupt Intrigues with the Spaniards.

He returned to Kentucky after some months' absence. He had greatly increased his reputation, and as substantial results of his voyage he showed permits to trade, and some special and exclusive commercial privileges, such as supplying the Mexican market with tobacco, and depositing it in the King's store at New Orleans. The Kentuckians were much excited by what he had accomplished. He bought goods himself and received goods from other merchants on commission; and a year after his first venture he sent a flotilla of heavy-laden flat-boats down the Mississippi, and disposed of their contents at a high profit in New Orleans.

The power this gave Wilkinson, the way he had obtained it, and the use he made of it, gave an impetus to the separatist party in Kentucky. He was by no means the only man, however, who was at this time engaged in the river trade to Louisiana; nor were his advantages over his commercial rivals as marked as he alleged. They, too, had discovered that the Spanish officials could be bribed to shut their eyes to smuggling, and that citizens of Natchez could be

The River Trade and the Separatist Spirit.

hired to receive property shipped thither as being theirs, so that it might be admitted on payment of twenty-five per cent. duty. Merchants gathered quantities of flour and bacon, but especially of tobacco, at Louisville, and thence shipped it in flatboats to Natchez, where it was received by their correspondents; and keel boats sometimes made the return journey, though the horses, cattle, and negro slaves were generally taken to Kentucky overland.[1] All these traders naturally felt the Spanish control of the navigation, and the intermittent but always possible hostility of the Spanish officials, to be peculiarly irksome. They were, as a rule, too short-sighted to see that the only permanent remedy for their troubles was their own absorption into a solid and powerful Union. Therefore they were always ready either to join a movement against Spain, or else to join one which seemed to promise the acquisition of special privileges from Spain.

The separatist feeling, and the desire to sunder the West from the East, and join hands with Spain or Britain, were not confined to Kentucky. Robertson In one shape or another, and with varying Talks of intensity, separatist agitations took place Disunion. in all portions of the West. In Cumberland, on the Holston, among the western mountains of Virginia proper, and in Georgia—which was practically a frontier community—there occurred manifestations of the separatist spirit. A curious feature of these various agitations was the slight extent to which a

[1] Draper MSS. John Williams to William Clark, New Orleans, Feb. 11, 1789 ; Girault to *Do.*, July 26, 1788, from Natchez ; *Do.* to *Do.*, Dec. 5, 1788 ; receipt of D. Brashear at Louisville, May 23, 1785.

separatist movement in any one of these localities depended upon or sympathized with a similar movement in any other. The national feeling among the separatists was so slight that the very communities which wished to break off from the Atlantic States were also quite indifferent to the deeds and fates of one another. The only bond among them was their tendency to break loose from the Central Government. The settlers on the banks of the Cumberland felt no particular interest in the struggle of those on the head-waters of the Tennessee to establish the State of Franklin; and the Kentuckians were indifferent to the deeds of both. In a letter written in 1788 to the Creek Chief McGillivray, Robertson alludes to the Holston men and the Georgians in precisely the language he might have used in speaking of foreign nations. He evidently took as a matter of course their waging war on their own account against, and making peace with, the Cherokees and Creeks, and betrayed little concern as to the outcome, one way or the other.

In this same letter,[1] Robertson frankly set forth his belief that the West should separate from the Union and join some foreign power, writing: "In all probability we can not long remain in our present state, and if the British, or any commercial nation which may be in possession of the Mississippi, would furnish us with trade and receive our produce, there cannot be a doubt but the people on the west side of the Apalachian mountains will open their eyes to their

Robert-
son's Letter
to Mac-
Gillivray.

---

[1] Robertson MSS., James Robertson to Alexander McGillivray, Nashville, Aug. 3, 1788.

real interests." At the same time Sevier was writing to Gardoqui, offering to put his insurrectionary
State of Franklin, then at its last gasp, under the
protection of Spain.[1]

Robertson spoke with indifference as to whether
the nation with which the Southerners allied themselves should happen to be Spain or Britain.
As a matter of fact, most of the intrigues   **British
Intrigue.**
carried on were with or against Spain ; but
in the fall of 1788 an abortive effort was made by a
British agent to arouse the Kentuckians against both
the Spaniards and the National Government, in the
interest of Great Britain. This agent was Conolly,
the unsavory hero of Lord Dunmore's war. He
went to Louisville, visited two or three prominent
men, and laid bare to them his plans. As he met
with no encouragement whatever, he speedily abandoned his efforts, and when the people got wind of
his design they threatened to mob him, while the
officers of the Continental troops made ready to
arrest him if his plans bore fruit, so that he was glad
to leave the country.[2]

These movements all aimed at a complete independence, but there were others which aimed merely
at separation from the parent States. The
efforts of Kentucky and Franklin in this   **Other
Separatist**
direction must be treated by themselves ;   **Movements.**
but those that were less important may be
glanced at in passing. The people in western Vir-

[1] Gardoqui MSS., Sevier to Gardoqui, Sept. 12, 1788.
[2] Do. Gardoqui to Florida Blanca, Jan. 12, 1789, inclosing a letter from
Col. George Moreau. See Green, p. 300. Also State Dept. MSS., No.
150, vol. iii., St. Clair to John Jay, Dec. 15, 1788. This letter and many
others of St. Clair are given in W. H. Smith's " St. Clair Papers."

ginia, as early as the spring of 1785, wished to erect themselves into a separate State, under Federal authority. Their desire was to separate from Virginia in peace and friendship, and to remain in close connection with the Union. A curious feature of the petition which they forwarded to the Continental Congress, was their proposition to include in the new State the inhabitants of the Holston territory, so that it would have taken in what is now West Virginia proper,[1] and also eastern Tennessee and Kentucky.

The originators of this particular movement meant to be friendly with Virginia, but of course friction was bound to follow. The later stages of the agitation, or perhaps it would be more correct to say the agitations, that sprang out of it, were marked by bitter feelings between the leaders of the movement and the Virginia authorities. Finding no heed paid to their requests for separation, some of the more extreme separatists threatened to refuse to pay taxes to Virginia; while the Franklin people proposed to unite with them into a new State, without regard to the wishes of Virginia or of North Carolina. Restless Arthur Campbell was one of the leaders of the separatists, and went so far as to acknowledge the authorship of the "State of Franklin," and to become one of its privy councillors, casting off his allegiance to the Virginian Government.[2] However, the whole movement soon collapsed, the collapse being inevitable when once it became evident that the Franklin experiment was doomed to failure.

[1] State Dept. MSS., Memorials, etc., No. 48, Thos. Cumings, on behalf of the deputies of Washington County, to the President of Congress, April 7, 1785.   [2] Va. State Papers, IV., pp. 5, 31, 32, 75, etc.

The West was thus seething with separatist agitations throughout the time of Gradoqui's residence as Spanish Envoy in America; and both Gardoqui and Miro, who was Governor of Louisiana all through these years, entered actively into intrigues with the more prominent separatist leaders.

Gardoqui's
Residence
in the
United
States.

Miro was a man of some ability, and Martin Navarro, the Spanish Intendant of Louisiana, possessed more; but they served a government almost imbecile in its fatuity. They both realized that Louisiana could be kept in possession of Spain only by making it a flourishing and populous province, and they begged that the Spanish authorities would remove the absurd commercial restrictions which kept it poor. But no heed was paid to their requests, and when they ventured to relax the severity of the regulations, as regards both the trade down the Mississippi and the sea-trade to Philadelphia, they were reprimanded and forced to reverse their policy. This was done at the instance of Gardoqui, who was jealous of the Louisiana authorities, and showed a spirit of rivalry towards them. Each side believed, probably with justice, that the other was influenced by corrupt motives.

Miro and
Navarro.

Miro and Navarro were right in urging a liberal commercial policy. They were right also in recognizing the Americans as the enemies of the Spanish power. They dwelt on the peril, not only to Louisiana but to New Mexico, certain to arise from the neighborhood of the backwoodsmen, whom they described as dangerous alike because of their poverty, their ambition, their restlessness, and their recklessness.[1]   They were at their wits' ends to know how to check these energetic foes.   They urgently asked for additional regular troops to increase the strength of the Spanish garrison.   They kept the creole militia organized.   But they relied mainly on keeping the southern Indians hostile to the Americans, on inviting the Americans to settle in Louisiana and become subjects of Spain, and on intriguing with the western settlements for the dissolution of the Union.   The Kentuckians, the settlers on the Holston and Cumberland, and the Georgians were the Americans with whom they had most friction and closest connection.   The Georgians, it is true, were only indirectly interested in the navigation question; but they claimed that the boundaries of Georgia ran west to the Mississippi, and that much of the eastern bank of the great river, including the fertile Yazoo lands, was theirs.

The Indians naturally sided with the Spaniards against the Americans; for the Americans were as eager to seize the possessions of Creek and Cherokee as they were to invade the dominions of the Catholic King.   Their friendship was sedulously fostered by the Spaniards.   Great councils were held with them, and their chiefs were bribed and flattered.   Every effort was made to prevent them from dealing with any traders who were not in the Spanish interest; New Orleans, Natchez, Mobile, and Pensacola were

Spaniards Incite the Indians to War.

[1] Guyarré, p. 190.   He was the first author who gave a full account of the relations between Miro and Wilkinson, and of the Spanish intrigues to dissever the West from the Union.

all centres for the Indian trade.   They were liberally
furnished with arms and munitions of war.   Finally
the Spaniards deliberately and treacherously incited
the Indians to war against the Americans, while
protesting to the latter that they were striving to
keep the savages at peace.   In answer to protests of
Robertson, setting forth that the Spaniards were
inciting the Indians to harry the Cumberland settlers,
both Miro and Gardoqui made him solemn denials.
Miro wrote him, in 1783, that so far from assisting
the Indians to war, he had been doing what he
could to induce McGillivray and the Creeks to
make peace, and that he would continue to urge
them not to trouble the settlers.[1]   Gardoqui, in
1788, wrote even more explicitly, saying that he was
much concerned over the reported outrages of the
savages, but was greatly surprised to learn that the
settlers suspected the Government of Spain of
fomenting the warfare, which, he assured Robertson,
was so far from the truth that the King was really
bent on treating the United States in general, and
the West in particular, with all possible benevolence
and generosity.[2]   Yet in 1786, midway between the
dates when these two letters were written, Miro, in
a letter to the Captain-General of the Floridas, set
forth that the Creeks, being desirous of driving
back the American frontiersmen by force of arms,
and knowing that this could be done only after
bloodshed, had petitioned him for fifty barrels of

[1] Robertson MSS., Miro to Robertson, New Orleans, April 20, 1783.
[2] Gardoqui MSS., Gardoqui to "Col. Elisha Robeson" of Cumberland,
April 18, 1788.

gunpowder and bullets to correspond, and that he had ordered the Governor of Pensacola to furnish McGillivray, their chief, these munitions of war, with all possible secrecy and caution, so that it should not become known.[1]   The Governor of Pensacola shortly afterwards related the satisfaction the Creeks felt at receiving the powder and lead, and added that he would have to furnish them additional supplies from time to time, as the war progressed, and that he would exercise every precaution so that the Americans might have no "just cause of complaint." [2]   There is an unconscious and somewhat gruesome humor in this official belief that the Americans could have "no just cause" for anger so long as the Spaniards' treachery was concealed.

Throughout these years the Spaniards thus secretly supplied the Creeks with the means of waging war Spanish   on the Americans, claiming all the time Duplicity.   that the Creeks were their vassals and that the land occupied by the southern Indians generally belonged to Spain and not to the United States.[3] They also kept their envoys busy among the Chickasaws, Choctaws, and even the Cherokees.

In fact, until the conclusion of Pinckney's treaty, the Spaniards of Louisiana pursued as a settled policy this· plan of inciting the Indians to war against the Americans.   Generally they confined

[1] *Do.*, Miro to Galvez, June 28, 1786, "que summistrase estas municiones à McGillivray Jefe principal to las Talapuches con toda la reserve y cantata posible de modo que ne se transiendiese la mano de este socorro."

[2] *Do.*, "sera necessaria la mayor precaucion, y maña para contenerle ciñendose à la suministracion de polvora, balas y efectos de treta con la cantata posible para no dar a los Americanos justos motivos de gueya."

[3] *Do.*

themselves to secretly furnishing the savages with guns, powder, and lead, and endeavoring to unite the tribes in a league; but on several occasions they openly gave them arms, when they were forced to act hurriedly. As late as 1794 the Flemish Baron de Carondelet, a devoted servant of Spain, and one of the most determined enemies of the Americans, instructed his lieutenants to fit out war parties of Chickasaws, Creeks, and Cherokees, to harass a fort the Americans had built near the mouth of the Ohio. Carondelet wrote to the Home Government that the Indians formed the best defence on which Louisiana could rely. By this time the Spaniards and English realized that, instead of showing hostility to one another, it behooved them to unite against the common foe; and their agents in Canada and Louisiana were beginning to come to an understanding. In another letter Carondelet explained that the system adopted by Lord Dorchester and the English officials in Canada in dealing with the savages was the same as that which he had employed, both the Spaniards and the British having found them the most powerful means with which to oppose the American advance. By the expenditure of a few thousand dollars, wrote the Spanish Governor,[1] he could always

[1] Draper Collection, Spanish MSS. State Documents.   Baron de Carondelet to Manuel Gayrso de Lemos, Aug. 20, 1794; Carondelet to Duke Alcudia, Sept. 25, 1795; Carondelet's Letter of July 9, 1795; Carondelet's Letter of Sept. 27, 1793.   These Spanish documents form a very important part of the manuscripts in the Library of the State Historical Society of Wisconsin.   I was able to get translations of them through the great courtesy of Mr. Reuben Gold Thwaites, the Secretary of the Society, to whom I must again render my acknowledgments for the generosity with which he has helped me.

rouse the southern tribes to harry the settlers, while at the same time covering his deeds so effectually that the Americans could not point to any specific act of which to complain.

There was much turbulence and some treachery exhibited by individual frontiersmen in their dealings with Spain, and the Americans of the Mississippi valley showed a strong tendency to win their way to the mouth of the river and to win the right to settle on its banks by sheer force of arms; but the American Government and its authorized representatives behaved with a straightforward and honorable good faith which offered a striking contrast to the systematic and deliberate duplicity and treachery of the Spanish Crown and the Spanish Governors. In truth, the Spaniards were the weakest, and were driven to use the pet weapons of weakness in opposing their stalwart and masterful foes. They were fighting against their doom, and they knew it. Already they had begun to fear, not only for Louisiana and Florida, but even for sultry Mexico and far-away golden California. It was hard, wrote one of the ablest of the Spanish Governors, to gather forces enough to ward off attacks from adventurers so hardy that they could go two hundred leagues at a stretch, or live six months in the wilderness, needing to carry nothing save some corn-meal, and trusting for everything solely to their own long rifles.

Next to secretly rousing the Indians, the Spaniards placed most reliance on intriguing with the Westerners, in the effort to sunder them from the seaboard

(Marginal note: Spanish Fear of the Americans.)

Americans. They also at times thought to bar the
American advance by allowing the frontiersmen
to come into their territory and settle on
condition of becoming Spanish subjects.   **Spaniards
Invite
Americans
to Become
Colonists.**
They hoped to make of these favored settlers a barrier against the rest of their kinsfolk. It was a foolish hope. A wild and
hardy race of rifle-bearing freemen, so intolerant of
restraint that they fretted under the slight bands
which held them to their brethren, were sure to
throw off the lightest yoke the Catholic King could
lay upon them, when once they gathered strength.
Under no circumstances, even had they profited by
Spanish aid against their own people, would the
Westerners have remained allied or subject to the
Spaniards longer than the immediate needs of the
moment demanded. At the bottom the Spaniards
knew this, and their encouragement of American immigration was fitful and faint-hearted.

Many Americans, however, were themselves eager
to enter into some arrangement of the kind; whether
as individual settlers, or, more often, as companies who
wished to form little colonies. Their eagerness in this
matter caused much concern to many of the Federal-
ists of the eastern States, who commented with bitterness upon the light-hearted manner in which these
settlers forsook their native land, and not only for-
swore their allegiance to it, but bound themselves to
take up arms against it in event of war. These critics
failed to understand that the wilderness dwellers of
that day, to whom the National Government was little more than a name, and the Union but a new idea,

could not be expected to pay much heed to the
imaginary line dividing one waste space from
another, and that, after all, their patriotism was dor-
mant, not dead.   Moreover, some of the Easterners
were as blind as the Spaniards themselves to the inevitable outcome of such settlements as those proposed, and were also alarmed at the mere natural
movement of the population, fearing lest it might result in crippling the old States, and in laying the
foundation of a new and possibly hostile country.
They themselves had not yet grasped the national
idea, and could not see that the increase in power of
any one quarter of the land, or the addition to it of
any new unsettled territory, really raised by so much
the greatness of every American.   However, there
was one point on which the more far-seeing of these
critics were right.   They urged that it would be better for the country not to try to sell the public land
speedily in large tracts, but to grant it to actual settlers in such quantity as they could use.[1]

The different propositions to settle large colonies
in the Spanish possessions came to naught, although
quite a number of backwoodsmen settled
there individually or in small bands.   One
great obstacle to the success of any such
movement was the religious intolerance of
the Spaniards.   Not only were they bigoted
adherents of the Church of Rome, but their ecclesiastical authorities were cautioned to exercise over all
laymen a supervision and control to which the few
Catholics among the American backwoodsmen would

Failure of These Coloniza- tion Schemes.

[1] St. Clair to Jay, Dec. 13, 1788.

have objected quite as strenuously as the Protestants. It is true that in trying to induce immigration they often promised religious freedom, but when they came to execute this promise they explained that it merely meant that the new-comers would not be compelled to profess the Roman Catholic faith, but that they would not be allowed the free exercise of their own religion, nor permitted to build churches nor pay ministers. This was done with the express purpose of weakening their faith, and rendering it easy to turn them from it, and the Spaniards brought Irish priests into the country and placed them among the American settlers with the avowed object of converting them.[1] Such toleration naturally appealed very little to men who were accustomed to a liberty as complete in matters ecclesiastical as in matters civil. When the Spanish authorities, at Natchez, or elsewhere, published edicts interfering with the free exercise of the Protestant religion, many of the settlers left,[2] while in regions remote from the Spanish centres of government the edicts were quietly disobeyed or ignored.

One of the many proposed colonies ultimately resulted in the founding of a town which to this day bears the name of New Madrid. This particular scheme originated in the fertile brain of one Col. George Morgan, a native of New Jersey, but long engaged in trading on the Mississippi. He originally organized a company to acquire lands under the United States, but meeting

Founding of New Madrid.

---

[1] Guyarré, III., 181, 200, 202.
[2] Va. State Papers, IV., 30.

with little response to his proposition from the Continental Congress, in 1788 he turned to Spain. With Gardoqui, who was then in New York, he was soon on a footing of intimacy, as their letters show; for these include invitations to dinner, to attend commencement at Princeton, to visit one another, and the like. The Spainard, a cultivated man, was pleased at being thrown in with an adventurer who was a college graduate and a gentleman; for many of the would-be colonizers were needy ne'er-do-wells, who were anxious either to borrow money, or else to secure a promise of freedom from arrest for debt when they should move to the new country. Morgan's plans were on a magnificent scale. He wished a tract of land as large as a principality on the west bank of the Mississippi. This he proposed to people with tens of thousands of settlers, whom he should govern under the commission of the King of Spain. Gardoqui entered into the plan with enthusiasm, but obstacles and delays of all kinds were encountered, and the dwindling outcome was the emigration of a few families of frontiersmen, and the founding of a squalid hamlet named after the Iberian capital.[1]

Another adventurer who at this time proposed to found a colony in Spanish terrritory was no less a Clark's person than George Rogers Clark. Clark Proposal. had indulged in something very like piracy at the expense of Spanish subjects but eighteen months previously. He was ready at any time to

[1] Gardoqui MSS., Gardoqui to Morgan, Sept. 2, 1788. Morgan to Gardoqui, Aug. 30, 1788. Letters of Sept. 9, 1788, Sept. 12, 1788; Gardoqui to Miro, Oct. 4, 1788, to Floridablanca, June 28, 1789. Letter to Gardoqui, Jan. 22, 1788.

lead the Westerners to the conquest of Louisiana; and a few years later he did his best to organize a freebooting expedition against New Orleans in the name of the French Revolutionary Government. But he was quite willing to do his fighting on behalf of Spain, instead of against her; for by this time he was savage with anger and chagrin at the indifference and neglect with which the Virginian and Federal Governments had rewarded his really great services. He wrote to Gardoqui in the spring of 1788, boasting of his feats of arms in the past, bitterly complaining of the way he had been treated, and offering to lead a large colony to settle in the Spanish dominions; for, he said, he had become convinced that neither property nor character was safe under a government so weak as that of the United States, and he therefore wished to put himself at the disposal of the King of Spain.[1] Nothing came of this proposal.

Another proposal which likewise came to nothing, is noteworthy because of the men who made it, and because of its peculiar nature. The pre- posers were all Kentuckians. Among them were Wilkinson, one Benjamin Sebastian, whom the Spaniards pensioned in the same manner they did Wilkinson, John Brown, the Kentucky delegate in Congress, and Harry Innes, the Attorney-General of Kentucky. All were more or less identified both with the obscure separatist movements in that commonwealth, and with the legit-

The Pro- posal of Wilkinson, Brown, and Innes.

[1] Gardoqui MSS., Clark to Gardoqui, Falls of the Ohio, March 15, 1788.

imate agitation for statehood into which some of these movements insensibly merged. In the spring of 1789 they proposed to Gardoqui to enter into an agreement somewhat similar to the one he had made with Morgan. But they named as the spot where they wished to settle the lands on the east bank of the Mississippi, in the neighborhood of the Yazoo, and they urged as a reason for granting the lands that they were part of the territory in dispute between Spain and the United States, and that the new settlers would hold them under the Spanish King, and would defend them against the Americans.[1]

This country was claimed by, and finally awarded to, the United States, and claimed by the State of Georgia in particular. It was here that the adventurers proposed to erect a barrier State which should be vassal to Spain, one of the chief purposes of the settlement being to arrest the Americans' advance. They thus deliberately offered to do all the damage they could to their own country, if the foreign country would give them certain advantages. The apologists for these separatist leaders often advance the excuse—itself not a weighty one—that they at least deserved well of their own section; but Wilkinson and his associates proposed a plan which was not only hostile to the interests of the American nation as a whole, but which was especially hostile to the interests of Kentucky, Georgia, and the other frontier communities. The men who proposed to enter into the scheme were certainly not loyal to their country; although the adventurers were not

[1] Gardoqui MSS., Gardoqui to Floridablanca, June 29, 1789.

actuated by hostile designs against it, engaging in the adventure simply from motives of private gain. The only palliation—there is no full excuse—for their offence is the fact that the Union was then so loose and weak, and its benefits so problematical, that it received the hearty and unswerving loyalty of only the most far-seeing and broadly patriotic men ; and that many men of the highest standing and of the most undoubted probity shared the views on which Brown and Innes acted.

Wilkinson was bitterly hostile to all these schemes in which he himself did not have a share, and protested again and again to Miro against their adoption. He protested no less strongly whenever the Spanish court or the Spanish authorities at New Orleans either relaxed their vigilant severity against the river smugglers, or for the time being lowered the duties ; whether this was done to encourage the Westerners in their hostilities to the East, or to placate them when their exasperation reached a pitch that threatened actual invasion. Wilkinson, in his protests, insisted that to show favors to the Westerners was merely to make them contented with the Union ; and that the only way to force them to break the Union was to deny them all privileges until they broke it.[1] He did his best to persuade the Spaniards to adopt measures which would damage both the East and West and would

Wilkinson's Advice to the Spaniards.

---

[1] *Guyarré*, iii., 30, 232, etc. Wilkinson's treachery dates from his first visit to New Orleans. Exactly when he was first pensioned outright is not certain ; but doubtless he was the corrupt recipient of money from the beginning.

increase the friction between them. He vociferously insisted that in going to such extremes of foul treachery to his country he was actuated only by his desire to see the Spanish intrigues attain their purpose; but he was probably influenced to a much greater degree by the desire to retain as long as might be the monopoly of the trade with New Orleans.

The Intendant Navarro, writing to Spain in 1788, dwelt upon the necessity of securing the separation of the Westerners from the old thirteen States; and to this end he urged that commercial privileges be granted to the West, and pensions and honors showered on its leaders. Spain readily adopted this policy of bribery. Wilkinson and Sebastian were at different times given sums of money, small portions of which were doubtless handed over to their own agents and subordinates and to the Spanish spies; and Wilkinson asked for additional sums, nominally to bribe leading Kentuckians, but very possibly merely with the purpose of pocketing them himself. In other words, Wilkinson, Sebastian, and their intimate associates on the one hand, and the Spanish officials on the other, entered into a corrupt conspiracy to dismember the Union.

Wilkinson took a leading part in the political agitations by which Kentucky was shaken throughout these years. He devoted himself to working for separation from both Virginia and the United States, and for an alliance with Spain. Of course he did not dare to avow his

The Spanish Conspiracy.

Wilkinson's Intrigues.

schemes with entire frankness, only venturing to advocate them more or less openly accordingly as the wind of popular opinion veered towards or away from disunion. Being a sanguine man, of bad judgment, he at first wrote glowing letters to his Spanish employers, assuring them that the Kentucky leaders enthusiastically favored his plans, and that the people at large were tending towards them. As time went on, he was obliged to change the tone of his letters, and to admit that he had been over-hopeful; he reluctantly acknowledged that Kentucky would certainly refuse to become a Spanish province, and that all that was possible to hope for was separation and an alliance with Spain. He was on intimate terms with the separatist leaders of all shades, and broached his views to them as far as he thought fit. His turgid oratory was admired in the backwoods, and he was much helped by his skill in the baser kinds of political management. He speedily showed all the familiar traits of the demagogue—he was lavish in his hospitality, and treated young and old, rich and poor, with jovial good-fellowship; so that all the men of loose habits, the idle men who were ready for any venture, and the men of weak character and fickle temper, swore by him, and followed his lead; while not a few straightforward, honest citizens were blinded by his showy ability and professions of disinterestedness.[1]

It is impossible to say exactly how far his different allies among the separatist leaders knew his real designs or sympathized with them. Their loosely

---

[1] Marshall, I., 245.

knit party was at the moment united for one ostensible purpose—that of separation from Virginia. The measures they championed were in effect revolutionary, as they wished to pay no regard to the action either of Virginia herself, or of the Federal Government. They openly advocated Kentucky's entering into a treaty with Spain on her own account. Their leaders must certainly have known Wilkinson's real purposes, even though vaguely. The probability is that they did not, either to him or in their own minds, define their plans with clearness, but awaited events before deciding on a definite policy. Meantime by word and act they pursued a course which might be held to mean, as occasion demanded, either mere insistence upon Kentucky's admission to the Union as a separate State, or else a movement for complete independence with a Spanish alliance in the background.

It was impossible to pursue a course so equivocal without arousing suspicion. In after years many who had been committed to it became ashamed of their actions, and loudly proclaimed that they had really been devoted to the Union; to which it was sufficient to answer that if this had been the case, and if they had been really loyal, no such deep suspicion could have been excited. A course of straightforward loyalty could not have been misunderstood. As it was, all kinds of rumors as to proposed disunion movements, and as to the intrigues with Spain, got afloat; and there was no satisfactory contradiction. The stanch Union men, the men who "thought continentally," as the phrase

went, took the alarm and organized a counter-movement. One of those who took prominent part in
this counter-movement was a man to whom Kentucky and the Union both owe much : Humphrey
Marshall, afterwards a Federalist senator from Kentucky, and the author of an interesting and amusing
and fundamentally sound, albeit somewhat rancor-
ous, history of his State. This loyal counter-movement hindered and hampered the separatists greatly,
and made them cautious about advocating outright
disunion. It was one of the causes which combined to render abortive both the separatist agitations, and the Spanish intrigues of the period.

While Miro was corresponding with Wilkinson
and arranging for pensioning both him and Sebastian, Gardoqui was busy at New York.
His efforts at negotiation were fruitless;   Gardoqui's
for his instructions positively forbade him   Intrigues.
to yield the navigation of the Mississippi, or to allow
the rectification of the boundary lines as claimed by
the United States;[1] while the representatives of the
latter refused to treat at all unless both of these
points were conceded.[2] Jay he found to be particularly intractable, and in one of his letters he expressed the hope that he would be replaced by
Richard Henry Lee, whom Gardoqui considered to
be in the Spanish interest. He was much interested
in the case of Vermont,[3] which at that time was in
doubt whether to remain an independent State, to

[1] Gardoqui MSS., Instructions, July 25 and October 2, 1784.
[2] *Do.*, Gardoqui's Letters, June 19, 1786, October 28, 1786, December 5,
1787, July 25, 1788, etc.
[3] *Do.*, May 11, 1787.

join the Union, or even possibly to form some kind of alliance with the British; and what he saw occurring in this New England State made him for the moment hopeful about the result of the Spanish designs on Kentucky.

Gardoqui was an over-hopeful man, accustomed to that diplomacy which acts on the supposition that every one has his price. After the manner of his kind, he was prone to ascribe absurdly evil motives to all men, and to be duped himself in consequence.[1] He never understood the people with whom he was dealing. He was sure that they could all be reached by underhand and corrupt influences of some kind, if he could only find out where to put on the pressure. The perfect freedom with which many loyal men talked to and before him puzzled him; and their characteristicly American habit of indulging in gloomy forebodings as to the nation's future—when they were not insisting that the said future would be one of unparalleled magnificence—gave him wild hopes that it might prove possible to corrupt them. He was confirmed in his belief by the undoubted corruption and disloyalty to their country, shown by a few of the men he met, the most important of those who were in his pay being an alleged Catholic, James White, once a North Carolina delegate and afterwards Indian agent. Moreover others who never indulged in overt disloyalty to the Union undoubtedly consulted and questioned Gardoqui about his proposals, while reserving their own decision; being men who let their loyalty be determined

[1] John Mason Brown, "Political Beginnings of Kentucky," 138.

by events. Finally some men of entire purity committed grave indiscretions in dealing with him.
Henry Lee, for instance, was so foolish as to borrow
five thousand dollars from this representative of a
foreign and unfriendly power; Gardoqui, of course,
lending the money under the impression that its
receipt would bind Lee to the Spanish interest.[1]

Madison, Knox, Clinton, and other men of position
under the Continental Congress, including Brown,
the delegate from Kentucky, were among those who
conferred freely with Gardoqui. In speaking with
several of them, including Madison and Brown, he
broached the subject of Kentucky's possible separation from the Union and alliance with Spain; and
Madison and Brown discussed his statements between themselves. So far there was nothing out of
the way in Brown's conduct; but after one of these
conferences, he wrote to Kentucky in terms which
showed that he was willing to entertain Gardoqui's
proposition if it seemed advisable to do so.

His letter, which was intended to be private, but
which was soon published, was dated July 10, 1788.
It advocated immediate separation from
Virginia without regard to constitutional
methods, and also ran in part as follows:
"In private conferences which I have had
with Mr. Gardoqui, the Spanish Minister, I have
been assured by him in the most explicit terms that
if Kentucky will declare her independence and em-

Brown and
His Party
Work for
Disunion.

---

[1] Gardoqui MSS., Gardoqui to Floridablanca, December 5, 1787; August
27, 1786; October 25, 1786; October 2, 1789, etc. In these letters White
is frequently alluded to as "Don Jaime."

power some proper person to negotiate with him, that he has authority and will engage to open the navigation of the Mississippi for the exportation of their produce on terms of mutual advantage. But this privilege never can be extended to them while part of the United States. . . . I have thought proper to communicate (this) to a few confidential friends in the district, with his permission, not doubting but that they will make a prudent use of the information."

At the outset of any movement which, whatever may be its form, is in its essence revolutionary, and only to be justified on grounds that justify a revolution, the leaders, though loud in declamation about the wrongs to be remedied, always hesitate to speak in plain terms concerning the remedies which they really have in mind. They are often reluctant to admit their purposes unequivocally, even to themselves, and may indeed blind themselves to the necessary results of their policy. They often choose their language with care, so that it may not commit them beyond all hope of explanation or retraction. Brown, Innes, and the other separatist leaders in Kentucky were not actuated by the motives of personal corruption which influenced Wilkinson, Sebastian, and White to conspire with Gardoqui and Miro for the break-up of the Union. Their position, as far as the mere separatist feeling itself was concerned, was not essentially different from that of George Clinton in New York or Sumter in South Carolina. Of course, however, their connection with a foreign power unpleasantly tainted their course,

exactly as a similar connection, with Great Britain
instead of with Spain, tainted the similar course of
action Ethan Allen was pursuing at this very time
in Vermont.[1] In after years they and their apologists
endeavored to explain away their deeds and words,
and tried to show that they were not disunionists;
precisely as the authors of the Kentucky and Virginia resolutions of 1798 and of the resolutions of
the Hartford Convention in 1814 tried in later years
to show that these also were not disunion movements.   The effort is as vain in one case as in the
other.   Brown's letter shows that he and the party
with which he was identified were ready to bring
about Kentucky's separation from the Union, if it
could safely be done; the prospect of a commercial
alliance with Spain being one of their chief objects,
and affording one of their chief arguments.

The publication of Brown's letter and the boldness
of the separatist party spurred to renewed effort the
Union men, one of whom, Col. Thomas   Failure of
Marshall, an uncle of Humphrey Marshall the Separa-
and father of the great Chief-Justice, sent tist Move-
a full account of the situation to Washing-   ments.
ton.   The more timid and wavering among the disunionists drew back; and the agitation was dropped
when the new National Government began to show
that it was thoroughly able to keep order at home,
and enforce respect abroad.[2]

These separatist movements were general in the
West, on the Holston and Cumberland, as well as on

---

[1] *Pennsylvania Magazine of History and Biography*, XI., No. 2, p. 165.
Ethan Allen's letter to Lord Dorchester.
[2] Letter of Col. T. Marshall, September 11, 1790.

the Ohio, during the troubled years immediately succeeding the Revolution; and they were furthered by the intrigues of the Spaniards. But the antipathy of the backwoodsmen to the Spaniards was too deep-rooted for them ever to effect a real combination. Ultimately the good sense and patriotism of the Westerners triumphed; and the American people continued to move forward with unbroken front towards their mighty future.

CHAPTER IV.

THE STATE OF FRANKLIN, 1784-1788.

THE separatist spirit was strong throughout the West. Different causes, such as the unchecked ravages of the Indians, or the refusal of the right to navigate the Mississippi, produced or accentuated different manifestations; but the feeling itself was latent everywhere. Its most striking manifestation occurred not in Kentucky, but in what is now the State of Tennessee; and was aimed not at the United States, but at the parent State of North Carolina.

In Kentucky the old frontiersmen were losing their grip on the governmental machinery of the district. The great flood of immigration tended to swamp the pioneers; and the leading parts in the struggle for statehood were played by men who had come to the country about the close of the Revolutionary War, and who were often related by ties of kinship to the leaders of the Virginia legislatures and conventions.

On the waters of the upper Tennessee matters were entirely different. Immigration had been slower, and the people who did come in were usually of the type of those who had first built their stockaded hamlets on the banks of the Watauga. The leaders of The Frontiersmen of the Upper Tennessee.

the early pioneers were still the leaders of the community, in legislation as in warfare. Moreover North Carolina was a much weaker and more turbulent State than Virginia, so that a separatist movement ran less risk of interference. Chains of forest-clad mountains severed the State proper from its western outposts. Many of the pioneer leaders were from Virginia — backwoodsmen who had drifted south along the trough-like valleys. These of course felt little loyalty to North Carolina. The others, who were North Carolinians by birth, had cast in their lot, for good or for evil, with the frontier communities, and were inclined to side with them in any contest with the parent State.

North Carolina herself was at first quite as anxious to get rid of the frontiersmen as they were to go. Not only was the central authority much weaker than in Virginia, but the people were less proud of their State and less jealously anxious to see it grow in power and influence. The over-mountain settlers had increased in numbers so rapidly that four counties had been erected for them; one, Davidson, taking in the Cumberland district, and the other three, Washington, Sullivan, and Greene, including what is now eastern Tennessee. All these counties sent representatives to the North Carolina legislature, at Hillsborough; but they found that body little disposed to consider the needs of the remote western colonists.

The State was very poor, and regarded the western settlements as mere burdensome sources of expense. In the innumerable Indian wars debts were contracted by the little pioneer communities with the faith that the State would pay them; but the payment was made grudgingly or not at all, and no measures were taken to provide for the protection of the frontier in the future. No provisions were made for the extension of the jurisdiction of the State courts over the western counties, and they became a refuge for outlaws, who could be dealt with only as the Indians were—that is, by the settlers acting on their own initiative, without the sanction of law. In short the settlers were left to themselves, to work out their own salvation as they best might, in peace or war; and as they bore most of the burdens of independence, they began to long for the privileges.

In June, 1784, the State Legislature passed an act ceding to the Continental Congress all the western lands, that is, all of what is now Tenessee. It was provided that the sovereignty of North Carolina over the ceded lands should continue in full effect until the United States accepted the gift; and that the act should lapse and become void unless Congress accepted within two years.[1]

North Carolina Cedes the West to Congress.

The western members were present and voted in favor of the cession, and immediately afterwards they returned to their homes and told the frontier people what had been done. There was a general feeling that some step should be taken forthwith to prevent

[1] Ramsey, 283. He is the best authority for the history of the curious state of Franklin.

the whole district from lapsing into anarchy. The frontiersmen did not believe that Congress, hampered as it was and powerless to undertake new responsibilities, could accept the gift until the two years were nearly gone; and meanwhile North Carolina would in all likelihood pay them little heed, so that they would be left a prey to the Indians without and to their own wrongdoers within. It was incumbent on them to organize for their own defence and preservation. The three counties on the upper Tennessee proceeded to take measures accordingly. The Cumberland people, however, took no part in the movement, and showed hardly any interest in it; for they felt as alien to the men of the Holston valley as to those of North Carolina proper, and watched the conflict with a tepid absence of friendship for, or hostility towards, either side. They had long practically managed their own affairs, and though they suffered from the lack of a strong central authority on which to rely, they did not understand their own wants, and were inclined to be hostile to any effort for the betterment of the national government.

The first step taken by the frontiersmen in the direction of setting up a new state was very characteristic, as showing the military structure of the frontier settlements. To guard against Indian inroad and foray, and to punish them by reprisals, all the able-bodied, rifle-bearing males were enrolled in the militia; and the divisions of this militia were territorial. The soldiers of each company represented

The Western Counties Set up a Separate State.

one cluster of rough little hamlets or one group of
scattered log houses. The company therefore formed
a natural division for purposes of representation.
It was accordingly agreed that " each captain's company " in the counties of Washington, Lincoln, and
Green should choose two delegates, who should all
assemble as committees in their respective counties
to deliberate upon some general plan of action.
The committees met and recommended the election
of deputies with full powers to a convention held at
Jonesboro.

This convention, of forty deputies or thereabouts,
met at Jonesboro, on August 23, 1784,   Meeting of
and appointed John Sevier President.   the Con-
The delegates were unanimous that the   stitutional
three counties represented should de-   Convention.
clare themselves independent of North Carolina, and
passed a resolution to this effect. They also resolved
that the three counties should form themselves into
an Association, and should enforce all the laws of
North Carolina not incompatible with beginning the
career of a separate state, and that Congress should
be petitioned to countenance them, and advise them
in the matter of their constitution. In addition,
they made provision for admitting to their state the
neighboring portions of Virginia, should they apply,
and should the application be sanctioned by the
State of Virginia, " or other power having cogni-
zance thereof." This last reference was, of course,
to Congress, and was significant. Evidently the
mountaineers ignored the doctrine of State Sovereignty. The power which they regarded as para-

mount was that of the Nation. The adhesion they
gave to any government was somewhat shadowy;
but such as it was, it was yielded to the United
States, and not to any one State. They wished to
submit their claim for independence to the judgment of Congress, not to the judgment of North
Carolina; and they were ready to admit into their
new state the western part of Virginia, on the assent, not of both Congress and Virginia, but of either
Congress or Virginia.

So far the convention had been unanimous; but a
split came on the question whether their declaration
of independence should take effect at once. The
majority held that it should, and so voted; while a
strong minority, amounting to one third of the
members, followed the lead of John Tipton, and
voted in the negative. During the session a crowd
of people, partly from the straggling little frontier
village itself, but partly from the neighboring
country, had assembled, and were waiting in the
street, to learn what the convention had decided.
A member, stepping to the door of the building,
announced the birth of the new state. The crowd,
of course, believed in strong measures, and expressed
its hearty approval. Soon afterwards the convention adjourned, after providing for the calling of a
new convention, to consist of five delegates from
each county, who should give a name to the state,
and prepare for it a constitution. The members of
this constitutional convention were to be chosen by
counties, and not by captain's companies.

There was much quarrelling over the choice of

members for the constitutional convention, the parties dividing on the lines indicated in the vote on the question of immediate independence. When the convention did meet, in November, it broke up in confusion. At the same time North Carolina, becoming alarmed, repealed her cession act; and thereupon Sevier himself counselled his fellow-citizens to abandon the movement for a new state. However, they felt they had gone too far to back out. The convention came together again in December, and took measures looking towards the assumption of full statehood. In the constitution they drew up they provided, among other things, for a Senate and a House of Commons, to form the legislative body, which should itself choose the Governor.[1] By an extraordinary resolution they further provided that the government should go into effect, and elections be held, at once; and yet that in the fall of 1785 a new convention should convene at which the very constitution under which the government had been carried on would be submitted for revision, rejection, or adoption.

Elections for the Legislature were accordingly held, and in March, 1785, the two houses of the new state of Franklin met, and chose Sevier as Governor. Courts were organized, and military and civil officials of every grade were provided, those holding commis-

Meeting of the Legislature.

---

[1] Haywood, 142; although Ramsey writes more in full about the Franklin government, it ought not to be forgotten that the groundwork of his history is from Haywood. Haywood is the original, and by far the most valuable authority on Tennessee matters, and he writes in a quaint style that is very attractive.

sions under North Carolina being continued in office
in almost all cases. The friction caused by the
change of government was thus minimized. Four
new counties were created, taxes were levied, and a
number of laws enacted. One of the acts was "for
the promotion of learning in the county of Washington." Under it the first academy west of the mountains was started; for some years it was the only
high school anywhere in the neighborhood where
Latin, or indeed any branch of learning beyond the
simplest rudiments, was taught. It is no small
credit to the backwoodsmen that in this their first
attempt at state-making they should have done what
they could to furnish their sons the opportunity of
obtaining a higher education.

One of the serious problems with which they had
to grapple was the money question. All through
Backwoods the United States the finances were in
Currency. utter disorder, the medium of exchange
being a jumble of almost worthless paper currency,
and of foreign coin of every kind, while the standard
of value varied from State to State. But in the
backwoods conditions were even worse, for there
was hardly any money at all. Transactions were
accomplished chiefly by the primeval method of
barter. Accordingly, this backwoods Legislature
legalized the payment of taxes and salaries in kind,
and set a standard of values. The dollar was declared equal to six shillings, and a scale of prices
was established. Among the articles which were
enumerated as being lawfully payable for taxes
were bacon at six pence a pound, rye whiskey at

two shillings and six pence a gallon, peach or apple brandy at three shillings per gallon, and country-made sugar at one shilling per pound. Skins, however, formed the ordinary currency; otter, beaver, and deer being worth six shillings apiece, and raccoon and fox one shilling and three pence. The Governor's salary was set at two hundred pounds, and that of the highest judge at one hundred and fifty.

The new Governor sent a formal communication to Governor Alexander Martin of North Carolina, announcing that the three counties beyond the mountains had declared their independence, and erected themselves into a separate state, and setting forth their reasons for the step. Governor Martin answered Sevier in a public letter, in which he went over his arguments one by one, and sought to refute them. He announced the willingness of the parent State to accede to the separation when the proper time came; but he pointed out that North Carolina could not consent to such irregular and unauthorized separation, and that Congress would certainly not countenance it against her wishes. In answering an argument drawn from the condition of affairs in Vermont, Martin showed that the Green Mountain State should not be treated as an example in point, because she had asserted her independence, as a separate commonwealth, before the Revolution, and yet had joined in the war against the British.

Correspondence with North Carolina.

One of the subjects on which he dwelt was the relations with the Indians. The mountain men accused North Carolina of not giving to the Cherokees a quantity of goods promised them, and asserted that this disappointment had caused the Indians to commit several murders.   In his answer the Governor admitted that the goods had not been given, but explained that this was because at the time the land had been ceded to Congress, and the authorities were waiting to see what Congress would do; and after the Cession Act was repealed the goods would have been given forthwith, had it not been for the upsetting of all legal authority west of the mountains, which brought matters to a standstill.   Moreover, the Governor in his turn made counter accusations, setting forth that the mountaineers had held unauthorized treaties with the Indians, and had trespassed on their lands, and even murdered them.   He closed by drawing a strong picture of the evils sure to be brought about by such lawless secession, and usurpation of authority.   He besought and commanded the revolted counties to return to their allegiance, and warned them that if they did not, and if peaceable measures proved of no avail, then the State of North Carolina would put down the rebellion by dint of arms.

At the same time, in the early spring of 1785, the authorities of the new state sent a memorial to the Continental Congress.[1]   Having found their natural civil chief and military leader in Sevier, the backwoodsmen now developed a diplomat in the person of one Willliam Cocke.   To

Petition to Congress.

---

[1] State Dept. MSS., Papers Continental Congress, Memorials, etc., No. 48.   State of Franklin, March 12, 1785.   Certificate that William Cocke is agent ; and memorial of the freemen, etc.

him they entrusted the memorial, together with a certificate, testifying, in the name of the state of Franklin, that he was delegated to present the memorial to Congress and to make what further representations he might find "conducive to the interest and independence of this country." The memorial set forth the earnest desire of the people of Franklin to be admitted as a State of the Federal Union, together with the wrongs they had endured from North Carolina, dwelling with particular bitterness upon the harm which had resulted from her failure to give the Cherokees the goods which they had been promised. It further recited how North Carolina's original cession of the western lands had moved the Westerners to declare their independence, and contended that her subsequent repeal of the act making this cession was void, and that Congress should treat the cession as an accomplished fact. However, Congress took no action either for or against the insurrectionary commonwealth.

The new state wished to stand well with Virginia, no less than with Congress. In July, 1785, Sevier wrote to Governor Patrick Henry, unsuccessfully appealing to him for sympathy. In this letter he insisted that he was doing all he could to restrain the people from encroaching on the Indian lands, though he admitted he found the task difficult. He assured Henry that he would on no account encourage the southwestern Virginians to join the new state, as some of them had proposed; and he added, what he evidently felt to be a needed explanation, "we hope to convince every one that we are not a banditti, but a people who mean to do right, as far as our knowledge will lead us."[1]

At the outset of its stormy career the new state had been named Franklin, in honor of Benjamin Franklin; but a large minority had wished to call it Frankland instead, and outsiders knew it as often by one title as the other.

Correspondence with Benjamin Franklin.

Benjamin Franklin himself did not know that it was named after him until it had been in existence eighteen months.[2]   The state was then in straits, and Cocke wrote Franklin, in the hope of some advice or assistance.   The prudent philosopher replied in conveniently vague and guarded terms.   He remarked that this was the first time he had been informed that the new state was named after him, he having always supposed that it was called Frankland.   He then expressed his high appreciation of the honor conferred upon him, and his regret that he could not show his appreciation by anything more substantial than good wishes.   He declined to commit himself as to the quarrel between Franklin and North Carolina, explaining that he could know nothing of its merits, as he had but just come home from abroad; but he warmly commended the proposition to submit the question to Congress, and urged that the disputants should abide by its decision.   He wound up his letter by some general remarks on the benefits of having a Congress which could act as a judge in such matters.

[1] Va. State Papers, IV., 42, Sevier to Henry, July 19, 1785.
[2] State Dept. MSS., Franklin Papers, Miscellaneous, vol. vii., Benj. Franklin to William Cocke, Philadelphia, Aug. 12, 1786.

While the memorial was being presented to Congress, Sevier was publishing his counter-manifesto to Governor Martin's in the shape of a letter to Martin's successor in the chair of the chief executive of North Carolina. In this letter Sevier justified at some length the stand the Franklin people had taken, and commented with lofty severity on Governor Martin's efforts "to stir up sedition and insurrection" in Franklin, and thus destroy the "tranquillity" of its "peaceful citizens." Sevier evidently shared to the full the horror generally felt by the leaders of a rebellion for those who rebel against themselves.

Sevier's Manifesto to North Carolina.

The new Governor of North Carolina adopted a much more pacific tone than his predecessor, and he and Sevier exchanged some further letters, but without result.

One of the main reasons for discontent with the parent State was the delay in striking an advantageous treaty with the Indians, and the Franklin people hastened to make up for this delay by summoning the Cherokees to a council.[1] Many of the chiefs, who were already under solemn agreement with the United States and North Carolina, refused to attend; but, as usual with Indians, they could not control all their people, some of whom were present at the time appointed. With the Indians who were thus present the whites went through the form of a treaty under which they received large cessions of Cherokee lands. The ordinary results of such a treaty followed. The

Treaty with the Cherokees.

[1] Virginia State Papers, IV., 25, 37, etc.

Indians who had not signed promptly repudiated as unauthorized and ineffective the action of the few who had ; and the latter asserted that they had been tricked into signing, and were not aware of the true nature of the document to which they had affixed their marks.[1] The whites heeded these protests not at all, but kept the land they had settled.

In fact the attitude of the Franklin people towards the Cherokees was one of mere piracy. In the August session of their legislature they passed a law to encourage an expedition to go down the Tennessee on the west side and take possession of the country in the great bend of that river under titles derived from the State of Georgia. The eighty or ninety men composing this expedition actually descended the river, and made a settlement by the Muscle Shoals, in what the Georgians called the county of Houston. They opened a land office, organized a county government, and elected John Sevier's brother, Valentine, to represent them in the Georgia Legislature ; but that body refused to allow him a seat. After a fortnight's existence the attitude of the Indians became so menacing that the settlement broke up and was abandoned.

In November, 1785, the convention to provide a permanent constitution for the state met at Greenville. There was already much discontent with the Franklin Government. The differences between its adherents and those of the old North Carolina Government were accentuated by bitter faction fights among the rivals

The Greenville Constitutional Convention.

[1] Talk of Old Tassel, September 19, 1785, Ramsey, 319.

for popular leadership, backed by their families and
followers.   Bad feeling showed itself at this convention, the rivalry between Sevier and Tipton
being pronounced.   Tipton was one of the mountain
leaders, second in influence only to Sevier, and his
bitter personal enemy.   At the convention a brand
new constitution was submitted by a delegate
named Samuel Houston.   The adoption of the new
constitution was urged by a strong minority.   The
most influential man of the minority party was
Tipton.

This written constitution, with its bill of rights
prefixed, was a curious document.   It provided that
the new state should be called the Commonwealth
of Frankland.   Full religious liberty was established,
so far as rites of worship went ; but no one was to
hold office unless he was a Christian who believed
in the Bible, in Heaven, in Hell, and in the Trinity.
There were other classes prohibited from holding
office,—immoral men and sabbath breakers, for
instance, and clergymen, doctors, and lawyers.   The
exclusion of lawyers from law-making bodies was
one of the darling plans of the ordinary sincere
rural demagogue of the day.   At that time lawyers,
as a class, furnished the most prominent and influential political leaders ; and they were, on the whole,
the men of most mark in the communities.   A
narrow, uneducated, honest countryman, especially
in the backwoods, then looked upon a lawyer,
usually with smothered envy and admiration, but
always with jealousy, suspicion, and dislike ; much
as his successors to this day look upon bankers and

railroad men. It seemed to him a praiseworthy thing to prevent any man whose business it was to study the law from having a share in making the law.

The proposed constitution showed the extreme suspicion felt by the common people for even their own elected lawmakers. It made various futile provisions to restrain them, such as providing that "except on occasions of sudden necessity," laws should only become such after being enacted by two successive Legislatures, and that a Council of Safety should be elected to look after the conduct of all the other public officials. Universal suffrage for all free-men was provided; the Legislature was to consist of but one body; and almost all offices were made elective. Taxes were laid to provide a state university. The constitution was tediously elaborate and minute in its provisions.

However, its only interest is its showing the spirit of the local "reformers" of the day and place in the matters of constitution-making and legislation. After a hot debate and some tumultuous scenes, it was rejected by the majority of the convention, and in its stead, on Sevier's motion, the North Carolina constitution was adopted as the groundwork for the new government. This gave umbrage to Tipton and his party, who for some time had been discontented with the course of affairs in Franklin, and had been grumbling about them.

The new constitution—which was in effect simply the old constitution with unimportant alterations—went into being, and under it the Franklin Legislature convened at Greenville, which was made the

permanent capital of the new state. The Commons
met in the court-house, a clapboarded building of
unhewn logs, without windows, the light
coming in through the door and through   Franklin
                                            Acts as
the chinks between the timbers. The Senate   an Inde-
met in one of the rooms of the town tavern.   pendent
                                               State.
The backwoods legislators lodged at this
tavern or at some other, at the cost of fourpence
a day, the board being a shilling for the man, and
sixpence for his horse, if the horse only ate hay ; a
half pint of liquor or a gallon of oats cost sixpence.[1]
Life was very rude and simple; no luxuries, and only
the commonest comforts, were obtainable.

The state of Franklin had now been in existence
over a year, and during this period the officers holding under it had exercised complete control in the
three insurrectionary counties. They had passed
laws, made treaties, levied taxes, recorded deeds, and
solemnized marriages. In short, they had performed
all the functions of civil government, and Franklin
had assumed in all respects the position of an independent commonwealth.

But in the spring of 1786 the discontent which
had smouldered burst into a flame. Tipton and his
followers openly espoused the cause of
North Carolina, and were joined, as time   Feuds of
                                               the Two
waned, by the men who for various reasons   Parties.
were dissatisfied with the results of the
trial of independent statehood. They held elections,
at the Sycamore Shoals and elsewhere, to choose representatives to the North Carolina Legislature, John

[1] Ramsey, 334.

Tipton being elected Senator. They organized the
entire local government over again in the interest of
the old State.

The two rival governments clashed in every way.
County courts of both were held in the same counties; the militia were called out by both sets of
officers; taxes were levied by both Legislatures.[1]
The Franklin courts were held at Jonesboro, the
North Carolina courts at Buffalo, ten miles distant;
and each court in turn was broken up by armed
bands of the opposite party. Criminals throve in
the confusion, and the people refused to pay taxes
to either party. Brawls, with their brutal accompaniments of gouging and biting, were common.
Sevier and Tipton themselves, on one occasion when
they by chance met, indulged in a rough-and-tumble
fight before their friends could interfere.

Throughout the year '86 the confusion gradually
grew worse. A few days after the Greenville con-
Growing vention met, the Legislature of North
Confusion. Carolina passed an act in reference to the
revolt. It declared that, at the proper time, the
western counties would be erected into an independent state, but that this time had not yet come;
until it did, they would be well cared for, but must
return to their ancient allegiance, and appoint and
elect their officers under the laws of North Carolina.
A free pardon and oblivion of all offences was
promised. Following this act came a long and
tedious series of negotiations. Franklin sent ambassadors to argue her case before the Legislature of

[1] Haywood, 160.

the mother State; the Governors and high officials exchanged long-winded letters and proclamations, and the rival Legislatures passed laws intended to undermine each other's influence. The Franklin Assembly tried menace, and threatened to fine any one who acted under a commission from North Carolina. The Legislature of the latter State achieved more by promises, having wisely offered to remit all taxes for the two troubled years to any one who would forthwith submit to her rule.

Neither side was willing to force the issue to trial by arms if it could be helped; and there was a certain pointlessness about the struggle, inasmuch as the differences between the contending parties were really so trifling. The North Carolinians kept protesting that they would be delighted to see Franklin set up as an independent state, as soon as her territory contained enough people; and the Franklin leaders in return were loud in their assurances of respect for North Carolina and of desire to follow her wishes. But neither would yield the points immediately at issue.

A somewhat comic incident of the affair occurred in connection with an effort made by Sevier and his friends to persuade old Evan Shelby to act as umpire. After a conference they signed a joint manifesto which aimed to preserve peace for the moment by the novel expedient of allowing the citizens of the disputed territory to determine, every man for himself, the government which he wished to own, and to pay his taxes to it accordingly. Nothing came of this manifesto.

During this time of confusion each party rallied
by turns, but the general drift was all in favor of
Decline of North Carolina. One by one the adher-
Franklin. ents of Franklin dropped away. The
revolt was essentially a frontier revolt, and Sevier
was essentially a frontier leader. The older and
longer-settled counties and parts of counties were
the first to fall away from him, while the settlers on
the very edge of the Indian country clung to him to
the last.

The neighboring States were more or less excited
over the birth of the little insurgent commonwealth.
Attitude of Virginia looked upon it with extreme dis-
Neighbor- favor, largely because her own western
ing States. counties showed signs of desiring to throw
in their fortunes with the Franklin people[1] Governor Patrick Henry issued a very energetic address
on the subject, and the authorities took effective
means to prevent the movement from gaining head.

Georgia, on the contrary, showed the utmost
friendliness towards the new state, and gladly en-
Franklin tered into an alliance with her.[2] Georgia
and had no self-assertive communities of her
Georgia. own children on her western border, as
Virginia and North Carolina had, in Kentucky and
Franklin. She was herself a frontier commonwealth,
challenging as her own lands that were occupied by
the Indians and claimed by the Spainards. Her interests were identical with those of Franklin. The
Governors of the two communities exchanged com-

[1] Va. State Papers, iv. 53.
[2] Stevens' "Georgia," II., 380.

plimentary addresses, and sent their rough ambassadors one to the other. Georgia made Sevier a brigadier-general in her militia, for the district she claimed
in the bend of the Tennessee; and her branch of the
Society of the Cincinnati elected him to membership.
In return Sevier, hoping to tighten the loosening
bonds of his authority by a successful Indian war,
entered into arrangements with Georgia for a combined campaign against the Creeks. For various
reasons the proposed campaign fell through, but the
mere planning of it shows the feeling that was, at
the bottom, the strongest of those which knit together the Franklin men and the Georgians.[1] They
both greedily coveted the Indians' land, and were
bent on driving the Indians off it. [2]

One of the Franklin judges, in sending a plea for
the independence of his state to the Governor of
North Carolina, expressed with unusual   The Frank-
frankness the attitude of the Holston   lin Men and
backwoodsmen towards the Indians. He   the Indians.
remarked that he supposed the Governor would be
astonished to learn that there were many settlers on
the land which North Carolina had by treaty
guaranteed to the Cherokees; and brushed aside all
remonstrances by simply saying that it was vain to
talk of keeping the frontiersmen from encroaching
on Indian territory. All that could be done, he
said, was to extend the laws over each locality as
rapidly as it was settled by the intruding pioneers;
otherwise they would become utterly lawless, and

---

[1] State Dept. MSS., No. 125, p. 163.

[2] Va. State Papers, IV., pp. 256, 353. Many of the rumors of defeats
and victories given in these papers were without foundation.

dangerous to their neighbors. As for laws and proclamations to restrain the white advance, he asked if
all the settlements in America had not been extended
in defiance of such. And now that the Indians
were cowed, the advance was certain to be faster,
and the savages were certain to be pushed back
more rapidly, and the limits of tribal territory more
narrowly circumscribed.[1]

This letter possessed at least the merit of express-
ing with blunt truthfulness the real attitude of the
Franklin people, and of the backwoodsmen generally,
towards the Indians. They never swerved from
their intention of seizing the Indian lands. They
preferred to gain their ends by treaty, and with the
consent of the Indians; but if this proved impossible, then they intended to gain them by force.

In its essence, and viewed from the standpoint of
abstract morality, their attitude was that of the free-
booter. The backwoodsmen lusted for the possessions of the Indian, as the buccaneers of the Spanish
main had once lusted for the possessions of the
Spaniard. There was but little more heed paid to
the rights of the assailed in one case than in the
other.

Yet in its results, and viewed from the standpoint
of applied ethics, the conquest and settlement by
the whites of the Indian lands was neces-
The Ethics
of Such Ter- sary to the greatness of the race and to the
ritorial Con- well-being of civilized mankind. It was as
quest.
ultimately beneficial as it was inevitable.
Huge tomes might be filled with arguments as to

[1] Ramsey, 350.

the morality or immorality of such conquests. But
these arguments appeal chiefly to the cultivated men
in highly civilized communities who have neither
the wish nor the power to lead warlike expeditions
into savage lands. Such conquests are commonly
undertaken by those reckless and daring adventurers
who shape and guide each race's territorial growth.
They are sure to come when a masterful people,
still in its raw barbarian prime, finds itself face to
face with a weaker and wholly alien race which
holds a coveted prize in its feeble grasp.

Many good persons seem prone to speak of all wars
of conquest as necessarily evil. This is, of course, a
shortsighted view. In its after effects a conquest
may be fraught either with evil or with good for
mankind, according to the comparative worth of the
conquering and conquered peoples. It is useless to
try to generalize about conquests simply as such in
the abstract; each case or set of cases must be judged
by itself. The world would have halted had it not
been for the Teutonic conquests in alien lands; but
the victories of Moslem over Christian have always
proved a curse in the end. Nothing but sheer evil
has come from the victories of Turk and Tartar.
This is true generally of the victories of barbarians
of low racial characteristics over gentler, more
moral, and more refined peoples, even though these
people have, to their shame and discredit, lost the
vigorous fighting virtues. Yet it remains no less
true that the world would probably have gone forward very little, indeed would probably not have
gone forward at all, had it not been for the displace-

ment or submersion of savage and barbaric peoples as a consequence of the armed settlement in strange lands of the races who hold in their hands the fate of the years. Every such submersion or displacement of an inferior race, every such armed settlement or conquest by a superior race, means the infliction and suffering of hideous woe and misery. It is a sad and dreadful thing that there should of necessity be such throes of agony; and yet they are the birth-pangs of a new and vigorous people. That they are in truth birth-pangs does not lessen the grim and hopeless woe of the race supplanted; of the race outworn or overthrown. The wrongs done and suffered cannot be blinked. Neither can they be allowed to hide the results to mankind of what has been achieved.

It is not possible to justify the backwoodsmen by appeal to principles which we would accept as binding on their descendants, or on the mighty nation which has sprung up and flourished in the soil they first won and tilled. All that can be asked is that they shall be judged as other wilderness conquerors, as other slayers and quellers of savage peoples, are judged. The same standards must be applied to Sevier and his hard-faced horse-riflemen that we apply to the Greek colonist of Sicily and the Roman colonist of the valley of the Po; to the Cossack rough-rider who won for Russia the vast and melancholy Siberian steppes, and to the Boer who guided his ox-drawn wagon-trains to the hot grazing lands of the Transvaal; to the founders of Massachusetts and Virginia, of Oregon and icy Saskatchewan;

and to the men who built up those far-off commonwealths whose coasts are lapped by the waters of the great South Sea.

The aggressions by the Franklin men on the Cherokee lands bore bloody fruit in 1786.[1] The young warriors, growing ever more alarmed and angered at the pressure of the settlers, could not be restrained. They shook off the control of the old men, who had seen the tribe flogged once and again by the whites, and knew how hopeless such a struggle was. The Chickamauga banditti watched from their eyries to pounce upon all boats that passed down the Tennessee, and their war bands harried the settlements far and wide, being joined in their work by parties from the Cherokee towns proper. Stock was stolen, cabins were burned, and settlers murdered. The stark riflemen gathered for revenge, carrying their long rifles and riding their rough mountain horses. Counterinroads were carried into the Indian country. On one, when Sevier himself led, two or three of the Indian towns were burned and a score or so of warriors killed. As always, it proved comparatively easy to deal a damaging blow to these southern Indians, who dwelt in well-built log-towns; while the widely scattered, shifting, wigwam-villages of the forest-nomads of the north rarely offered a tangible mark at which to strike. Of course, the retaliatory blows of the whites, like the strokes of the Indians, fell as often on the innocent as on the guilty. During this

Indian Hostilities.

---

[1] State Dept. MSS. vol. ii., No. 71, Arthur Campbell to Joseph Martin, June 16, 1786; Martin to the Governor of Virginia, June 25, 1786, etc.

summer, to revenge the death of a couple of settlers, a backwoods Colonel, with the appropriate name of Outlaw, fell on a friendly Cherokee town and killed two or three Indians, besides plundering a white man, a North Carolina trader, who happened to be in the town. Nevertheless, throughout 1786 the great majority of the Cherokees remained quiet.[1]

Early in 1787, however, they felt the strain so severely that they gathered in a great council and deliberated whether they should not abandon their homes and move far out into the western wilderness; but they could not yet make up their minds to leave their beloved mountains. The North Carolina authorities wished to see them receive justice, but all they could do was to gather the few Indian prisoners who had been captured in the late wars and return them to the Cherokees. The Franklin Government had opened a land office and disposed of all the lands between the French Broad and the Tennessee,[2] which territory North Carolina had guaranteed the Cherokees; and when, on the authority of the Governor of North Carolina, his representative ordered the settlers off the invaded land, they treated his command with utter defiance. Not only the Creeks, but even the distant Choctaws and Chickasaws became uneasy and irritated over the American encroachments, while the French traders who came up the Tennessee preached war to the Indians, and the Spanish Government ordered all the American

[1] Va. State Papers, IV., pp. 162, 164, 176.

[2] State Dept. MSS., vol. ii. No. 71. Letter to Edmund Randolph, Feb. 10, 1787; Letter of Joseph Martin, of March 25, 1787; Talk from Piominigo, the Chickasaw Chief, Feb. 15, 1787.

traders to be expelled from among the southern tribes unless they would agree to take commissions from Spain and throw off their allegiance to the United States.

In this same year the Cherokees became embroiled, not only with the Franklin people but with the Kentuckians. The Chickamaugas, who were mainly renegade Cherokees, were always ravaging in Kentucky. Colonel John Logan had gathered a force to attack one of their war bands, but he happened instead to stumble on a Cherokee party, which he scattered to the winds with loss. The Kentuckians wrote to the Cherokee chiefs explaining that the attack was an accident, but that they did not regret it greatly, inasmuch as they found in the Cherokee camp several horses which had been stolen from the settlers. They then warned the Cherokees that the outrages by the Chickamaugas must be stopped; and if the Cherokees failed to stop them they would have only themselves to thank for the woes that would follow, as the Kentuckians could not always tell the hostile from the friendly Indians, and were bent on taking an exemplary, even if indiscriminate revenge. The Council of Virginia, on hearing of this announced intention of the Kentuckians " highly disapproved of it," [1] but they could do nothing except disapprove. The governmental authorities of the eastern States possessed but little more power to restrain the backwoodsmen than the sachems had to restrain the young braves. Virginia and

[1] State Dept. MSS., No. 71.   Resolutions of Kentucky Committee, June 5, 1787.

North Carolina could no more control Kentucky and Franklin than the Cherokees could control the Chickamaugas.

In 1787 the state of Franklin began to totter to its fall. In April[1] Sevier, hungering for help or friendly advice, wrote to the gray statesman after whom his state was named. The answer did not come for several months, and when it did come it was not very satisfactory. The old sage repeated that he knew too little of the circumstances to express an opinion, but he urged a friendly understanding with North Carolina, and he spoke with unpalatable frankness on the subject of the Indians. At that very time he was writing to a Cherokee chief[2] who had come to Congress in the vain hope that the Federal authorities might save the Cherokees from the reckless backwoodsmen; he had promised to try to obtain justice for the Indians, and he was in no friendly mood towards the backwoods aggressors.

Growing Weakness of the New State.

Prevent encroachments on Indian lands, Franklin wrote to Sevier,—Sevier, who, in a last effort to rally his followers, was seeking a general Indian war to further these very encroachments,—and remember that they are the more unjustifiable because the Indians usually give good bargains in the way of purchase, while a war with them costs more than any possible price they may ask. This advice was based on Franklin's usual principle of merely mercantile

[1] State Dept. MSS. Franklin Papers, VIII., Benjamin Franklin to His Excellency Governor Sevier, Philadelphia, June 30, 1787.

[2] *Do.* Letter to the Chief "Cornstalk" (Corntassel ?), same date and place.

morality; but he was writing to a people who stood in sore need of just the teaching he could furnish and who would have done well to heed it. They were slow to learn that while sober, debt-paying thrift, love of order, and industry, are perhaps not the loftiest virtues and are certainly not in themselves all sufficient, they yet form an indispensable foundation, the lack of which is but ill supplied by other qualities even of a very noble kind.

Sevier, also in the year 1787, carried on a long correspondence with Evan Shelby, whose adherence to the state of Franklin he much desired, as the stout old fellow was a power not only among the frontiersmen but with the Virginian and North Carolinian authorities likewise. Sevier persuaded the Legislature to offer Shelby the position of chief magistrate of Franklin, and pressed him to accept it, and throw in his lot with the Westerners, instead of trying to serve men at a distance. Shelby refused; but Sevier was bent upon being pleasant, and thanked Shelby for at least being neutral, even though not actively friendly. In another letter, however, when he had begun to suspect Shelby of positive hostility, he warned him that no unfriendly interference would be tolerated.[1]

Shelby could neither be placated nor intimidated. He regarded with equal alarm and anger the loosening of the bands of authority and order among the Franklin frontiersmen. He bitterly disapproved of their lawless encroachments on the Indian lands,

[1] Tennessee Hist. Soc. MSS.   Letters of Sevier to Evan Shelby, Feb. 11, May 20, May 30, and Aug. 12, 1787.

which he feared would cause a general war with the
savages.[1]   At the very time that Sevier was writing
to him, he was himself writing to the North Carolina
Government, urging them to send forward troops
who would put down the rebellion by force, and
was requesting the Virginians to back up any such
movement with their militia.   He urged that the
insurrection threatened not only North Carolina, but
Virginia and the Federal Government itself ; and in
phrases like those of the most advanced Federalist
statesman, he urged the Federal Government to
interfere.   The Governor of Virginia was inclined
to share his views, and forwarded his complaints and
requests to the Continental Congress.

However, no action was necessary.   The Franklin
Government collapsed of itself.   In September, 1787,
Collapse of the Legislature met for the last time, at
Franklin. Greenville.   There was a contested election case for senator from the county of Hawkins,
which shows the difficulties under which the members had labored in carrying their elections, and
gives a hint of the anarchy produced by the two
contending Governments.   In this case the sheriff
of the county of Hawkins granted the certificate of
election to one man, and the three inspectors of the
poll granted it to another.   On investigation by a
committee of the Senate, it appeared that the poll
was opened by the sheriff " on the third Friday and
Saturday in August," as provided by law, but that
in addition to the advertisement of the election

[1] State Dept. MSS., No. 71.   Evan Shelby to General Russell, April 27,
1787.   Beverly Randolph to Virginia Delegates, June 2, 1787.

which was published by the sheriff of Hawkins, who held under the Franklin Government, another proclamation, advertising the same election, was issued by the sheriff of the North Carolina county of Spencer, which had been recently created by North Carolina out of a portion of the territory of Hawkins County. The North Carolina sheriff merely wished to embarrass his Franklin rival, and he succeeded admirably. The Franklin man proclaimed that he would allow no one to vote who had not paid taxes to Franklin; but after three or four votes had been taken the approach of a body of armed adherents of the North Carolina interest caused the shutting of the polls. The Franklin authorities then dispersed, the North Carolina sheriff having told them plainly that the matter would have to be settled by seeing which party was strongest. One or two efforts were made to have an adjourned election elsewhere in the neighborhood, with the result that in the confusion certificates were given to two different men [1] Such disorders showed that the time had arrived when the authorities of Franklin either had to begin a bloody civil war or else abandon the attempt to create a new state; and in their feebleness and uncertainty they adopted the latter alternative.

When in March, 1788, the term of Sevier as Governor came to an end, there was no one to take his place, and the officers of North Carolina were left in undisputed possession of whatever governmental authority there was.

[1] Tennessee Hist. Soc. MSS. Report of " Committee of Privileges and Elections " of Senate of Franklin, Nov. 23, 1787.

The North Carolina Assembly which met in
November, 1787, had been attended by regularly
elected members from all the western counties, Tipton being among them; while the far-off log hamlets
on the banks of the Cumberland sent Robertson himself. [1] This assembly once more offered full pardon
and oblivion of past offences to all who would
again become citizens; and the last adherents of the
insurrectionary Government reluctantly accepted the
terms. Franklin had been in existence for three
years, during which time she had exercised all the
powers and functions of independent statehood.
During the first year her sway in the district was
complete; during the next she was forced to hold
possession in common with North Carolina; and then,
by degrees her authority lapsed altogether.

Sevier was left in dire straits by the falling of
the state he had founded; for not only were the
North Carolina authorities naturally bitter
against him, bnt he had to count on the
personal hostility of Tipton. In his distress he wrote to one of the opposing
party, not personally unfriendly to him, that he had
been dragged into the Franklin movement by the
people of the county; that he wished to suspend
hostilities, and was ready to abide by the decision
of the North Carolina Legislature, but that he was
determined to share the fate of those who had stood
by him, whatever it might be. [2] About the time that
his term as Governor expired, a writ, issued by the

Fight be-
tween Tip-
ton and
Sevier.

[1] Haywood, 174.
[2] Va. State Papers, IV., 416, 421. Sevier to Martin, April 3 and May 27,
1788.

North Carolina courts, was executed against his estate. The sheriff seized all his negro slaves, as they worked on his Nolichucky farm, and bore them for safe-keeping to Tipton's house, a rambling cluster of stout log buildings, on Sinking Creek of the Watauga. Sevier raised a hundred and fifty men and marched to take them back, carrying a light fieldpiece. Tipton's friends gathered, thirty or forty strong, and a siege began. Sevier hesitated to push matters to extremity by charging home. For a couple of days there was some skirmishing and two or three men were killed or wounded. Then the county-lieutenant of Sullivan, with a hundred and eighty militia, came to Tipton's rescue. They surprised Sevier's camp at dawn on the last day of February,[1] while the snow was falling heavily; and the Franklin men fled in mad panic, only one or two being slain. Two of Sevier's sons were taken prisoners, and Tipton was with difficulty dissuaded from hanging them. This scrambling fight marked the ignoble end of the state of Franklin. Sevier fled to the uttermost part of the frontier, where no writs ran, and the rough settlers were devoted to him. Here he speedily became engaged in the Indian war.

Early in the spring of 1788, the Indians renewed their ravages.[2] The Chickamaugas were the leaders, but there were among them a few Creeks, and they were also joined by some of the Cherokees proper, goaded to anger by the encroach-

Indian Ravages.

---

[1] State Dept. MSS., No. 150, vol. iii. Armstrong to Wyllys, April 28, 1788.   [2] Va. State Papers, IV., 396, 432.

ments of the whites on their lands. Many of the settlers were killed, and the people on the frontier began to gather into their stockades and block-houses. The alarm was great. One murder was of peculiar treachery and atrocity. A man named John Kirk[1] lived on a clearing on Little River, seven miles south of Knoxville. One day when he was away from home, an Indian named Slim Tom, well-known to the family, and believed to be friendly, came to the cabin and asked for food. The food was given him and he withdrew. But he had come merely as a spy; and seeing that he had to deal only with helpless women and children, he returned with a party of Indians who had been hiding in the woods. They fell on the wretched creatures, and butchered them all, eleven in number, leaving the mangled bodies in the court-yard. The father and eldest boy were absent and thus escaped. It would have been well had the lad been among the slain, for his coarse and brutal nature was roused to a thirst for indiscriminate revenge, and shortly afterwards he figured as chief actor in a deed of retaliation as revolting and inhuman as the original crime.

At the news of the massacres the frontiersmen gathered, as was their custom, mounted and armed, and ready either to follow the marauding parties or to make retaliatory inroads on their own account. Sevier, their darling leader, was among them, and to him they gave the command.

Another frontier leader and Indian fighter of note

[1] State Dept. MSS., No. 150, vol. ii., p. 435. Proclamation of Thos. Hutchings, June 3, 1788.

was at this time living among the Cherokees. He
was Joseph Martin, who had dwelt much
among the Indians, and had great influence over them, as he always treated them
justly; though he had shown in more
than one campaign that he could handle them in
war as well as in peace.   Early in 1788, he had been
appointed by North Carolina Brigadier-General of
the western counties lying beyond the mountains.
In the military organization, which was really the
most important side of the Government to the frontiersmen, this was the chief position; and Martin's
duties were not only to protect the border against
Indian raids, but also to stamp out any smouldering
embers of insurrection, and see that the laws of the
State were again put in operation.

*Joseph Mar-
tin Tries to
Keep the
Peace.*

In April he took command, and on the 24th
of the month reached the lower settlements on the
Holston River.[1] Here he found that a couple of
settlers had been killed by Indians a few days before, and he met a party of riflemen who had
gathered to avenge the death of their friends by a
foray on the Cherokee towns.   Martin did not
believe that the Cherokees were responsible for the
murder.   After some talk he persuaded the angry
whites to choose four of their trusted men to accom-
pany him as ambassadors to the Cherokee towns in
order to find out the truth.

Accordingly they all went forward together.
Martin sent runners ahead to the Cherokees,

[1] State Dept. MSS., No. 150, vol. ii. Joseph Martin to H. Knox, July
15, 1788.

and their chiefs and young warriors gathered to meet him. The Indians assured him that they were guiltless of the recent murder; that it should doubtless be laid at the door of some Creek war party. The Creeks, they said, kept passing through their villages to war on the whites, and they had often turned them back. The frontier envoys at this professed themselves satisfied, and returned to their homes, after begging Martin to stay among the Cherokees; and he stayed, his presence giving confidence to the Indians, who forthwith began to plant their crops.

Mutual Outrages.

Unfortunately, about the middle of May, the murders again began, and again parties of riflemen gathered for vengeance. Martin intercepted one of these parties ten miles from a friendly Cherokee town; but another attacked and burned a neighboring town, the inhabitants escaping with slight loss. For a time Martin's life was jeopardized by this attack; the Cherokees, who swore they were innocent of the murders, being incensed at the counter attack. They told Martin that they thought he had been trying to gentle them, so that the whites might take them unawares. After a while they cooled down; and explained to Martin that the outrages were the work of the Creeks and Chickamaugas, whom they could not control, and whom they hoped the whites would punish; but that they themselves were innocent and friendly. Then the whites sent messages to express their regret; and though Martin declined longer to be responsible for the deeds of men of his own color, the Indians consented to patch up another truce.[1]

[1] State Dept MSS., No. 71, vol. ii. Martin to Randolph, June 11, 1788.

The outrages, however, continued; among others, a big boat was captured by the Chickamaugas, and all but three of the forty souls on board were killed. The settlers drew no fine distinctions between different Indians; they knew that their friends were being murdered by savages who came from the direction of the Cherokee towns; and they vented their wrath on the Indians who dwelt in these towns because they were nearest to hand.

On May 24th Martin left the Indian town of Chota, the beloved town, where he had been staying, and rode to the French Broad. There he found that a big levy of frontier militia, with Sevier at their head, were preparing to march against the Indians; Sevier having been chosen general, as mentioned above. Realizing that it was now hopeless to try to prevent a war, Martin hurried back to Chota, and removed his negroes, horses, and goods.

Sevier, heedless of Martin's remonstrances, hurried forward on his raid, with a hundred riders. He struck a town on Hiawassee and destroyed it, killing a number of the warriors. This feat, and two or three others like it, made the frontiersmen flock to his standard[1]; but before any great number were embodied under him, he headed a small party on a raid which was sullied by a deed of atrocious treachery and cruelty. He led some forty men to Chilhowa[2] on the Tennessee; opposite a small town of Cherokees, who were well known to have been friendly to the whites. Among

Sevier's Crime.

[1] State Dept. MSS., No. 150, vol. iii.   Geo. Maxwell to Martin, July 9, 1788.

[2] State Dept. MSS., No. 150, vol. iii.   Thos. Hutchings to Martin, July 11, 1788

them were several chiefs, including an old man named the Corn Tassel, who for years had been foremost in the endeavor to keep the peace, and to prevent raids on the settlers. They put out a white flag; and the whites then hoisted one themselves. On the strength of this one of the Indians crossed the river, and on demand of the whites ferried them over.[1] Sevier put the Indians in a hut, and then a horrible deed of infamy was perpetrated. Among Sevier's troops was young John Kirk, whose mother, sisters, and brothers had been so foully butchered by the Cherokee Slim Tom and his associates. Young Kirk's brutal soul was parched with longing for revenge, and he was, both in mind and heart, too nearly kin to his Indian foes greatly to care whether his vengeance fell on the wrongdoers or on the innocent. He entered the hut where the Cherokee chiefs were confined and brained them with his tomahawk, while his comrades looked on without interfering. Sevier's friends asserted that at the moment he was absent; but this is no excuse. He knew well the fierce blood lust of his followers, and it was criminal negligence on his part to leave to their mercy the friendly Indians who had trusted to his good faith; and, moreover, he made no effort to punish the murderer.

As if to show the futility of the plea that Sevier was powerless, a certain Captain Gillespie successfully protected a captive Indian from militia violence at this very time. He had come into the Indian

---

[1] State Dept. MSS., No. 150, vol. iii. Hutchings to Maxwell, June 20, 1788. Hutchings to Martin, July 11, 1788.

country with one of the parties which intended to join Sevier, and while alone he captured a Cherokee. When his troops came up they immediately proposed to kill the Indian, and told him they cared nothing for his remonstrances; whereupon he sprang from his horse, cocked his rifle, and told them he would shoot dead the first man who raised a hand to molest the captives. They shrank back, and the Indian remained unharmed.[1]

As for young Kirk all that need be said is that he stands in the same category with Slim Tom, the Indian murderer. He was a fair type of the low-class, brutal white borderer, whose inhumanity almost equalled that of the savage. *Misconduct of the Frontiersmen.* But Sevier must be judged by another standard. He was a member of the Cincinnati, a correspondent of Franklin, a follower of Washington. He sinned against the light, and must be condemned accordingly. He sank to the level of a lieutenant of Alva, Guise, or Tilly, to the level of a crusading noble of the middle ages. It would be unfair to couple even this crime with those habitually committed by Sidney and Sir Peter Carew, Shan O'Neil and Fitzgerald, and the other dismal heroes of the hideous wars waged between the Elizabethan English and the Irish. But it is not unfair to compare this border warfare in the Tennessee mountains with the border warfare of England and Scotland two centuries earlier. There is no blinking the fact that in this instance Sevier and his followers stood on the same level of brutality with

[1] Haywood, p. 183.

"keen Lord Evers," and on the same level of
treachery with the "assured" Scots at the battle of
Ancram Muir.

Even on the frontier, and at that time, the better
class of backwoodsmen expressed much horror at the
murder of the friendly chiefs. Sevier had
planned to march against the Chickamaugas with the levies that were thronging
to his banner; but the news of the murder
provoked such discussion and hesitation
that his forces melted away. He was obliged to
abandon his plan, partly owing to this disaffection among the whites, and partly owing to what
one of the backwoodsmen, in writing to General
Martin, termed "the severity of the Indians,"[1]—a
queer use of the word severity which obtains to
this day in out-of-the-way places through the Alleghanies, where people style a man with a record for
desperate fighting a " severe man," and speak of big,
fierce dogs, able to tackle a wolf, as "severe" dogs.

The Better-
Class Fron-
tiersmen
Condemn
the Deed.

Elsewhere throughout the country the news of
the murder excited great indignation. The Continental Congress passed resolutions condemning acts which they had been powerless to prevent and were powerless to
punish.[2] The Justices of the Court of Abbeville
County, South Carolina, with Andrew Pickens at
their head, wrote "to the people living on Nole-
chucke, French Broad, and Holstein," denouncing
in unmeasured terms the encroachments and out-

It is Con-
demned
Elsewhere.

---

[1] State Department MSS., 150, iii., Maxwell to Martin, July 7, 1788.
[2] *Do.*, No. 27, p. 359, and No. 151, p. 351.

rages of which Sevier and his backwoods troopers had been guilty.[1] In their zeal the Justices went a little too far, painting the Cherokees as a harmless people, who had always been friendly to the Americans,—a statement which General Martin, although he too condemned the outrages openly and with the utmost emphasis, felt obliged to correct, pointing out that the Cherokees had been the inveterate and bloody foes of the settlers throughout the Revolution.[2] The Governor of North Carolina, as soon as he heard the news, ordered the arrest of Sevier and his associates—doubtless as much because of their revolt against the State as because of the atrocities they had committed against the Indians.[3]

In their panic many of the Indians fled across the mountains and threw themselves on the mercy of the North and South Carolinians, by whom they were fed and protected. Others immediately joined the Chickamaugas in force, and the frontier districts of the Franklin region were harried with vindictive ferocity. The strokes fell most often and most heavily on the innocent. Half of the militia were called out, and those who most condemned the original acts of aggression committed by their neighbors were obliged to make common cause with these neighbors, so as to save their own lives and the lives of their families.[4] The officers of the district ordered a

[1] *Do.*, No. 56, Andrew Pickens to Thos. Pinckney, July 11, 1788; No. 150, vol. iii., Letter of Justices, July 9th.

[2] *Do.*, No. 150, vol. iii., Martin to Knox, Aug. 23, 1788.

[3] *Do.*, No. 72, Samuel Johnston to Sec'y of Congress, Sept. 29, 1788.

[4] *Do.*, Hutchings to Maxwell, June 20th, and to Martin, July 11th.

VOL. III.—13

general levy of the militia to march against the Indian towns, and in each county the backwoodsmen began to muster.[1]

Before the troops assembled many outrages were committed by the savages. Horses were stolen, peo-
The Indian ple were killed in their cabins, in their fields,
War. on the roads, and at the ferries; and the settlers nearest the Indian country gathered in their forted stations, and sent earnest appeals for help to their unmolested brethren. The stations were attacked, and at one or two the Indians were successful; but generally they were beaten off, the militia marching promptly to the relief of each beleaguered garrison. Severe skirmishing took place between the war parties and the bands of militia who first reached the frontier; and the whites were not always successful. Once, for instance, a party of militia, greedy for fruit, scattered through an orchard, close to an Indian town which they supposed to be deserted; but the Indians were hiding near by and fell upon them, killing seventeen. The savages mutilated the dead bodies in fantastic ways, with ferocious derision, and left them for their friends to find and bury.[2] Sevier led parties against the Indians without ceasing; and he and his men by their conduct showed that they waged the war very largely for profit. On a second incursion, which he made with canoes, into the Hiawassee country, his followers made numerous tomahawk claims, or "improve-

---

[1] *Do.,* No. 150, vol. ii., Daniel Kennedy to Martin, June 6, 1788; Maxwell to Martin, July 9th, etc. No. 150, vol. iii., p. 357: Result of Council of Officers of Washington District, August 19, 1788.

[2] *Do.,* Martin to Knox, August 23, 1788.

ments," as they were termed, in the lands from
which the Indians fled; hoping thus to establish a
right of ownership to the country they had overrun.[1]

The whites speedily got the upper hand, ceasing
to stand on the defensive; and the panic disappeared.
When the North Carolina Legislature met, the members, and the people of the seaboard generally, were
rather surprised to find that the over-hill men
talked of the Indian war as troublesome rather than
formidable.[2]

The militia officers holding commissions from
North Carolina wished Martin to take command of
the retaliatory expeditions against the Cherokees;
but Martin, though a good fighter on occasions, preferred the arts of peace, and liked best treating with
and managing the Indians. He had already acted
as agent to different tribes on behalf of Virginia,
North Carolina, and Georgia; and at this time he
accepted an offer from the Continental Congress
to serve in the same capacity for all the Southern
Indians.[3] Nevertheless he led a body of militia
against the Chickamauga towns. He burnt a couple,
but one of his detachments was driven back in a
fight on Lookout Mountain; his men became discontented, and he was forced to withdraw, followed
and harassed by the Indians. On his retreat the Indians attacked the settlements in force, and captured
Gillespie's station.

Sevier was the natural leader of the Holston rifle-

---

[1] *Do.*, Hutchings to Martin, July 11, 1788.

[2] *Columbian Magazine*, ii., 472.

[3] State Dep. MSS., No. 50, vol. ii., p. 505 etc.

men in such a war ; and the bands of frontiersmen in-
Sevier's sisted that he should take the command
Feats. whenever it was possible. Sevier swam well
in troubled waters, and he profited by the storm he
had done so much to raise. Again and again during
the summer of 1788 he led his bands of wild horsemen on forays against the Cherokee towns, and
always with success. He followed his usual tactics,
riding hard and long, pouncing on the Indians in
their homes before they suspected his presence, or
intercepting and scattering their war parties ; and
he moved with such rapidity that they could not
gather in force sufficient to do him harm. Not
only was the fame of his triumphs spread along the
frontier, but vague rumors reached even the old
settled States of the seaboard,[1] rumors that told of
the slight loss suffered by his followers, of the head-
long hurry of his marches, of the fury with which
his horsemen charged in the skirmishes, of his successful ambuscades and surprises, and of the heavy
toll he took in slain warriors and captive women
and children, who were borne homewards to exchange for the wives and little ones of the settlers
who had themselves been taken prisoners.

Sevier's dashing and successful leadership wiped
out in the minds of the backwoodsmen the memory
of all his shortcomings and misdeeds ; even the
memory of that unpunished murder of friendly Indians which had so largely provoked the war. The
representatives of the North Carolina Government
and his own personal enemies were less forgetful.

[1] *Columbian Magazine* for 1789, p. 204. Also letter from French Broad,
December 18, 1788.

The Governor of the State had given orders to seize him because of his violation of the laws and treaties in committing wanton murder on friendly Indians; and a warrant to arrest him for high treason was issued by the courts.

As long as "Nolichucky Jack" remained on the border, among the rough Indian fighters whom he had so often led to victory, he was in no Sevier is danger. But in the fall, late in October, Arrested. he ventured back to the longer settled districts. A council of officers with Martin presiding and Tipton present as one of the leading members, had been held at Jonesboro, and had just broken up when Sevier and a dozen of his followers rode into the squalid little town.[1] He drank freely and caroused with his friends; and he soon quarrelled with one of the other side who denounced him freely and justly for the murder of Corn Tassel and the other peaceful chiefs. Finally they all rode away, but when some miles out of town Sevier got into a quarrel with another man; and after more drinking and brawling he went to pass the night at a house, the owner of which was his friend. Meanwhile one of the men with whom he had quarrelled informed Tipton that his foe was in his grasp. Tipton gathered eight or ten men and early next morning surprised Sevier in his lodgings.

Sevier could do nothing but surrender, and Tipton put him in irons and sent him across the mountains to Morgantown, in North Carolina, where Sevier's he was kindly treated and allowed much Escape. liberty. Most of the inhabitants sympathized with

[1] Haywood, 190.

him, having no special repugnance to disorder, and no special sympathy even for friendly Indians. Meanwhile a dozen of his friends, with his two sons at their head, crossed the mountains to rescue their beloved leader. They came into Morgantown while court was sitting and went unnoticed in the crowds. In the evening, when the court adjourned and the crowds broke up, Sevier's friends managed to get near him with a spare horse; he mounted and they all rode off at speed. By daybreak they were out of danger.[1] Nothing further was attempted against him. A year later he was elected a member of the North Carolina Legislature; after some hesitation he was allowed to take his seat, and the last trace of the old hostility disappeared.

Neither the North Carolinians, nor any one else, knew that there was better ground for the charge of treason against Sevier than had appeared in his overt actions. He was one of those who had been in correspondence with Gardoqui on the subject of an alliance between the Westerners and Spain.

The year before this Congress had been much worked up over the discovery of a supposed move-

Alleged Filbuster-ing Movement.

ment in Franklin to organize for the armed conquest of Louisiana. In September 1787 a letter was sent by an ex-officer of the Continental line named John Sullivan, writing from Charleston, to a former comrade in

---

[1] Ramsey first copies Haywood and gives the account correctly. He then adds a picturesque alternative account—followed by later writers,—in which Sevier escapes in open court on a celebrated race mare. The basis for the last account, so far as it has any basis at all, lies on statements made nearly half a century after the event, and entirely unknown to Haywood. There is no evidence of any kind as to its truthfulness. It must be set down as mere fable.

arms; and this letter in some way became public. Sullivan had an unpleasant reputation. He had been involved in one of the mutinies of the under-paid Continental troops, and was a plotting, shifty, violent fellow. In his letter he urged his friend to come west forthwith and secure lands on the Tennessee; as there would soon be work cut out for the men of that country; and, he added: "I want you much—by God—take my word for it that we will speedily be in possession of New Orleans." [1]

The Secretary of War at once directed General Harmar to interfere, by force if necessary, with the execution of any such plan, and an officer of the regular army was sent to Franklin to find out the truth of the matter. This officer visited the Holston country in April, 1788, and after careful inquiry came to the conclusion that Sullivan had no backing, and that no movement against Spain was contemplated; the settlers being absorbed in the strife between the followers of Sevier and of Tipton. [2]

The real danger for the moment lay, not in a movement by the backwoodsmen against Spain, but Intrigues in a conspiracy of some of the backwoods with leaders with the Spanish authorities. Just Spain. at this time the unrest in the West had taken the form, not of attempting the capture of Louisiana by force, but of obtaining concessions from the Spaniards in return for favors to be rendered them. Clark and Robertson, Morgan, Brown and Innes, Wilkinson and Sebastian, were all in

[1] State Dept. MSS., No. 150, vol. iii., John Sullivan to Major Wm. Brown, September 24, 1787.

[2] *Do.*, Lieutenant John Armstrong to Major John P. Wyllys, April 28, 1788.

correspondence with Gardoqui and Miro, in the
endeavor to come to some profitable agreement with
them.   Sevier now joined the number.   His new-
born state had died; he was being prosecuted for
high treason; he was ready to go to any lengths
against North Carolina; and he clutched at the
chance of help from the Spaniard.   At the time
North Carolina was out of the Union, so that Sevier
committed no offence against the Federal Government.

Gardoqui was much interested in the progress of
affairs in Franklin ; and in the effort to turn them
Gardoqui to the advantage of Spain he made use of
and Sevier. James White, the Indian agent who was
in his pay.   He wrote[1] home that he did not believe Spain could force the backwoodsmen out of
Franklin (which he actually claimed as Spanish territory), but that he had secret advices that they could
easily be brought over to the Spanish interest by
proper treatment.   When the news came of the fight
between Sevier's and Tipton's men, he judged the
time to be ripe, and sent White to Franklin to sound
Sevier and bring him over; but he did not trust
White enough to give him any written directions,
merely telling him what to do and furnishing him
with three hundred dollars for his expenses.   The
mission was performed with such guarded caution that
only Sevier and a few of his friends ever knew of
the negotiations, and these kept their counsel well.

Sevier was in the mood to grasp a helping hand
stretched out from no matter what quarter.   He had

---

[1] Gardoqui MSS., Gardoqui to Floridablanca, April 18, 1788.

no organized government back of him; but he was in the midst of his successful Cherokee campaigns, and he knew the reckless Indian fighters would gladly follow him in any movement, if he had a chance of success. He felt that if he were given money and arms, and the promise of outside assistance, he could yet win the day. He jumped at Gardoqui's cautious offers; though careful not to promise to subject himself to Spain, and doubtless with no idea of playing the part of Spanish vassal longer than the needs of the moment required.

In July he wrote to Gardoqui, eager to strike a bargain with him; and in September sent him two letters by the hand of his son James Sevier who accompanied White when the latter made his return journey to the Federal capital.[1] One letter, which was not intended to be private, formally set forth the status of Franklin with reference to the Indians, and requested the representatives of the Catholic king to help keep the peace with the southern tribes. The other letter was the one of importance. In it he assured Gardoqui that the western people had grown to know that their hopes of prosperity rested on Spain, and that the principal people of Franklin were anxious to enter into an alliance with, and obtain commercial concessions from, the Spaniards. He importuned Gardoqui for money and for military aid, assuring him that the Spaniards could best accomplish their ends by furnishing these supplies immediately, especially as the struggle over the adoption of the Federal Constitution made the time opportune for revolt.

[1] Gardoqui MSS., Sevier to Gardoqui, Sept. 12, 1788.

Gardoqui received White and James Sevier with much courtesy, and was profuse, though vague, in his promises. He sent them both to New Orleans that Miro might hear and judge of their plans.[1] Nevertheless nothing came of the project, and doubtless only a few people in Franklin ever knew that it existed. As for Sevier, when he saw that he was baffled he suddenly became a Federalist and an advocate of a strong Central Government; and this, doubtless, not because of love for Federalism, but to show his hostility to North Carolina, which had at first refused to enter the new Union.[2] This particular move was fairly comic in its abrupt unexpectedness.

Thus the last spark of independent life flickered out in Franklin proper. The people who had settled on the Indian borders were left without government, North Carolina regarding them as trespassers on the Indian territory.[3] They accordingly met and organized a rude governmental machine, on the model of the Commonwealth of Franklin; and the wild little state existed as a separate and independent republic until the new Federal Government included it in the territory south of the Ohio.[4]

An Independent Frontier State.

[1] Gardoqui MSS., Gardoqui to Miro, Oct. 10, 1788.

[2] *Columbian Magazine*, Aug. 27, 1788, vol. ii., 542.

[3] Haywood, 195.

[4] In my first two volumes I have discussed, once for all, the worth of Gilmore's "histories" of Sevier and Robertson and their times. It is unnecessary further to consider a single statement they contain.

CHAPTER V.

KENTUCKY'S STRUGGLE FOR STATEHOOD.
1784–1790.

WHILE the social condition of the communities on the Cumberland and the Tennessee had changed very slowly, in Kentucky the changes had been rapid.

Col. William Fleming, one of the heroes of the battle of the Great Kanawha, and a man of note on the border, visited Kentucky on sur- Colonel veying business in the winter of 1779–80. Fleming's His journal shows the state of the new Journal. settlements as seen by an unusually competent observer; for he was an intelligent, well-bred, thinking man. Away from the immediate neighborhood of the few scattered log hamlets, he found the wilderness absolutely virgin. The easiest way to penetrate the forest was to follow the "buffalo paths," which the settlers usually adopted for their own bridle trails, and finally cut out and made into roads. Game swarmed. There were multitudes of swans, geese, and ducks on the river; turkeys and the small furred beasts, such as coons, abounded. Big game was almost as plentiful. Colonel Fleming shot, for the subsistence of himself and his party, many buffalo, bear, and deer, and some elk. His attention was drawn by the great flocks of parroquets, which appeared even in winter, and by the big, boldly colored, ivory-billed woodpeckers — birds which have long drawn back to the most remote swamps of the hot Gulf-coast, fleeing before man precisely as the buffalo and elk have fled.

Like all similar parties he suffered annoyance from the horses straying. He lost much time in hunting up the strayed beasts, and frequently had to pay the settlers for helping find them. There were no luxuries to be had for any money, and even such common necessaries as corn and salt were scarce and dear. Half a peck of salt cost a little less than eight pounds, and a bushel of corn the same. The surveying party, when not in the woods, stayed at the cabins of the more prominent settlers, and had to pay well for board and lodging, and for washing too.

Fleming was much struck by the misery of the settlers. At the Falls they were sickly, suffering **Kentucky** with fever and ague; many of the children **during the** were dying. Boonsboro and Harrodsburg **Revolution.** were very dirty, the inhabitants were sickly, and the offal and dead beasts lay about, poisoning the air and the water. During the winter no more corn could be procured than was enough to furnish an occasional hoe-cake. The people sickened on a steady diet of buffalo-bull beef, cured in smoke without salt, and prepared for the table by boiling. The buffalo was the stand-by of the settlers; they used his flesh as their common food, and his robe for covering; they made moccasins of his hide and fiddle-strings of his sinews, and combs of his horns.

They spun his winter coat into yarn, and out of it they made coarse cloth, like wool. They made a harsh linen from the bark of the rotted nettles. They got sugar from the maples. There were then, Fleming estimated, about three thousand souls in Kentucky. The Indians were everywhere, and all men lived in mortal terror of their lives; no settlement was free from the dread of the savages.[1]

Half a dozen years later all this was changed. The settlers had fairly swarmed into the Kentucky country, and the population was so dense that the true frontiersmen, the real pioneers, were already wandering off to Illinois and elsewhere ; every man of them desiring to live on his own land, by his own labor, and scorning to work for wages. The unexampled growth had wrought many changes ; not the least was the way in which it lessened the importance of the first hunter-settlers and hunter-soldiers. The great herds of game had been woefully thinned, and certain species, as the buffalo, practically destroyed. The killing of game was no longer the chief industry, and the flesh and hides of wild beasts were no longer the staples of food and clothing. The settlers already raised crops so large that they were anxious to export the surplus. They no longer clustered together in palisaded hamlets. They had cut out trails and roads in every direction from one to another of the many settlements. The scattered clearings on which they generally lived dotted the forest everywhere, and the

Immense and Rapid Changes.

[1] Draper MSS., Colonel Wm. Fleming, " MS. Journal in Kentucky," Nov. 12, 1779, to May 27, 1780.

towns, each with its straggling array of log cabins, and its occasional frame houses, did not differ materially from those in the remote parts of Pennsylvania and Virginia. The gentry were building handsome houses, and their amusements and occupations were those of the up-country planters of the seaboard.

The Indians were still a scourge to the settlements;[1] but, though they caused much loss of life, there was not the slightest danger of their imperilling the existence of the settlements as a whole, or even of any considerable town or group of clearings. Kentucky was no longer all a frontier. In the thickly peopled districts life was reasonably safe, though the frontier proper was harried and the remote farms jeopardized and occasionally abandoned,[2] while the river route and the wilderness road were beset by the savages. Where the country was at all well settled, the Indians did not attack in formidable war bands, like those that had assailed the forted villages in the early years of their existence; they skulked through the woods by twos and threes, and pounced only upon the helpless or the unsuspecting.

The Indian Ravages.

Nevertheless, if the warfare was not dangerous to the life and growth of the Commonwealth, it was fraught with undreamed-of woe and hardship to individual settlers and their families. On the outlying farms no man could tell when the blow would fall. Thus, in one backwoodsman's written reminiscences,

[1] State Department MSS., No. 151, p. 259, Report of Secretary of War, July 10, 1787 ; also, No. 60, p. 277.

[2] Virginia State Papers, iv., 149, State Department MSS., No. 56, p. 271.

there is a brief mention of a settler named Israel
Hart, who, during one May night, in 1787, suffered
much from a toothache. In the morning he went to
a neighbor's, some miles away through the forest, to
have his tooth pulled, and when he returned he
found his wife and his five children dead and cut to
pieces.[1] Incidents of this kind are related in every
contemporary account of Kentucky; and though they
commonly occurred in the thinly peopled districts,
this was not always the case. Teamsters and travellers were killed on the highroads near the towns—
even in the neighborhood of the very town where
the constitutional convention was sitting.

In all new-settled regions in the United States, so
long as there was a frontier at all, the changes in the
pioneer population proceeded in a certain Shifting of
definite order, and Kentucky furnished an the Fron-
example of the process. Throughout our tiersmen.
history as a nation the frontiersmen have always been
mainly native Americans, and those of European
birth have been speedily beaten into the usual frontier type by the wild forces against which they waged
unending war. As the frontiersmen conquered and
transformed the wilderness, so the wilderness in its
turn created and preserved the type of man who
overcame it. Nowhere else on the continent has so
sharply defined and distinctively American a type
been produced as on the frontier, and a single generation has always been more than enough for its pro-
duction. The influence of the wild country upon the
man is almost as great as the effect of the man upon

[1] Draper MSS., Whitely MS. Narrative.

the country.   The frontiersman destroys the wilderness, and yet its destruction means his own.   He
passes away before the coming of the very civilization whose advance guard he has been.   Nevertheless, much of his blood remains, and his striking characteristics have great weight in shaping the development of the land.   The varying peculiarities of the
different groups of men who have pushed the frontier westward at different times and places remain
stamped with greater or less clearness on the people
of the communities that grow up in the frontier's
stead.[1]

In Kentucky, as in Tennessee and the western portions of the seaboard States, and as later in the great
Succession West, different types of settlers appeared
of Types on successively on the frontier.   The hunter or
Frontier. trapper came first.   Sometimes he combined
with hunting and trapping the functions of an Indian
trader, but ordinarily the American, as distinguished
from the French or Spanish frontiersman, treated the
Indian trade as something purely secondary to his
more regular pursuits.   In Kentucky and Tennessee
the first comers from the East were not traders at
all, and were hunters rather than trappers.   Boone
was a type of this class, and Boone's descendants
went westward generation by generation until they
reached the Pacific.

Close behind the mere hunter came the rude hunter-
settler.   He pastured his stock on the wild range,

---

[1] Frederick Jackson Turner: " The Significance of the Frontier in
American History."   A suggestive pamphlet, published by the State Historical Society of Wisconsin.

and lived largely by his skill with the rifle. He worked with simple tools and he did his work roughly. His squalid cabin was destitute of the commonest comforts; the blackened stumps and dead, girdled trees stood thick in his small and badly tilled field. He was adventurous, restless, shiftless, and he felt ill at ease and cramped by the presence of more industrious neighbors. As they pressed in round about him he would sell his claim, gather his cattle and his scanty store of tools and household goods, and again wander forth to seek uncleared land. The Lincolns, the forbears of the great President, were a typical family of this class.

Most of the frontiersmen of these two types moved fitfully westward with the frontier itself, or near it, but in each place where they halted, or where the advance of the frontier was for the moment stayed, some of their people remained to grow up and mix with the rest of the settlers.

The third class consisted of the men who were thrifty, as well as adventurous, the men who were even more industrious than restless. These were they who entered in to hold the land, and who handed it on as an inheritance to their children and their children's children. Often, of course, these settlers of a higher grade found that for some reason they did not prosper, or heard of better chances still farther in the wilderness, and so moved onwards, like their less thrifty and more uneasy brethren, the men who half-cleared their lands and half-built their cabins. But, as a rule, these better-class settlers were not mere life-long pioneers.

The Permanent Settlers.

They wished to find good land on which to build, and plant, and raise their big families of healthy children, and when they found such land they wished to make thereon their permanent homes. They did not share the impulse which kept their squalid, roving fellows of the backwoods ever headed for the vague beyond. They had no sympathy with the feeling which drove these humbler wilderness-wanderers always onwards, and made them believe, wherever they were, that they would be better off somewhere else, that they would be better off in that somewhere which lay in the unknown and untried. On the contrary, these thriftier settlers meant to keep whatever they had once grasped. They got clear title to their lands. Though they first built cabins, as soon as might be they replaced them with substantial houses and barns. Though they at first girdled and burnt the standing timber, to clear the land, later they tilled it as carefully as any farmer of the seaboard States. They composed the bulk of the population, and formed the backbone and body of the State. The McAfees may be taken as a typical family of this class.

Yet a fourth class was composed of the men of means, of the well-to-do planters, merchants, and The lawyers, of the men whose families already Gentry. stood high on the Atlantic slope. The Marshalls were such men; and there were many other families of the kind in Kentucky. Among them were an unusually large proportion of the families who came from the fertile limestone region of Botetourt County in Virginia, leaving behind them, in the hands of their kinsmen, their roomy, comfortable houses, which stand to this day. These men soon grew to take the leading places in the new commonwealth. They were of good blood—using the words as they should be used, as meaning blood that has flowed through the veins of generations of self-restraint and courage and hard work, and careful training in mind and in the manly virtues. Their inheritance of sturdy and self-reliant manhood helped them greatly; their blood told in their favor as blood generally does tell when other things are equal. If they prized intellect they prized character more; they were strong in body and mind, stout of heart, and resolute of will. They felt that pride of race which spurs a man to effort, instead of making him feel that he is excused from effort. They realized that the qualities they inherited from their forefathers ought to be further developed by them as their forefathers had originally developed them. They knew that their blood and breeding, though making it probable that they would with proper effort succeed, yet entitled them to no success which they could not fairly earn in open contest with their rivals.

Such were the different classes of settlers who successively came into Kentucky, as into other western lands. There were of course no sharp lines of cleavage between the classes. They merged insensibly into one another, and the same individual might, at different times, stand in two or three. As a rule the individuals composing the first two were crowded out by their successors, and, after doing the roughest of the pioneer work, moved westward with the frontier; but some families were of course continually turning into permanent abodes what were merely temporary halting places of the greater number.

With the change in population came the corresponding change in intellectual interests and in Change in material pursuits. The axe was the tool, Subjects of and the rifle the weapon, of the early set-Interest. tlers; their business was to kill the wild beasts, to fight the savages, and to clear the soil; and the enthralling topics of conversation were the game and the Indians, and, as the settlements grew, the land itself. As the farms became thick, and towns throve, and life became more complex, the chances for variety in work and thought increased likewise. The men of law sprang into great prominence, owing in part to the interminable litigation over the land titles. The more serious settlers took about as much interest in matters theological as in matters legal; and the congregations of the different churches were at times deeply stirred by quarrels over questions of church discipline and doctrine.[1] Most of the books were either text-books of the simpler kinds or else theological.

Except when there was an Indian campaign, politics and the river commerce formed the two chief interests for all Kentuckians, but especially for the well-to-do.

In spite of all the efforts of the Spanish officials

---

[1] Durrett Collection ; see various theological writings, *e.g.*, " A Progress," etc., by Adam Rankin, Pastor at Lexington. Printed "at the Sign of the Buffalo," Jan. 1, 1793.

the volume of trade on the Mississippi grew steadily.
Six or eight years after the close of the   Features
Revolution the vast stretches of brown of the River
water, swirling ceaselessly between the   Travel.
melancholy forests, were already furrowed everywhere by the keeled and keelless craft.   The hol-
lowed log in which the Indian paddled; the same
craft, the pirogue, only a little more carefully made,
and on a little larger model, in which the creole
trader carried his load of paints and whiskey and
beads and bright cloths to trade for the peltries of
the savage ; the rude little scow in which some backwoods farmer drifted down stream with his cargo,
the produce of his own toil; the keel boats which,
with square-sails and oars, plied up as well as down
the river; the flotilla of huge flat boats, the property of some rich merchant, laden deep with tobacco
and flour, and manned by crews who were counted
rough and lawless even in the rough and lawless
backwoods—all these, and others too, were familiar
sights to every traveller who descended the Mississippi from Pittsburgh to New Orleans,[1] or who was
led by business to journey from Louisville to St.
Louis or to Natchez or New Madrid.

   The fact that the river commerce throve was
partly the cause and partly the consequence of the
general prosperity of Kentucky.   The pioneer days,
with their fierce and squalid struggle for bare life,
were over.   If men were willing to work, and
escaped the Indians, they were sure to succeed in
earning a comfortable livelihood in a country so rich.

   [1] John Pope's " Tour," in 1790.   Printed at Richmond in 1792.

"The neighbors are doing well in every sense of the word," wrote one Kentuckian to another, "they get children and raise crops."[1] Like all other successful and masterful people the Kentuckians fought well and bred well, and they showed by their actions their practical knowledge of the truth that no race can ever hold its own unless its members are able and willing to work hard with their hands.

The general prosperity meant rude comfort everywhere; and it meant a good deal more than rude Standard comfort for the men of greatest ability. of Living. By the time the river commerce had become really considerable, the rich merchants, planters, and lawyers had begun to build two-story houses of brick or stone, like those in which they had lived in Virginia. They were very fond of fishing, shooting, and riding, and were lavishly hospitable. They sought to have their children well taught, not only in letters but in social accomplishments like dancing; and at the proper season they liked to visit the Virginian watering-places, where they met "genteel company" from the older States, and lodged in good taverns in which "a man could have a room and a bed to himself."[2]

An agreement entered into about this time between one of the Clarks and a friend shows that Kentuckians were already beginning to appreciate the merits of neat surroundings even for a rather humble town-house. This particular house, together

[1] Draper MSS., Jonathan Clark Papers. O'Fallen to Clark, Isles of Ohio, May 30, 1791.

[2] Letter of a young Virginian, L. Butler, April 13, 1790. *Magazine of Amer. Hist.*, i., 113.

with the stable and lot, was rented for " one cow " for the first eight months, and two dollars a month after that—certainly not an excessive rate ; and it was covenanted that everything should be kept in good repair, and particularly that the grass plots around the house should not be " trod on or tore up."[1]

All Kentuckians took a great interest in politics, as is the wont of self-asserting, independent freemen, living under a democratic government. But the gentry and men of means and the law- **Interest in** yers very soon took the lead in political affairs. A **Politics.** larger proportion of these classes came from Virginia than was the case with the rest of the population, and they shared the eagerness and aptitude for political life generally shown by the leading families of Virginia. In many cases they were kin to these families ; not, however, as a rule, to the families of the tidewater region, the aristocrats of colonial days, but to the families—so often of Presbyterian Irish stock—who rose to prominence in western Virginia at the time of the Revolution. In Kentucky all were mixed together, no matter from what State they came, the wrench of the break from their home ties having shaken them so that they readily adapted themselves to new conditions, and easily assimilated with one another. As for their differences of race origin, these had ceased to influence their lives even before they came to Kentucky. They were all Americans, in feeling as well as in name, by habit as well as by birth ; and the positions they

---

[1] Draper MSS. Wm. Clark Papers. Agreement between Clark and Bagley, April 1, 1790.

took in the political life of the West was determined partly by the new conditions surrounding them, and partly by the habits bred in them through generations of life on American soil.

One man, who would naturally have played a prominent part in Kentucky politics, failed to do so

Clark's Breakdown.
from a variety of causes. This was George Rogers Clark. He was by preference a military rather than a civil leader; he belonged by choice and habit to the class of pioneers and Indian fighters whose influence was waning; his remarkable successes had excited much envy and jealousy, while his subsequent ignominious failure had aroused contempt; and, finally, he was undone by his fondness for strong drink. He drew himself to one side, though he chafed at the need, and in his private letters he spoke with bitterness of the " big little men," the ambitious nobodies, whose jealousy had prompted them to destroy him by ten thousand lies; and, making a virtue of necessity, he plumed himself on the fact that he did not meddle with politics, and sneered at the baseness of his fellow-citizens, whom he styled " a swarm of hungry persons gaping for bread." [1]

Benjamin Logan, who was senior colonel and county lieutenant of the District of Kentucky,

Logan's Prominence.
stood second to Clark in the estimation of the early settlers, the men who, riding their own horses and carrying their own rifles, had so often followed both commanders on their swift

---

[1] Draper MSS., G. R. Clark to J. Clark, April 20, 1788, and September 2, 1791.

raids against the Indian towns. Logan naturally took the lead in the first serious movement to make Kentucky an independent state. In its beginnings this movement showed a curious parallelism to what was occurring in Franklin at the same time, though when once fairly under way the difference between the cases became very strongly marked. In each case the prime cause in starting the movement was trouble with the Indians. In each, the first steps were taken by the commanders of the local militia, and the first convention was summoned on the same plan, a member being elected by every militia company. The companies were territorial as well as military units, and the early settlers were all, in practice as well as in theory, embodied in the militia. Thus in both Kentucky and Franklin the movements were begun in the same way by the same class of Indian-fighting pioneers; and the method of organization chosen shows clearly the rough military form which at that period settlement in the wilderness, in the teeth of a hostile savagery, always assumed.

In 1784 fear of a formidable Indian invasion—an unwarranted fear, as the result showed—became general in Kentucky, and in the fall Logan summoned a meeting of the field officers to discuss the danger and to provide against it. When the officers gathered and tried to evolve some plan of operations, they found that they were helpless. They were merely the officers of one of the districts of Virginia; they could take no proper steps of their own motion, and Virginia was too far

Conference of Militia Officers.

away and her interests had too little in common with theirs, for the Virginian authorities to prove satisfactory substitutes for their own. [1]   No officials in Kentucky were authorized to order an expedition against the Indians, or to pay the militia who took part in it, or to pay for their provisions and munitions of war.   Any expedition of the kind had to be wholly voluntary, and could of course only be undertaken under the strain of a great emergency; as a matter of fact the expeditions of Clark and Logan in 1786 were unauthorized by law, and were carried out by bodies of mere volunteers, who gathered only because they were forced to do so by bitter need. Confronted by such a condition of affairs, the militia officers issued a circular-letter to the people of the district, recommending that on December 24, 1784, a convention should be held at Danville further to consider the subject, and that this convention should consist of delegates elected one from each militia company.

The recommendation was well received by the people of the district; and on the appointed date First Con- the convention met at Danville.   Col. vention William Fleming, the old Indian fighter Elected by Militia and surveyor, was again visiting Kentucky, Companies. and he was chosen President of the convention.   After some discussion the members concluded that, while some of the disadvantages under which they labored could be remedied by the action of the Virginia Legislature, the real trouble was

---

[1] Marshall, himself an actor in these events, is the best authority for this portion of Kentucky history ; see also Green ; and compare Collins, Butler, and Brown

deep-rooted, and could only be met by separation
from Virginia and the erection of Kentucky into a
state. There was, however, much opposition to this
plan, and the convention wisely decided to dissolve,
after recommending to the people to elect, by counties, members who should meet in convention at
Danville in May for the express purpose of deciding
on the question of addressing to the Virginia
Assembly a request for separation.[1]

The convention assembled accordingly, Logan being one of the members, while it was presided over
by Col. Samuel McDowell, who, like Flem-   Second
ing, was a veteran Indian fighter and hero Convention
of the Great Kanawha. Up to this point   Held.
the phases through which the movement for statehood in Kentucky had passed were almost exactly
the same as the phases of the similar movement in
Franklin. But the two now entered upon diverging
lines of progression. In each case the home government was willing to grant the request for separation,
but wished to affix a definite date to their consent,
and to make the fulfilment of certain conditions a
prerequisite. In each case there were two parties in
the district desiring separation, one of them favoring
immediate and revolutionary action, while the other,
with much greater wisdom and propriety, wished to
act through the forms of law and with the consent
of the parent State. In Kentucky the latter party
triumphed. Moreover, while up to the time of this
meeting of the May convention the leaders in the

[1] State Dep. MSS. Madisòn Papers, Wallace to Madison, Sept. 25,
1785.

movement had been the old Indian fighters, after
this date the lead was taken by men who had come
to Kentucky only after the great rush of immigrants
began.   The new men were not backwoods hunter-
warriors, like Clark and Logan, Sevier, Robertson, and
Tipton.   They were politicians of the Virginia stamp.
They founded political clubs, one of which, the Danville club, became prominent, and in them they discussed with fervid eagerness the public questions of
the day, the members showing a decided tendency
towards the Jeffersonian school of political thought.

The convention, which met at Danville, in May,
1785, decided unanimously that it was desirable to
separate, by constitutional methods, from
Virginia, and to secure admission as a separate state into the Federal Union.   Accordingly, it directed the preparation of a
petition to this effect, to be sent to the Virginia
Legislature, and prepared an address to the people in
favor of the proposed course of action.   Then, in a
queer spirit of hesitancy, instead of acting on its own
responsibility, as it had both the right and power to
do, the convention decided that the issuing of the address, and the ratification of its own actions generally,
should be submitted to another convention, which
was summoned to meet at the same place in August
of the same year.   The people of the district were as
yet by no means a unit in favor of separation, and
this made the convention hesitate to take any ir-
revocable step.

Convention Urges Indepen- dence.

One of the members of this convention was Judge
Caleb Wallace, a recent arrival in Kentucky, and a
representative of the new school of Kentucky poli-

ticians. He was a friend and ally of Brown and Innes. He was also a friend of Madison, and to him he wrote a full account of the reasons which actuated the Kentuckians in the step they had taken.[1] He explained that he and the people of the district generally felt that they did not " enjoy a greater portion of liberty than an American colony might have done a few years ago had she been allowed a representation in the British Parliament." He complained bitterly that some of the taxes were burdensome and unjust, and that the money raised for the expenses of government all went to the east, to Virginia proper, while no corresponding benefits were received; and insisted that the seat of government was too remote for Kentucky ever to get justice from the rest of the State. Therefore, he said, he thought it would be wiser to part in peace rather than remain together in discontented and jealous union. But he frankly admitted that he was by no means sure that the people of the district possessed sufficient wisdom and virtue to fit them for successful self-government, and he anxiously asked Madison's advice as to several provisions which it was thought might be embodied in the constitution of the new state.

In the August convention Wilkinson sat as a member, and he succeeded in committing his colleagues to a more radical course of action than that of the preceding convention. The resolutions they forwarded to the Virginia Legislature, asked the immediate erection of Kentucky into an independent state, and

The Separatists Urge Immediate Revolution.

[1] State Department MSS. Madison Papers, Caleb Wallace to Madison, July 12, 1785.

expressed the conviction that the new commonwealth would undoubtedly be admitted into the Union. This, of course, meant that Kentucky would first become a power outside and independent of the Union; and no provision was made for entry into the Union beyond the expression of a hopeful belief that it would be allowed.

Such a course would have been in the highest degree unwise; and the Virginians refused to allow it to be followed. Their Legislature, in January, 1786, provided that a new convention should be held in Kentucky in September, 1786, and that, if it declared for independence, the state should come into being after the 1st of September, 1787, provided, however, that Congress, before June 1, 1787, consented to the erection of the new state, and agreed to its admission into the Union. It was also provided that another convention should be held, in the summer of 1787, to draw up a constitution for the new state.[1]

Virginia thus, with great propriety, made the acquiescence of Congress a condition precedent for the formation of the new State. Wilkinson immediately denounced this condition and demanded that Kentucky declare herself an independent State forthwith, no matter what Congress or Virginia might say. All the disorderly, unthinking, and separatist elements followed his lead. Had his policy been adopted the result would probably have been a civil war; and at the least there would have followed a period of anarchy and confusion, and a condition of things similar to that obtaining at this very time in

Virginia Wisely Affixes Conditions to her Consent.

[1] Marshall, i., 224.

the territory of Franklin.   The most enlightened
and far-seeing men of the district were alarmed at
the outlook; and a vigorous campaign in favor of
orderly action was begun, under the lead of men like
the Marshalls.   These men were themselves uncom-
promisingly in favor of statehood for Kentucky;
but they insisted that it should come in an orderly
way, and not by a silly and needless revolution,
which could serve no good purpose and was certain
to entail much disorder and suffering upon the community.   They insisted, furthermore, that there should
be no room for doubt in regard to the new state's
entering the Union.

There were thus two well defined parties, and
there were hot contests for seats in the convention.
One unforeseen event delayed the organization of
that body.   When the time that it should have convened arrived, Clark and Logan were making their
raids against the Shawnees and the Wabash Indians.
So many members-elect were absent in command of
their respective militia companies that the convention merely met to adjourn, no quorum to transact
business being obtained until January, 1787.   The
convention then sent to the Virginian Legislature
explaining the reason for the delay, and requesting
that the terms of the act of separation already passed
should be changed to suit the new conditions.

Virginia had so far acted wisely; but now she in
her turn showed unwisdom, for her Legislature
passed a new act, providing for another   Virginia
convention, to be held in August, 1787,   Makes
the separation from Virginia only to be   Needless
                                          Delay.
consummated if Congress, prior to July 4, 1788,

should agree to the erection of the state and provide for its admission to the Union. When news of this act, with its requirement of needless and tedious delay, reached the Kentucky convention, it adjourned for good, with much chagrin.

Wilkinson and the other separatist leaders took advantage of this very natural chagrin to inflame the minds of the people against both Virginia and Congress. It was at this time that the Westerners became deeply stirred by exaggerated reports of the willingness of Congress to yield the right to navigate the Mississippi; and the separatist chiefs fanned their discontent by painting the danger as real and imminent, although they must speedily have learned that it had already ceased to exist. Moreover, there was much friction between the Federal and Virginian authorities and the Kentucky militia officers in reference to the Indian raids. The Kentuckians showed a disposition to include all Indians, good and bad alike, in the category of foes. On the other hand the home authorities were inclined to forbid the Kentuckians to make the offensive return-forays which could alone render successful their defensive warfare against the savages. All these causes combined to produce much irritation, and the separatists began to talk rebellion. One of their leaders, Innes, in a letter to the Governor of Virginia, threatened that Kentucky would revolt not only from the parent State but from the Union, if heed were not paid to her wishes and needs. [1]

However, at this time Wilkinson started on his

[1] Green, 83.

first trading voyage to New Orleans, and the district
was freed from his very undesirable presence. He was the main-spring of the
movement in favor of lawless separation;
for the furtive, restless, unscrupulous man
had a talent for intrigue which rendered
him dangerous at a crisis of such a kind. In his
absence the feeling cooled. The convention met
in September, 1787, and acted with order and propriety, passing an act which provided for statehood
upon the terms and conditions laid down by Virginia.
The act went through by a nearly unanimous vote,
only two members dissenting, while three or four
refused to vote either way. Both Virginia and the
Continental Congress were notified of the action
taken.

The Ken-
tuckians
Grumble
but Acqui-
esce.

The only adverse comment that could be made on
the proceedings was that in the address to Congress
there was expressed a doubt, which was almost
equivalent to a threat, as to what the district would
do if it was not given full life as a state. But this
fear as to the possible consequences was real, and
many persons who did not wish for even a constitutional separation, nevertheless favored it because
they dreaded lest the turbulent and disorderly elements might break out in open violence if they saw
themselves chained indefinitely to those whose interests were, as they believed, hostile to theirs. The
lawless and shiftless folk, and the extreme separatists,
as a whole, wished for complete and absolute independence of both State and Nation, because it would
enable them to escape paying their share of the

Federal and State debts, would permit them to confiscate the lands of those whom they called "nonresident monopolizers," and would allow of their treating with the Indians according to their own desires. The honest, hardworking, forehanded, and farsighted people thought that the best way to defeat these mischievous agitators was to take the matter into their own hands, and provide for Kentucky's being put on an exact level with the older States.[1]

With Wilkinson's return to Kentucky, after his successful trading trip to New Orleans, the disunion agitation once more took formidable form. The news of his success excited the cupidity of every mercantile adventurer, and the whole district became inflamed with desire to reap the benefits of the rich river-trade; and naturally the people formed the most exaggerated estimate of what these benefits would be. Chafing at the way the restrictions imposed by the Spanish officials hampered their commerce, the people were readily led by Wilkinson and his associates to consider the Federal authorities as somehow to blame because these restrictions were not removed.

Renewal of the Disunion Agitation.

The discontent was much increased by the growing fury of the Indian ravages. There had been a lull in the murderous woodland warfare during the years immediately succeeding the close of the Revolution, but the storm had again gathered. The hostility of the savages had grown steadily. By the summer of 1787 the Kentucky fron-

The Indian Ravages.

[1] State Dep. MSS. Madison Papers, Wallace to Madison, Nov. 12, 1787.

tier was suffering much. The growth of the district was not stopped, nor were there any attempts made against it by large war bands; and in the thickly settled regions life went on as usual. But the out-lying neighborhoods were badly punished, and the county lieutenants were clamorous in their appeals for aid to the Governor of Virginia. They wrote that so many settlers had been killed on the frontier that the others had either left their clearings and fled to the interior for safety, or else had gathered in the log forts, and so were unable to raise crops for the support of their families. Militia guards and small companies of picked scouts were kept continu-ally patrolling the exposed regions near the Ohio, but the forays grew fiercer, and the harm done was great.[1] In their anger the Kentuckians denounced the Federal Government for not aiding them, the men who were loudest in their denunciations being the very men who were most strenuously bent on refusing to adopt the new Constitution, which alone could give the National Government the power to act effectually in the interest of the people.

While the spirit of unrest and discontent was high, the question of ratifying or rejecting this new Federal Constitution came up for decision. The Wilkinson party, and all the men who believed in a weak central government, or who wished the Federal tie dissolved out-right, were, of course, violently opposed to ratifica-tion. Many weak or short-sighted men, and the doctrinaires and theorists—most of the members of

Ratification of the Fed-eral Con-stitution.

---

[1] State Dept. MSS., No. 71, vol. ii., pp. 561, 563.

the Danville political club, for instance—announced that they wished to ratify the Constitution, but only after it had been amended. As such prior amendment was impossible, this amounted merely to playing into the hands of the separatists; and the men who followed it were responsible for the by no means creditable fact that most of the Kentucky members in the Virginia convention voted against ratification. Three of them, however, had the patriotism and foresight to vote in favor of the Constitution.

Another irritating delay in the march toward statehood now occurred. In June, 1788, the Con-

Further Delay. tinental Congress declared that it was expedient to erect Kentucky into a state.[1] But immediately afterwards news came that the Constitution had been ratified by the necessary nine States, and that the new government was, therefore, practically in being. This meant the dissolution of the old Confederation, so that there was no longer any object in admitting Kentucky to membership, and Congress thereupon very wisely refused to act further in the matter. Unfortunately Brown, who was the Kentucky delegate in Congress, was one of the separatist leaders. He wrote home an account of the matter, in which he painted the refusal as due to the jealousy felt by the East for the West. As a matter of fact the delegates from all the States, except Virginia, had concurred in the action taken. Brown suppressed this fact, and used language carefully calculated to render the Kentuckians hostile to the Union.

---

[1] State Dep. MSS., No. 20, vol. i., p. 341 etc.

Naturally all this gave an impetus to the separatist movement. The district held two conventions, in July and again in November, during the year 1788; and in both of them the separatist leaders made determined efforts to have Kentucky forthwith erect herself into an independent state. In uttering their opinions and desires they used vague language as to what they would do when once separated from Virginia. It is certain that they bore in mind at the time at least the possibility of separating outright from the Union and entering into a close alliance with Spain. The moderate men, headed by those who were devoted to the national idea, strenuously opposed this plan; they triumphed and Kentucky merely sent a request to Virginia for an act of separation in accordance with the recommendations of Congress.[1]

It was in connection with these conventions that there appeared the first newspaper ever printed in this new west; the west which lay no longer among the Alleghanies, but beyond them. It was a small weekly sheet called the *Kentucke Gazette*, and the first number appeared in August, 1787. The editor and publisher was one John Bradford, who brought his printing press down the river on a flat-boat; and some of the type were cut out of dogwood. In politics the paper sided with the separatists and clamored for revolutionary action by Kentucky.[2]

The Kentucke Gazette.

The purpose of the extreme separatist was, un-

---

[1] See Marshall and Green for this year.
[2] Durrett Collection, *Kentucke Gazette*, September 20, 1788.

questionably, to keep Kentucky out of the Union

Failure of the Separatist Movement. and turn her into a little independent nation,—a nation without a present or a future, an English-speaking Uraguay or Ecuador. The back of this separatist movement was broken by the action of the fall convention of 1788, which settled definitely that Kentucky should become a state of the Union. All that remained was to decide on the precise terms of the separation from Virginia. There was at first a hitch over these, the Virginia Legislature making terms to which the district convention of 1789 would not consent; but Virginia then yielded the points in dispute, and the Kentucky convention of 1790 provided for the admission of the state to the Union in 1792, and for holding a constitutional convention to decide upon the form of government, just before the admission.[1]

Thus Kentucky was saved from the career of ignoble dishonor to which she would have been doomed by the success of the disunion faction. She was saved from the day of small things. Her interests became those of a nation which was bound to succeed greatly or to fail greatly. Her fate was linked for weal or for woe with the fate of the mighty Republic.

[1] Marshall, i., 342 etc.

CHAPTER VI.

THE NORTHWEST TERRITORY; OHIO. 1787–1790.

So far the work of the backwoodsmen in exploring, conquering, and holding the West had been
work undertaken solely on individual initiative. The nation as a whole had not
directly shared in it. The frontiersmen
who chopped the first trails across the
Alleghanies, who earliest wandered through the
lonely western lands, and who first built stockaded
hamlets on the banks of the Watauga, the Kentucky,
and the Cumberland, acted each in consequence of
his own restless eagerness for adventure and possible
gain. The nation neither encouraged them to undertake the enterprises on which they embarked, nor
protected them for the first few years of uncertain
foothold in the new-won country. Only the backwoodsmen themselves felt the thirst for exploration
of the unknown, the desire to try the untried, which
drove them hither and thither through the dim
wilderness. The men who controlled the immediate
destinies of the confederated commonwealths knew
little of what lay in the forest-shrouded country
beyond the mountains, until the backwoods explorers
of their own motion penetrated its hidden and in-

most fastnesses. Singly or in groups, the daring hunters roved through the vast reaches of sombre woodland, and pitched their camps on the banks of rushing rivers, nameless and unknown. In bands of varying size the hunter-settlers followed close behind, and built their cabins and block-houses here and there in the great forest land. They elected their own military leaders, and waged war on their own account against their Indian foes. They constructed their own governmental systems, on their own motion, without assistance or interference from the parent States, until the settlements were firmly established, and the work of civic organization well under way.

Of course some help was ultimately given by the parent States; and the indirect assistance rendered by the nation had been great. The West **Help Rendered by National Government.** could neither have been won nor held by the frontiersmen, save for the backing given by the Thirteen States. England and Spain would have made short work of the men whose advance into the lands of their Indian allies they viewed with such jealous hatred, had they not also been forced to deal with the generals and soldiers of the Continental army, and the statesmen and diplomats of the Continental Congress. But the real work was done by the settlers themselves. The distinguishing feature in the exploration, settlement, and up-building of Kentucky and Tennessee was the individual initiative of the backwoodsmen.

The direct reverse of this was true of the settle-

ment of the country northwest of the Ohio. Here,
also, the enterprise, daring, and energy of
the individual settlers were of the utmost
consequence; the land could never have
been won had not the incomers possessed
these qualities in a very high degree. But
the settlements sprang directly from the action of
the Federal Government, and the first and most
important of them would not have been undertaken
save for that action. The settlers were not the first
comers in the wilderness they cleared and tilled.
They did not themselves form the armies which met
and overthrew the Indians. The regular forces led
the way in the country north of the Ohio. The Federal forts were built first; it was only afterwards
that the small towns sprang up in their shadow.
The Federal troops formed the vanguard of the white
advance. They were the mainstay of the force behind which, as behind a shield, the founders of the
commonwealths did their work.

> The North-
> west Won
> by the
> Nation as
> a Whole.

Unquestionably many of the settlers did their full
share in the fighting; and they and their descendants, on many a stricken field, and through many a
long campaign, proved that no people stood above
them in hardihood and courage; but the land on
which they settled was won less by themselves than
by the statesmen who met in the national capital,
and the scarred soldiers who on the frontier upbore
the national colors. Moreover, instead of being
absolutely free to choose their own form of government, and shape their own laws and social conditions
untrammelled by restrictions, the Northwesterners

were allowed to take the land only upon certain definite conditions. The National Government ceded to settlers part of its own domain, and provided the terms upon which states of the Union should afterwards be made out of this domain; and with a wisdom and love of righteousness which have been of incalculable consequence to the whole nation, it stipulated that slavery should never exist in the States thus formed. This condition alone profoundly affected the whole development of the Northwest, and sundered it by a sharp line from those portions of the new country which, for their own ill fortune, were left free from all restriction of the kind. The Northwest owes its life and owes its abounding strength and vigorous growth to the action of the nation as a whole. It was founded not by individual Americans, but by the United States of America. The mighty and populous commonwealths that lie north of the Ohio and in the valley of the Upper Mississippi are in a peculiar sense the children of the National Government, and it is no mere accident that has made them in return the especial guardians and protectors of that government; for they form the heart of the nation.

Before the Continental Congress took definite action concerning the Northwest, there had been settlements within its borders, but these settle-
Unorganized Settlements West of the Ohio. ments were unauthorized and illegal, and had little or no effect upon the aftergrowth of the region. Wild and lawless adventurers had built cabins and made tomahawk claims on the west bank of the Upper Ohio. They lived

in angry terror of the Indians, and they also had
cause to dread the regular army; for wherever the
troops discovered their cabins, they tore them down,
destroyed the improvements, and drove off the sullen
and threatening squatters. As the tide of settlement
increased in the neighboring country these trespassers
on the Indian lands and on the national domain
became more numerous. Many were driven off,
again and again; but here and there one kept his
foothold. It was these scattered few successful ones
who were the first permanent settlers in the present
State of Ohio, coming in about the same time that
the forts of the regular troops were built. They
formed no organized society, and their presence was
of no importance whatever in the history of the
State.

The American settlers who had come in round the
French villages on the Wabash and the Illinois were
of more consequence. In 1787 the adult males
among these American settlers numbered 240, as
against 1040 French of the same class.[1] They had
followed in the track of Clark's victorious march.
They had taken up land, sometimes as mere squatters,
sometimes under color of title obtained from the
French courts which Clark and Todd had organized
under what they conceived to be the authority of
Virginia. They were for the most part rough, enterprising men ; and while some of them behaved well,
others proved very disorderly and gave much trouble

[1] State Dept. MSS., No. 48, p. 165. Of adult males there were among
the French 520 at Vincennes, 191 at Kaskaskia, 239 at Cahokia, 11 at St.
Phillippe, and 78 at Prairie du Rocher. The American adult males numbered 103 at Vincennes and 137 in the Illinois.

to the French; so that both the Creoles and the Indians became exasperated with them and put them in serious jeopardy just before Clark undertook his expedition in the fall of 1786.

The Creoles had suffered much from the general misrule and anarchy in their country, and from the disorderly conduct of some of the American settlers, and of not a few of the ragged volunteer soldiery as well. They hailed with sincere joy the advent of the disciplined Continental troops, commanded by officers who behaved with rigid justice towards all men and put down disorder with a strong hand. They were much relieved to find themselves under the authority of Congress, and both to that body and to the local Regular Army officers, they sent petitions setting forth their grievances and hopes. In one petition to Congress they recited at length the wrongs done them, dwelling especially upon the fact that they had gladly furnished the garrison established among them with poultries and provisions of every kind, for which they had never received a dollar's payment. They remarked that the stores seemed to disappear in a way truly marvellous, leaving the backwoods soldiers who were to have benefited by them "as ragged as ever." The petitioners complained that the undisciplined militia quartered among them, who on their arrival were "in the most shabby and wretched state," and who had "rioted in abundance and unaccustomed luxury" at the expense of the Creoles, had also maltreated and insulted them; as for instance they had at times wantonly shot the

The French Villages.

cattle merely to try their rifles. "Ours was the task of hewing and carting them firewood to the barracks," continued the petition, complaining of the way the Virginians had imposed on the submissiveness and docility of the inhabitants, "ours the drudgery of raising vegetables which we did not eat, poultry for their kitchen, cattle for the diversion of their marksmen."

The petitioners further asked that every man among them should be granted five hundred acres. They explained that formerly they had set no value on the land, occupying themselves chiefly with the Indian trade, and raising only the crops they absolutely needed for food; but that now they realized the worth of the soil, and inasmuch as they had various titles to it, under lost or forgotten charters from the French kings, they would surrender all the rights these titles conveyed, save only what belonged to the Church of Cahokia, in return for the above named grant of five hundred acres to each individual.[1]

The memorialists alluded to their explanation of the fact that they had lost all the title-deeds to the land, that is all the old charters granted them, as "ingenuous and candid"; and so it was. The immense importance of having lost all proof of their rights did not strike them. There was an almost

[1] State Department MSS., No. 48, " Memorial of the French Inhabitants of Post Vincennes, Kaskaskia, La Prairie du Rocher, Cahokia, and Village of St. Philip to Congress." By Bartholemew Tardiveau, agent. New York, February 26, 1788. Tardiveau was a French mercantile adventurer, who had relations with Gardoqui and the Kentucky separatists, and in a petition presented by him it is not easy to discriminate between the views that are really those of the Creoles, and the views which he deemed it for his own advantage to have expressed.

pathetic childishness in the request that the United
States authorities should accept oral tradition in lieu
of the testimony of the lost charters, and in the way
they dwelt with a kind of humble pride upon their
own "submissiveness and docility." In the same
spirit the inhabitants of Vincennes surrendered
their charter, remarking "accustomed to mediocrity,
we do not wish for wealth but for mere competency."[1]
Of course the "submissiveness" and the light-
heartedness of the French did not prevent their
being also fickle; and their "docility" was varied
by fits of violent quarrelling with their American
neighbors and among themselves. But the quarrels
of the Creoles were those of children, compared with
the ferocious feuds of the Americans.

Sometimes the trouble was of a religious nature.
The priest at Vincennes, for instance, bitterly assailed
the priest at Cahokia, because he married a Catholic
to a Protestant; while all the people of the Cahokia
church stoutly supported their pastor in what he had
done.[2] This Catholic priest was Clark's old friend
Gibault. He was suffering from poverty, due to his
loyal friendship to the Americans; for he had advanced Clark's troops both goods and peltries, for
which he had never received payment. In a petition
to Congress he showed how this failure to repay him
had reduced him to want, and had forced him to sell
his two slaves, who otherwise would have kept and
tended him in his old age.[3]

---

[1] *Do.*, July 26, 1787.   [2] *Do.*, p. 85.
[3] American State Papers, Public Lands, I., Gibault's Memorial, May 1,
1790.

The Federal General Harmar, in the fall of 1787, took formal possession, in person, of Vincennes and the Illinois towns ; and he commented upon the good behavior of the Creoles, and their respect for the United States Government, and laid stress upon the fact that they were entirely unacquainted with what the Americans called liberty, and could best be governed in the manner to which they were accustomed —" by a commandant with a few troops."[1]

The American pioneers, on the contrary, were of all people the least suited to be governed by a commandant with troops. They were much better stuff out of which to make a free, self-governing nation, and they were much better able to hold their own in the world, and to shape their own destiny; but they were far less pleasant people to govern. To this day the very virtues of the pioneers—not to speak of their faults—make it almost impossible for them to get on with an ordinary army officer, accustomed as he is to rule absolutely, though justly and with a sort of severe kindness. Army officers on the frontier —especially when put in charge of Indian reservations or of French or Spanish communities—have almost always been more or less at swords-points with the stubborn, cross-grained pioneers. The borderers are usually as suspicious as they are independent, and their self-sufficiency and self-reliance often degenerate into mere lawlessness and defiance of all restraint.

Contrast between the French and Americans.

[1] St. Clair Papers, Harmar's Letters, August 7th and November 24th, 1787.

The Federal officers in the backwoods north of the Ohio got on badly with the backwoodsmen. Harmar took the side of the French Creoles, and warmly denounced the acts of the frontiersmen who had come in among them.[1] In his letter to the Creoles he alluded to Clark's Vincennes garrison as "a set of lawless banditti," and explained that his own troops were regulars, who would treat with justice both the French and Indians. Harmar never made much effort to conceal his dislike of the borderers. In one letter he alludes to a Delaware chief as "a manly old fellow, and much more of a gentleman than the generality of these frontier people."[2] Naturally, there was little love lost between the bitterly prejudiced old army officer, fixed and rigid in all his ideas, and the equally prejudiced backwoodsmen, whose ways of looking at almost all questions were antipodal to his.

The Regular Officers Side with the French against the Americans.

The Creoles of the Illinois and Vincennes sent warm letters of welcome to Harmar. The American settlers addressed him in an equally respectful but very different tone, for, they said, their hearts were filled with "anxiety, gloominess, and dismay." They explained the alarm they felt at the report that they were to be driven out of the country, and protested— what was doubtless true—that they had settled on the land in entire good faith, and with the assent of the French inhabitants. The latter themselves bore testi-

[1] State Dept. MSS., No. 150, vol. ii., Harmar to Le Grasse and Busseron, June 29, 1787.
[2] *Do.*, Harmar to the Secretary of War, March 9, 1788.

mony to the good faith and good behavior of many of the settlers, and petitioned that these should not be molested,[1] explaining that the French had been benefited by their industry, and had preserved a peaceable and friendly intercourse with them. In the end, while the French villagers were left undisturbed in their ancient privileges, and while they were granted or were confirmed in the possession of the land immediately around them, the Americans and the French who chose to go outside the village grants were given merely the rights of other settlers.

The Continental officers exchanged courtesies with the Spanish commandants of the Creole villages on the west bank of the Mississippi, but kept a sharp eye on them, as these commandants endeavored to persuade all the French inhabitants to move west of the river by offering them free grants of land.[2]

But all these matters were really of small consequence. The woes of the Creoles, the trials of the American squatters, the friction between the regular officers and the backwoodsmen, the jealousy felt by both for the Spaniards —all these were of little real moment at this period of the history of the Northwest. The vital point in its history was the passage by Congress of the Ordinance of 1787, and the doings of the various land companies under and in consequence of this ordinance.

The Real Founders of the Northwest.

[1] *Do.*, Address of American Inhabitants of Vincennes, August 4, 1787; Recommendation by French Inhabitants in Favor of American Inhabitants, August 2d ; Letter of Le Chamy and others, Kaskaskia, August 25th ; Letter of J. M. P. Le Gras, June 25th.

[2] Hamtranck to Harmar, October 13, 1788.

16

The wide gap between the ways in which the Northwest and the Southwest were settled is made plain by such a statement. In the Northwest, it was the action of Congress, the action of the representatives of the nation acting as a whole, which was all-important. In the Southwest, no action of Congress was of any importance when compared with the voluntary movements of the backwoodsmen themselves. In the Northwest, it was the nation which acted. In the Southwest, the determining factor was the individual initiative of the pioneers. The most striking feature in the settlement of the Southwest was the free play given to the workings of extreme individualism. The settlement of the Northwest represented the triumph of an intelligent collectivism, which yet allowed to each man a full measure of personal liberty.

Individualism in the Southwest, Collectivism in the Northwest.

Another difference of note was the difference in stock of the settlers. The Southwest was settled by the true backwoodsmen, the men who lived on their small clearings among the mountains of western Pennsylvania, Virginia, and North Carolina. The first settlement in Ohio, the settlement which had most effect upon the history of the Northwest, and which largely gave it its peculiar trend, was the work of New Englanders. There was already a considerable population in New England; but the rugged farmers with their swarming families had to fill up large waste spaces in Maine and in Northern New Hampshire and Vermont, and there was a very marked

Difference in Stock of the Settlers.

movement among them towards New York, and especially into the Mohawk valley, all west of which was yet a wilderness. In consequence, during the years immediately succeeding the close of the Revolutionary War, the New England emigrants made their homes in those stretches of wilderness which were nearby, and did not appear on the western border. But there had always been enterprising individuals among them desirous of seeking a more fertile soil in the far west or south, and even before the Revolution some of these men ventured to Louisiana itself, to pick out a good country in which to form a colony. After the close of the war the fame of the lands along the Ohio was spread abroad; and the men who wished to form companies for the purposes of adventurous settlement began to turn their eyes thither.

The first question to decide was the ownership of the wished-for country. This decision had to be made in Congress by agreement among the representatives of the different States. Seven States—Massachusetts, Connecticut, New York, Virginia, Georgia, and both Carolinas —claimed portions of the western lands. New York's claim was based with entire solemnity on the ground that she was the heir of the Iroquois tribes, and therefore inherited all the wide regions overrun by their terrible war-bands. The other six States based their claims on various charters, which in reality conferred rights not one whit more substantial.

These different claims were not of a kind to which any outside power would have paid heed. Their usefulness came in when the States bargained among themselves. In the bargaining, both among the claimant States, and between the claimant and the non-claimant States, the charter titles were treated as of importance, and substantial concessions were exacted in return for their surrender. But their value was really inchoate until the land was reduced to possession by some act of the States or the Nation.

At the close of the Revolutionary War there existed wide differences between the various States Virginia as to the actual ownership and possession and North of the lands they claimed. Virginia and Carolina. North Carolina were the only two who had reduced to some kind of occupation a large part of the territory to which they asserted title. Their backwoodsmen had settled in the lands so that they already held a certain population. Moreover, these same backwoodsmen, organized as part of the militia of the parent States, had made good their claim by successful warfare. The laws of the two States were executed by State officials in communities scattered over much of the country claimed. The soldier-settlers of Virginia and North Carolina had actually built houses and forts, tilled the soil, and exercised the functions of civil government, on the banks of the Wabash and the Ohio, the Mississippi, the Cumberland, and the Tennessee. Counties and districts had been erected by the two States on the western waters; and representatives of the civil divisions thus constituted sat in the State Legislatures. The claims of Virginia and North Carolina to much of the territory had behind them the substantial element of armed possession. The settlement and conquest of the lands had been achieved without direct intervention by the Federal Government; though of course it was only the ultimate success of the nation in its contest with the foreign foe that gave the settlement and conquest any value.

As much could not be said for the claims of the other States. South Carolina's claim was to a mere ribbon of land south of the North Caro- **Georgia.** lina territory, and need not be considered ; it was ceded to the Government about the time the Northwest was organized.[1] Georgia asserted that her boundaries extended due west to the Mississippi, and that all between was hers. But the entire western portion of the territory was actually held by the Spaniards and by the Indian tribes tributary to the Spaniards. No subjects of Georgia lived on it, or were allowed to live on it. The few white inhabitants were subjects of the King of Spain, and lived under Spanish law ; the Creeks and Choctaws were his subsidized allies; and he held the country by right of conquest. Georgia, a weak and turbulent, though a growing State, was powerless to enforce her claims. Most of the territory to which she asserted title did not in truth become part of the United States until Pinckney's treaty went into effect. It was the United States and not Georgia that actually won and held the land in dispute; and it was a discredit to Georgia's patriotism that she so long wrangled about it, and ultimately drove

[1] For an account of this cession see Mr. Garrett's excellent paper in the publications of the Tennessee Historical Society.

so hard a bargain concerning it with the National Government.

There was a similar state of affairs in the far Northwest. No New Yorkers lived in the region Claims to bounded by the shadowy and wavering the North- lines of the Iroquois conquests. The lands west. claimed under ancient charters by Massachusetts and Connecticut were occupied by the British and their Indian allies, who held adverse possession. Not a single New England settler lived in them; no New England law had any force in them; no New England soldier had gone or could go thither. They were won by the victory of Wayne and the treaty of Jay. If Massachusetts and Connecticut had stood alone, the lands would never have been yielded to them at all; they could not have enforced their claim, and it would have been scornfully disregarded. The region was won for the United States by the arms and diplomacy of the United States. Whatever of reality there was in the titles of Massachusetts and Connecticut came from the existence and actions of the Federal Union.[1]

[1] For this northwestern history see " The Life, Journal, and Correspondence of Manasseh Cutler," by Wm. Parker Cutler and Julia Perkins Cutler ; "The St. Clair Papers," by W. H. Smith ; " The Old Northwest," by B. A. Hinsdale ; " Maryland's Influence upon Land Cessions," by Herbert Adams. See also Donaldson's " Public Domain," Hildreth's " History of Washington County," and the various articles by Poole and others. In Prof. Hinsdale's excellent book, on p. 200, is a map of the " Territory of the Thirteen Original States in 1783." This map is accurate enough for Virginia and North Carolina ; but the lands in the west put down as belonging to Massachusetts, Connecticut, and Georgia, did not really belong to them at all in 1783 ; they were held by the British and Spaniards, and were ultimately surrendered to the United States, not to individual States. These States did not surrender the land ; they merely surrendered a disputed title to the lands.

All the States that did not claim lands beyond the mountains were strenuous in belittling the claims of those that did, and insisted that the **The Non-**title to the western territory should be **claimant** vested in the Union. Not even the danger **States.** from the British armies could keep this question in abeyance, and while the war was at its height the States were engaged in bitter wrangles over the subject; for the weakness of the Federal tie rendered it always probable that the different members of the Union would sulk or quarrel with one another rather than oppose an energetic resistance to the foreign foe. At different times different non-claimant States took the lead in pushing the various schemes for nationalizing the western lands; but Maryland was the first to take action in this direction, and was the most determined in pressing the matter to a successful issue. She showed the greatest hesitation in joining the Confederation at all while the matter was allowed to rest unsettled; and insisted that the titles of the claimant States were void, that there was no need of asking them to cede what they did not possess, and that the West should be declared outright to be part of the Federal domain.

Maryland was largely actuated by fear of her neighbor Virginia. Virginia's claims were the most considerable, and if they had all been allowed, hers would have been indeed an empire. Maryland's fears were twofold. She dreaded the mere growth of Virginia in wealth, power, and population in the first place; and in the second she feared lest her own population might be drained into these vacant

lands, thereby at once diminishing her own, and
building up her neighbor's, importance. Each State,
at that time, had to look upon its neighbors as
probable commercial rivals and possible armed enemies. This is a feeling which we now find difficulty
in understanding. At present no State in the Union
fears the growth of a neighbor, or would ever dream
of trying to check that growth. The direct reverse
was the case during and after the Revolution ; for
the jealousy and distrust which the different States
felt for one another were bitter to a degree.

The Continental Congress was more than once at
its wits' ends in striving to prevent an open break
The Contin- over the land question between the more
ental Con- extreme States on the two sides. The
gress Advo- wisest and coolest leaders saw that the
cates a
Com-   matter could never be determined on a
promise.   mere consideration of the abstract rights,
or even of the equities, of the case. They saw that
it would have to be decided, as almost all political
questions of great importance must be decided, by
compromise and concession. The foremost statesmen of the Revolution were eminently practical
politicians. They had high ideals, and they strove
to realize them, as near as might be ; otherwise they
would have been neither patriots nor statesmen. But
they were not theorists. They were men of affairs,
accustomed to deal with other men ; and they understood that few questions of real moment can be decided on their merits alone. Such questions must
be dealt with on the principle of getting the greatest
possible amount of ultimate good, and of surrender-

ing in return whatever must be surrendered in order to attain this good.   There was no use in learned arguments to show that Maryland's position was the proper one for a far-sighted American patriot, or that Virginia and North Carolina had more basis for their claims than Connecticut or Georgia.   What had to be done was to appeal to the love of country and shrewd common-sense of the people in the different States, and persuade them each to surrender on certain points, so that all could come to a common agreement.

New York's claim was the least defensible of all, but, on the other hand, New York led the way in vesting whatever title she might have in the Federal Government.   In 1780 she gave proof of the growth of the national idea among her citizens by abandoning all her claim to western lands in favor of the Union.   Congress used this surrender as an argument by which to move the other States to action.   It issued an earnest appeal to them to follow New York's example without regard to the value of their titles, so that the Federal Union might be put on a firm basis. Congress did not discuss its own rights, nor the rights of the States ; it simply asked that the cessions be made as a matter of expediency and patriotism ; and announced that the policy of the Government would be to divide this new territory into districts of suitable size, which should be admitted as States as soon as they became well settled.   This last proposition was important, as it outlined the future policy of the Government, which was to

Land Cessions by the Claimant States.

admit the new communities as States, with all the rights of the old States, instead of treating them as subordinate and dependent, after the manner of the European colonial systems.

Maryland then joined the Confederation, in 1781. Virginia and Connecticut had offered to cede their claims but under such conditions that it was impossible to close with the offers.   Congress accepted the New York cession gratefully, with an eye to the effect on the other States; but for some time no progress was made in the negotiations with the latter. Finally, early in 1784, the bargain with Virginia was consummated.   She ceded to Congress her rights to the territory northwest of the Ohio, except a certain amount retained as a military reserve for the use of her soldiers, while Congress tacitly agreed not to question her right to Kentucky.   A year later Massachusetts followed suit, and ceded to Congress her title to all the lands lying west of the present western boundary of New York State.   Finally, in 1786, a similar cession was made by Connecticut.   But Connecticut's action was not much more patriotic or less selfish than Georgia's.   Throughout the controversy she showed a keen desire to extract from Congress all that could possibly be obtained, and to delay action as long as might be; though, like Georgia, Connecticut could by rights claim nothing that was not in reality obtained for the Union by the Union itself.   She made her grant conditionally upon being allowed to reserve for her own profit about five thousand square miles in what is now northern Ohio.   This tract was afterwards known as the

Western Reserve. Congress was very reluctant to accept such a cession, with its greedy offset, but there was no wise alternative, and the bargain was finally struck.

The non-claimant states had attained their object, and yet it had been obtained in a manner that left the claimant States satisfied. The project for which Maryland had contended was realized, with the difference that Congress accepted the Northwest as a gift coupled with conditions, instead of taking it as an unconditional right. The lands became part of the Federal domain, and were nationalized so far as they could be under the Confederation; but there was no national treasury into which to turn the proceeds from the sale until the Constitution was adopted.[1]

Having got possession of the land, Congress proceeded to arrange for its disposition, even before providing the outline of the governmental system for the states that might grow up therein. Congress regarded the territory as forming a treasury chest, and was anxious to sell the land in lots, whether to individuals or to companies. In 1785 it passed an ordinance of singular wisdom, which has been the basis of all our subsequent legislation on the subject.

The Land Policy of Congress.

This ordinance was another proof of the way in which the nation applied its collective power to the subdual and government of the Northwest, instead of leaving the whole matter to the working of unrestricted individualism, as in the Southwest. The pernicious system of acquiring title to public lands in vogue among the

[1] Hinsdale, 250.

Virginians and North Carolinians was abandoned. Instead of making each man survey his own land, and allowing him to survey it when, how, and where he pleased, with the certainty of producing endless litigation and trouble, Congress provided for a corps of government surveyors, who were to go about this work systematically. It provided further for a known base line, and then for division of the country into ranges of townships six miles square, and for the subdivision of these townships into lots ("sections") of one square mile—six hundred and forty acres— each. The ranges, townships, and sections were duly numbered. The basis for the whole system of public education in the Northwest was laid by providing that in every township lot No. 16 should be reserved for the maintenance of public schools therein. A minimum price of a dollar an acre was put on the land.

Congress hoped to find in these western lands a source of great wealth. The hope was disappointed. The task of subduing the wilderness is not very remunerative. It yields a little more than a livelihood to men of energy, resolution, and bodily strength and address; but it does not yield enough for men to be able to pay heavily for the privilege of undertaking the labor. Throughout our history the pioneer has found that by taking up wild land at a low cost he can make a rough living, and keep his family fed, clothed, and housed; but it is only by very hard work that he can lay anything by, or materially better his condition. Of course, the few very successful do much more, and the unsuccessful

do even less; but the average pioneer can just man-
age to keep continually forging a little ahead, in matters material and financial. Under such conditions
a high price cannot be obtained for public lands;
and when they are sold, as they must be, at a low
price, the receipts do little more than offset the
necessary outlay. The truth is that people have a
very misty idea as to the worth of wild lands. Even
when the soil is rich they only possess the capacity
of acquiring value under labor. All their value
arises from the labor done on them or in their
neighborhood, except that it depends also upon the
amount of labor which must necessarily be expended
in transportation.

It is the fashion to speak of the immense opportunity offered to any race by a virgin continent. In
one sense the opportunity is indeed great; but in
another sense it is not, for the chance of failure is
very great also. It is an opportunity of which advantage can be taken only at the cost of much hardship and much grinding toil.

It remained for Congress to determine the conditions under which the settlers could enter the new
land, and under which new States should The Ordi-
spring up therein. These conditions were nance of
fixed by the famous Ordinance of 1787; 1787.
one of the two or three most important acts ever
passed by an American legislative body, for it determined that the new northwestern States, the children, and the ultimate leaders, of the Union, should
get their growth as free commonwealths, untainted
by the horrible curse of negro slavery.

Several ordinances for the government of the Northwest were introduced and carried through Congress in 1784–1786, but they were never put into operation. In 1784 Jefferson put into his draft of the ordinance of that year a clause prohibiting slavery in all the western territory, south as well as north of the Ohio River, after the beginning of the year 1801. This clause was struck out; and even if adopted it would probably have amounted to nothing, for if slavery had been permitted to take firm root it could hardly have been torn up. In 1785 Rufus King advanced a proposition to prohibit all slavery in the Northwest immediately, but Congress never acted on the proposal.

The next movement in the same direction was successful, because when it was made it was pushed by a body of well-known men who were anxious to buy the lands that Congress was anxious to sell, but who would not buy them until they had some assurance that the governmental system under which they were to live would meet their ideas. This body was composed of New Englanders, mostly veterans of the Revolutionary War, and led by officers who had stood well in the Continental army.

When, in the fall of 1783, the Continental army was disbanded, the war-worn and victorious soldiers, who had at last wrung victory from the reluctant years of defeat, found themselves fronting grim penury. Some were worn with wounds and sickness; all were poor and unpaid; and Congress had no means to pay them. Many among them felt that they had small chance to repair their broken fortunes if they returned to the homes they had aban-

doned seven weary years before, when the guns of the
minute-men first called them to battle.

These heroes of the blue and buff turned their
eyes westward to the fertile lands lying beyond the
mountains. They petitioned Congress to
mark out a territory, in what is now the   The Ohio
State of Ohio, as the seat of a distinct   Company.
colony, in time to become one of the confederated
States; and they asked that their bounty lands
should be set off for them in this territory. Two
hundred and eighty-five officers of the Continental
line joined in this petition; one hundred and fifty-
five, over half, were from Massachusetts, the State
which had furnished more troops than any other to
the Revolutionary armies. The remainder were from
Connecticut, New Hampshire, New Jersey, and
Maryland.

The signers of this petition desired to change the
paper obligations of Congress, which they held, into
fertile wild lands which they should themselves
subdue by their labor; and out of these wild lands
they proposed to make a new State. These two
germ ideas remained in their minds, even though
their petition bore no fruit. They kept before their
eyes the plan of a company to undertake the work,
after getting the proper cession from Congress.
Finally, in the early spring of 1786, some of the New
England officers met at the "Bunch of Grapes" tavern in Boston, and organized the Ohio Company of
Associates. They at once sent one of their number
as a delegate to New York, where the Continental
Congress was in session, to lay their memorial before
that body.

Congress was considering another ordinance for the government of the Northwest when the memo-
Congress and the Ohio Company.
rial was presented, and the former was delayed until the latter could be consid-ered by the committee to which it had been referred. In July, Dr. Manasseh Cutler, of Ipswich, Massachusetts, arrived as a second delegate to look after the interests of the company. He and they were as much concerned in the terms of the governmental ordinance, as in the conditions on which the land grant was to be made. The orderly, liberty-loving, keen-minded New Englanders who formed the company, would not go to a land where the form of government was hostile to their ideas of righteousness and sound public policy.

The one point of difficulty was the slavery ques-tion. Only eight States were at the time represented
The Prohi-bition of Slavery.
in the Congress; these were Massachusetts, New York, New Jersey, Delaware, Vir-ginia, North and South Carolina, and Georgia—thus five of the eight States were southern. But the Federal Congress rose in this, almost its last act, to a lofty pitch of patriotism; and the Southern States showed a marked absence of sec-tional feeling in the matter. Indeed, Cutler found that though he was a New England man, with a New England company behind him, many of the Eastern people looked rather coldly at his scheme, fearing lest the settlement of the West might mean a rapid drainage of population from the East. Nathan Dane, a Massachusetts delegate, favored it, in part because he hoped that planting such a colony in the West might keep at least that part of it true to

"Eastern politics." The Southern members, on the other hand, heartily supported the plan. The committee that brought in the ordinance, the majority being Southern men, also reported an article prohibiting slavery. Dane was the mover, while the rough draft may have been written by Cutler; and the report was vigorously pushed by the two Virginians on the committee, William Grayson and Richard Henry Lee. The article was adopted by a vote unanimous, except for the dissent of one delegate, a nobody from New York.

The ordinance established a territorial government, with a governor, secretary, and judges. A General Assembly was authorized as soon as there should be five thousand free male inhabitants in the district. The lower house was elective, the upper house, or council, was appointive. The Legislature was to elect a territorial delegate to Congress. The governor was required to own a freehold of one thousand acres in the district, a judge five hundred, and a representative two hundred; and no man was allowed to vote unless he possessed a freehold of fifty acres.[1] These provisions would seem strangely undemocratic if applied to a similar territory in our own day.

The all-important features of the ordinance were contained in the six articles of compact between the confederated States and the people and states of the territory, to be forever unalterable, save by the consent of both parties. The first guaranteed complete freedom of worship and religious belief to all peaceable and

Features of the Ordinance of 1787.

---

[1] "St. Clair Papers," ii., 603.

orderly persons. The second provided for trial by jury, the writ of habeas corpus, the privileges of the common law, and the right of proportional legislative representation. The third enjoined that faith should be kept with the Indians, and provided that "schools and the means of education" should forever be encouraged, inasmuch as "religion, morality, and knowledge" were necessary to good government. The fourth ordained that the new states formed in the Northwest should forever form part of the United States, and be subject to the laws, as were the others. The fifth provided for the formation and admission of not less than three or more than five states, formed out of this northwestern territory, whenever such a putative state should contain sixty thousand inhabitants; the form of government to be republican, and the state, when created, to stand on an equal footing with all the other States.

The sixth and most important article declared that there should never be slavery or involuntary servitude in the Northwest, otherwise than for the punishment of convicted criminals, provided, however, that fugitive slaves from the older States might lawfully be reclaimed by their owners. This was the greatest blow struck for freedom and against slavery in all our history, save only Lincoln's emancipation proclamation, for it determined that in the final struggle the mighty West should side with the right against the wrong. It was in its results a deadly stroke against the traffic in and ownership of human beings, and the blow was dealt by southern men, to whom all honor should ever be given.

This anti-slavery compact was the most important feature of the ordinance, yet there were many other features only less important.

In truth the ordinance of 1787 was so wide-reaching in its effects, was drawn in accordance with so lofty a morality and such far-seeing states- *Importance* manship, and was fraught with such weal *of the* for the nation, that it will ever rank *Ordinance.* among the foremost of American state papers, coming in that little group which includes the Declaration of Independence, the Constitution, Washington's Farewell Address, and Lincoln's Emancipation Proclamation and Second Inaugural. It marked out a definite line of orderly freedom along which the new States were to advance. It laid deep the foundation for that system of widespread public education so characteristic of the Republic and so essential to its healthy growth. It provided that complete religious freedom and equality which we now accept as part of the order of nature, but which were then unknown in any important European nation. It guaranteed the civil liberty of all citizens. It provided for an indissoluble Union, a Union which should grow until it could relentlessly crush nullification and secession; for the States founded under it were the creatures of the Nation, and were by the compact declared forever inseparable from it.

In one respect the ordinance marked a new departure of the most radical kind. The adoption of the policy therein outlined has worked a *New Method* complete revolution in the way of looking *of Creating* at new communities formed by coloniza- *Colonies.*

tion from the parent country. Yet the very completeness of this revolution to a certain extent veils
from us its importance. We cannot realize the
greatness of the change because of the fact that the
change was so great; for we cannot now put ourselves in the mental attitude which regarded the old
course as natural. The Ordinance of 1787 decreed
that the new States should stand in every respect
on an equal footing with the old; and yet should
be individually bound together with them. This
was something entirely new in the history of colonization. Hitherto every new colony had either been
subject to the parent state, or independent of it.
England, Holland, France, and Spain, when they
founded colonies beyond the sea, founded them for
the good of the parent state, and governed them as
dependencies. The home country might treat her
colonies well or ill, she might cherish and guard
them, or oppress them with harshness and severity,
but she never treated them as equals. Russia, in
pushing her obscure and barbarous conquest and
colonization of Siberia,—a conquest destined to be
of such lasting importance in the history of Asia,—
pursued precisely the same course.

In fact, this had been the only kind of colonization known to modern Europe. In the ancient
world it had also been known, and it was only
through it that great empires grew. Each Roman
colony that settled in Gaul or Iberia founded a
city or established a province which was tributary
to Rome, instead of standing on a footing of equality
in the same nation with Rome. But the other great

colonizing peoples of antiquity, the Greeks and
Phœnicians, spread in an entirely different way.
Each of their colonies became absolutely independent of the country whence it sprang. Carthage
and Syracuse were as free as Tyre or Sidon, as Cor-
inth or Athens. Thus under the Roman method
the empire grew, at the cost of the colonies losing
their independence. Under the Greek and Carthaginian method the colonies acquired the same freedom that was enjoyed by the mother cities; but
there was no extension of empire, no growth of a
great and enduring nationality. The modern European nations had followed the Roman system. Until
the United States sprang into being every great
colonizing people followed one system or the other.

The American Republic, taking advantage of its
fortunate federal features and of its strong central
government, boldly struck out on a new path, which
secured the freedom-giving properties of the Greek
method, while preserving national Union as carefully as it was preserved by the Roman Empire.
New States were created, which stood on exactly
the same footing as the old ; and yet these new
States formed integral and inseparable parts of a
great and rapidly growing nation. This movement
was original with the American Republic ; she was
dealing with new conditions, and on this point the
history of England merely taught her what to avoid.
The English colonies were subject to the British
Crown, and therefore to Great Britain. The new
American States, themselves colonies in the old
Greek sense, were subject only to a government

which they helped administer on equal terms with
the old States.   No State was subject to another,
new or old.   All paid a common allegiance to a central power which was identical with none.

The absolute novelty of this feature, as the world
then stood, fails to impress us now because we are
so used to it.   But it was at that time without precedent; and though since then the idea has made
rapid progress, there seems in most cases to have
been very great difficulty in applying it in practice.
The Spanish-American states proved wholly unable
to apply it at all.   In Australia and South Africa
all that can be said is that events now apparently
show a trend in the direction of adopting this
system.   At present all these British colonies, as
regards one another, are independent but disunited;
as regards the mother country, they remain united
with her, but in the condition of dependencies.

The vital feature of the ordinance was the prohibition of slavery.   This prohibition was not retro-
The Ques- active; the slaves of the French villagers,
tion of   and of the few American slaveholders who
Slavery.   had already settled round them, were not
disturbed in their condition.   But all further im-
portation of slaves, and the holding in slavery of
any not already slaves, were prohibited.   The prohibition was brought about by the action of the
Ohio Company.   Without the prohibition the company would probably not have undertaken its experiment in colonization; and save for the pressure
of the company slavery would hardly have been
abolished.   Congress wished to sell the lands, and

was much impressed by the solid worth of the founders of the association. The New Englanders were anxious to buy the lands, but were earnest in their determinating to exclude slavery from the new territory. The slave question was not at the time a burning issue between North and South ; for no Northerner thought of crusading to destroy the evil, while most enlightened Southerners were fond of planning how to do away with it. The tact of the company's representative before Congress, Dr. Cutler, did the rest. A compromise was agreed to ; for, like so many other great political triumphs, the passage of the Ordinance of 1787 was a compromise. Slavery was prohibited, on the one hand; and on the other, that the territory might not become a refuge for runaway negroes, provision was made for the return of such fugitives. The popular conscience was yet too dull about slavery to be stirred by the thought of returning fugitive slaves into bondage.

A fortnight after the passage of the ordinance, the transaction was completed by the sale of a million and a half acres, north of the Ohio, to the Ohio Company. Three million and a half more, known as the Sciato purchase, **Land Purchase.** were authorized to be sold to a purely speculative company, but the speculation ended in nothing save financial disaster. The price was nominally seventy cents an acre ; but as payment was made in depreciated public securities, the real price was only eight or nine cents an acre. The sale illustrated the tendency of Congress at that time to sell the land in large tracts ; a most unwholesome tendency, fruitful of evil to the whole community. It was only by degrees that the wisdom of selling the land in small plots, and to actual occupiers, was recognized.

Together with the many wise and tolerant measures included in the famous Ordinance of 1787, and in the land Ordinance of 1785, there were one or two which represented the feelings of the past, not the future. One of them was a regulation which reserved a lot in every township to be given for the purposes of religion. Nowadays, and rightfully, we regard as peculiarly American the complete severance of Church and State, and refuse to allow the State to contribute in any way towards the support of any sect.

A regulation of a very different kind provided that two townships should be set apart to endow a university. These two townships now endow the University of Ohio, placed in a town which, with queer poverty of imagination, and fatuous absence of humor, has been given the name of Athens.

The company was well organized, the founders showing the invaluable New England aptitude for **Organiza-** business, and there was no delay in getting **tion of the** the settlement started. After some delib- **Company.** eration the lands lying along the Ohio, on both sides of, but mainly below, the Muskingum, were chosen for the site of the new colony. There was some delay in making the payments subsequent to the first, and only a million and some odd acres were patented. One of the reasons for choosing the mouth of the Muskingum as the site for the town was the neighborhood of Fort Harmar, with its strong Federal garrison, and the spot was but a short distance beyond the line of already existing settlement.

As soon as enough of the would-be settlers were ready, they pushed forward in parties towards the headwaters of the Ohio, struggling along Founding the winter-bound roads of western Penn-of Marietta. sylvania. In January and February they began to reach the banks of the Youghioghany, and set about building boats to launch when the river opened. There were forty-eight settlers in all who started down stream, their leader being General Rufus Putnam. He was a tried and gallant soldier, who had served with honor not only in the Revolutionary armies, but in the war which crushed the French power in America. On April 7, 1788, he stepped from his boat, which he had very appropriately named the Mayflower, on to the bank of the Muskingum. The settlers immediately set to work felling trees, building log houses and a stockade, clearing fields, and laying out the ground-plan of Marietta; for they christened the new town after the French Queen, Marie Antoinette.[1] It was laid out in the untenanted wilderness; yet near by was the proof that ages ago the wilderness had been tenanted, for close at hand were huge embankments, marking the site of a town of the long-vanished mound-builders. Giant trees grew on the mounds; all vestiges of the builders had vanished, and the

[1] "St. Clair Papers," i., 139. It was at the beginning of the dreadful pseudo-classic cult in our intellectual history, and these honest soldiers and yeomen, with much self-complacency, gave to portions of their little raw town such ludicrously inappropriate names as the Campus Martius and Via Sacra.

solemn forest had closed above every remembrance of their fate.

The day of the landing of these new pilgrims was a day big with fate not only for the Northwest but Beginning for the Nation. It marked the beginning of Ohio. of the orderly and national conquest of the lands that now form the heart of the Republic. It marked the advent among the pioneers of a new element, which was to leave the impress of its strong personality deeply graven on the institutions and the people of the great States north of the Ohio ; an element which in the end turned their development in the direction towards which the parent stock inclined in its home on the North Atlantic seaboard. The new settlers were almost all soldiers of the Revolutionary armies ; they were hardworking, orderly men of trained courage and of keen intellect. An outside observer speaks of them as being the best informed, the most courteous and industrious, and the most lawabiding of all the settlers who had come to the frontier, while their leaders were men of a higher type than was elsewhere to be found in the West.[1] No better material for founding a new State existed anywhere. With such a foundation the State was little likely to plunge into the perilous abysses of anarchic license or of separatism and disunion. Moreover, to plant a settlement of this kind on the edge of the Indian-haunted wilderness showed that the founders possessed both hardihood and resolution.

Yet it must not be forgotten that the daring

[1] " Denny's Military Journal," May 28 and June 15, 1789.

needed for the performance of this particular deed
can in no way be compared with that
shown by the real pioneers, the early explorers and Indian fighters. The very
fact that the settlement around Marietta
was national in its character, that it was
the outcome of national legislation, and was undertaken under national protection, made the work of
the individual settler count for less in the scale.
The founders and managers of the Ohio Company
and the statesmen of the Federal Congress deserve
much of the praise that in the Southwest would have
fallen to the individual settlers only. The credit to
be given to the nation in its collective capacity was
greatly increased, and that due to the individual
was correspondingly diminished.

Contrast
with the
Deeds of
the Old
Pioneers.

Rufus Putnam and his fellow New Englanders
built their new town under the guns of a Federal
fort, only just beyond the existing boundary of
settlement, and on land guaranteed them by the
Federal Government. The dangers they ran and
the hardships they suffered in no wise approached
those undergone and overcome by the iron-willed,
iron-limbed hunters who first built their lonely
cabins on the Cumberland and Kentucky. The
founders of Marietta trusted largely to the Federal
troops for protection, and were within easy reach of
the settled country ; but the wild wood-wanderers
who first roamed through the fair lands south of
the Ohio built their little towns in the heart of the
wilderness, many scores of leagues from all assistance, and trusted solely to their own long rifles in

time of trouble. The settler of 1788 journeyed at ease over paths worn smooth by the feet of many thousands of predecessors; but the early pioneers cut their own trails in the untrodden wilderness, and warred single-handed against wild nature and wild man.

In the summer of 1788 Dr. Manasseh Cutler visited the colony he had helped to found, and Cutler kept a diary of his journey. His trip Visits through Pennsylvania was marked merely Marietta. by such incidents as were common at that time on every journey in the United States away from the larger towns. He travelled with various companions, stopping at taverns and private houses; and both guests and hosts were fond of trying their skill with the rifle, either at a mark or at squirrels. In mid-August he reached Coxe's fort, on the Ohio, and came for the first time to the frontier proper. Here he embarked on a big flat boat, with on board forty-eight souls all told, besides cattle. They drifted and paddled down stream, and on the evening of the second day reached the Muskingum. Here and there along the Virginian shore the boat passed settlements, with grain fields and orchards; the houses were sometimes squalid cabins, and sometimes roomy, comfortable buildings. When he reached the newly built town he was greeted by General Putnam, who invited Cutler to share the marquee in which he lived; and that afternoon he drank tea with another New England general, one of the original founders.

The next three weeks he passed very comfortably

with his friends, taking part in the various social entertainments, walking through the woods, and visiting one or two camps of friendly Indians with all the curiosity of a pleasure-tourist. He greatly admired the large cornfields, proof of the industry of the settlers. Some of the cabins were already comfortable; and many families of women and children had come out to join their husbands and fathers.

The newly appointed Governor of the territory, Arthur St. Clair, had reached the place in July, and formally assumed his task of government. St. Clair Both Governor St. Clair and General Har- Made mar were men of the old Federalist school, Governor. utterly unlike the ordinary borderers; and even in the wilderness they strove to keep a certain stateliness and formality in their surroundings. They speedily grew to feel at home with the New England leaders, who were gentlemen of much the same type as themselves, and had but little more in common with the ordinary frontier folk. Dr. Cutler frequently dined with one or other of them. After dining with the Governor at Fort Harmar, he pronounced it in his diary a " genteel dinner "; and he dwelt on the grapes, the beautiful garden, and the good looks of Mrs. Harmar. Sometimes the leading citizens gave a dinner to " His Excellency," as Dr. Cutler was careful to style the Governor, and to " General Harmar and his Lady." On such occasions the visitors were rowed from the fort to the town in a twelve-oared barge with an awning; the drilled crew rowed well, while a sergeant stood in the stern to steer. On each oar blade was painted the word

" Congress "; all the regular army men were devout believers in the Union. The dinners were handsomely served, with punch and wine; and at one Dr. Cutler records that fifty-five gentlemen sat down, together with three ladies. The fort itself was a square, with block-houses, curtains, barracks, and artillery.

After three weeks' stay the Doctor started back, up stream, in the boat of a well-to-do Creole trader from the Illinois. This trader was no less **Cutler's Trip up the Ohio.** a person than Francis Vigo, who had welcomed Clark when he took Kaskaskia, and who at that time rendered signal service to the Americans, advancing them peltries and goods. To the discredit of the nation be it said, he was never repaid what he had advanced. When Cutler joined him he was making his way up the Ohio in a big keel-boat, propelled by ten oars and a square sail. The Doctor found his quarters pleasant; for there was an awning and a cabin, and Vigo was well equipped with comforts and even luxuries. In his travelling-chest he carried his silver-handled knives and forks, and flasks of spirits. The beds were luxurious for the frontier; in his journal the Doctor mentions that one night he had to sleep in "wet sheets." The average pioneer knew nothing whatever of sheets, wet or dry. Often the voyagers would get out and walk along shore, shooting pigeons or squirrels and plucking bunches of grapes. On such occasions if they had time they would light a fire and have " a good dish of tea and a french fricassee." Once they saw some Indians; but the latter were merely chasing a bear, which they killed, giving the travellers some of the meat.

Cutler and his companions caught huge catfish in the river; they killed game of all kinds in the forest; and they lived very well indeed. In the morning they got under way early, after a "bitter and a biscuit," and a little later breakfasted on cold meat, pickles, cabbage, and pork. Between eleven and twelve they stopped for dinner; usually of hot venison or wild turkey, with a strong "dish of coffee" and loaf-sugar. At supper they had cold meat and tea. Here and there on the shore they passed settlers' cabins, where they obtained corn and milk, and sometimes eggs, butter, and veal. Cutler landed at his starting-point less than a month after he had left it to go down stream.[1]

Another Massachusetts man, Col. John May, had made the same trip just previously. His experiences were very like those of Dr. Cutler; but in his journal he told them more entertainingly, being a man of considerable humor and sharp observation. He travelled on horseback from Boston. In Philadelphia he put up "at the sign of the Connastago Wagon" —the kind of wagon then used in the up country, and afterwards for two generations the wheeled-house with which the pioneers moved westward across plain and prairie. He halted for some days in the log-built town of Pittsburg, and, like many other travellers of the day, took a dislike to the place and to its inhabitants, who were largely Pennsylvania Germans. He mentions that he had reached it in thirty days from Boston, and had not lost a pound of his baggage, which had accompanied him in a wagon under the care of some of his hired men. At Pittsburg he was

[1] Cutler, p. 420.

much struck by the beauty of the mountains and the river, and also by the numbers of flat-boats, loaded with immigrants, which were constantly drifting and rowing past on their way to Kentucky. From the time of reaching the river his journal is filled with comments on the extraordinary abundance and great size of the various kinds of food fishes.

At last, late in May, he started in a crowded flat-boat down the Ohio, and was enchanted with the wild and beautiful scenery. He was equally pleased with the settlement at the mouth of the Muskingum; and he was speedily on good terms with the officers of the fort, who dined and wined him to his heart's content. There were rumors of savage warfare from below; but around Marietta the Indians were friendly. May and his people set to work to clear land and put up buildings; and they lived sumptuously, for game swarmed. The hunters supplied them with quantities of deer and wild turkeys, and occasionally elk and buffalo were also killed; while quantities of fish could be caught without effort, and the gardens and fields yielded plenty of vegetables. On July 4th the members of the Ohio Company entertained the officers from Fort Harmar, and the ladies of the garrison, at an abundant dinner, and drank thirteen toasts,—to the United States, to Congress, to Washington, to the King of France, to the new Constitution, to the Society of the Cincinnati, and various others.

Colonel May built him a fine "mansion house," thirty-six feet by eighteen, and fifteen feet high, with a good cellar underneath, and in the windows panes of glass he had brought all the way from Boston. He continued to enjoy the life in all its phases, from hunting in the woods to watching the sun rise, and making friends with the robins, which, in the wilderness, always followed the settlements. In August he went up the river, without adventure, and returned to his home.[1]

Such a trip as either of these was a mere holiday picnic. It offers as striking a contrast as well could be offered to the wild and lonely journeyings of the stark wilderness-hunters and Indian fighters, who first went west of the mountains. General Rufus Putnam and his associates did a deed the consequences of which were of vital importance. They showed that they possessed the highest attributes of good citizenship—resolution and sagacity, stern morality, and the capacity to govern others as well as themselves. But they performed no pioneer feat of any note as such, and they were not called upon to display a tithe of the reckless daring and iron endurance of hardship which characterized the conquerors of the Illinois and the founders of Kentucky and Tennessee. This is in no sense a reflection upon them. They did not need to give proof of a courage they had shown time and again in bloody battles against the best troops of Europe. In this particular enterprise, in which they showed so many admirable qualities, they had little chance to show the quality of adventurous bravery. They drifted comfortably down stream, from the log fort whence they started,

Contrasts with Travels of Early Explorers.

[1] Journal and Letters of Colonel John May ; one of the many valuable historical publications of Robert Clarke & Co., of Cincinnati.

past many settlers' houses, until they came to the post of a small Federal garrison, where they built their town. Such a trip is not to be mentioned in the same breath with the long wanderings of Clark and Boone and Robertson, when they went forth un-assisted to subdue the savage and make tame the shaggy wilderness.

St. Clair, the first Governor, was a Scotchman of good family. He had been a patriotic but unsuccess-ful general in the Revolutionary army. He **St. Clair.** was a friend of Washington, and in politics a firm Federalist; he was devoted to the cause of Union and Liberty, and was a conscientious, high-minded man. But he had no aptitude for the in-credibly difficult task of subduing the formidable forest Indians, with their peculiar and dangerous system of warfare; and he possessed no capacity for getting on with the frontiersmen, being without sympathy for their virtues while keenly alive to their very unattractive faults.

In the fall of 1787 another purchase of public lands was negotiated, by the Miami Company. The chief **The Miami** personage in this company was John **Purchase.** Cleves Symmes, one of the first judges of the Northwestern Territory. Rights were acquired to take up one million acres, and under these rights three small settlements were made towards the close of the year 1788. One of them was chosen by St. Clair to be the seat of government. This little town had been called Losantiville in its first infancy, but St. Clair re-christened it Cincinnati, in honor of the Society of the officers of the Continental army.

The men who formed these Miami Company colonies came largely from the Middle States. Like
the New England founders of Marietta, very many
of them, if not most, had served in the Continental
army. They were good settlers; they made good
material out of which to build up a great state.
Their movement was modelled on that of Putnam
and his associates. It was a triumph of collectivism
rather than of individualism. The settlers were
marshalled in a company, instead of moving freely
by themselves, and they took a territory granted
them by Congress, under certain conditions, and defended for them by the officers and troops of the
regular army.

Civil government was speedily organized. St.
Clair and the judges formed the first legislature; in
theory they were only permitted to adopt Establish-
laws already in existence in the old States, ment of Civil
but as a matter of fact they tried any legis- Govern-
lative experiments they saw fit. St. Clair was an
autocrat both by military training and by political
principles. He was a man of rigid honor, and he
guarded the interests of the territory with jealous
integrity, but he exercised such a rigorous supervision over the acts of his subordinate colleagues,
the judges, that he became involved in wrangles at
the very beginning of his administration. To prevent the incoming of unauthorized intruders, he
issued a proclamation summoning all newly arrived
persons to report at once to the local commandants,
and, with a view of keeping the game for the use of
the actual settlers, and also to prevent as far as pos-

sible fresh irritation being given the Indians, he forbade all hunting in the territory for hides or flesh save
by the inhabitants proper.[1]   Only an imperfect obedience was rendered either proclamation.

Thus the settlement of the Northwest was fairly
begun, on a system hitherto untried.   The fates and
the careers of all the mighty states which yet lay
formless in the forest were in great measure determined by what was at this time done.   The nation
had decreed that they should all have equal rights
with the older States and with one another, and yet
that they should remain forever inseparable from the
Union ; and above all, it had been settled that the
bondman should be unknown within their borders.
Their founding represented the triumph of the principle of collective national action over the spirit of
intense individualism displayed so commonly on the
frontier.   The uncontrolled initiative of the individual, which was the chief force in the settlement of
the Southwest, was given comparatively little play in
the settlement of the Northwest.   The Northwest
owed its existence to the action of the nation as a
whole.

[1] Draper MSS. Wm. Clark Papers. Proclamation, Vincennes, June
28, 1790.

CHAPTER VII.

THE WAR IN THE NORTHWEST. 1787-1790

THE Federal troops were camped in the Federal territory north of the Ohio. They garrisoned the forts and patrolled between the little log-towns. They were commanded by the Federal General Harmar, and the territory was ruled by the Federal Governor St. Clair. Thenceforth the national authorities and the regular troops played the chief parts in the struggle for the Northwest. The frontier militia became a mere adjunct—often necessary, but always untrustworthy—of the regular forces.

For some time the regulars fared ill in the warfare with the savages; and a succession of mortifying failures closed with a defeat more ruinous than any which had been experienced since the days of the "iron-tempered general with the pipe-clay brain,"—for the disaster which befell St. Clair was as overwhelming as that wherein Braddock met his death. The continued checks excited the anger of the Eastern people, and the dismay and derision of the Westerners. They were keenly felt by the officers of the army; and they furnished an excuse for those who wished to jeer at regular troops, and exalt the militia. Jeffer-

The Regular Army in the Northwest.

277

son, who never understood anything about warfare, being a timid man, and who belonged to the visionary school which always denounced the army and navy, was given a legitimate excuse to criticise the tactics of the regulars [1]; and of course he never sought occasion to comment on the even worse failings of the militia.

The truth was that the American military authorities fell into much the same series of errors as their
Shortcomings of the Regulars. predecessors, the British, untaught by the dreary and mortifying experience of the latter in fighting these forest foes. The War Department at Washington, and the Federal generals who first came to the Northwest, did not seem able to realize the formidable character of the Indian armies, and were certainly unable to teach their own troops how to fight them. Harmar and St. Clair were both fair officers, and in open country were able to acquit themselves respectably in the face of civilized foes. But they did not have the peculiar genius necessary to the successful Indian fighter, and they never learned how to carry on a campaign in the woods.

They had the justifiable distrust of the militia felt by all the officers of the Continental Army. In the long campaigns waged against Howe, Clinton, and Cornwallis they had learned the immense superiority of the Continental troops to the local militia. They knew that the Revolution would have failed had it not been for the continental troops. They knew also, by the bitter experience common to

[1] Draper MSS., G. R. Clark Papers. Jefferson to Innes, March 7, 1791.

all officers who had been through the war, that, though the militia might on occasion do well, yet they could never be trusted; they were certain to desert or grow sulky and mutinous if exposed to the fatigue and hardship of a long campaign, while in a pitched battle in the open they never fought as stubbornly as the regulars, and often would not fight at all.

All this was true; yet the officers of the regular army failed to understand that it did not imply the capacity of the regular troops to fight savages on their own ground. They showed little real comprehension of the extraordinary difficulty of such warfare against such foes, and of the reasons which made it so hazardous. The Regulars in Indian Warfare. They could not help assigning other causes than the real ones for every defeat and failure. They attributed each in turn to the effects of ambuscade or surprise, instead of realizing that in each the prime factor was the formidable fighting power of the individual Indian warrior, when in the thick forest which was to him a home, and when acting under that species of wilderness discipline which was so effective for a single crisis in his peculiar warfare. The Indian has rarely shown any marked excellence as a fighter in mass in the open; though of course there have been one or two brilliant exceptions. At times in our wars we have tried the experiment of drilling bodies of Indians as if they were whites, and using them in the ordinary way in battle. Under such conditions, as a rule, they have shown themselves inferior to the white troops against whom they were pitted. In the same way they failed to show themselves a match for the white hunters of the great plains when on equal terms. But their marvellous faculty for taking advantage of cover, and for fighting in concert when under cover, has always made the warlike tribes foes to be dreaded beyond all others when in the woods, or among wild broken mountains.

The history of our warfare with the Indians during the century following the close of the Revolution Striking is marked by curiously sharp contrasts in Contrasts the efficiency shown by the regular troops in our In- in campaigns carried on at different times dian Wars. and under varying conditions. These contrasts are due much more to the difference in the conditions under which the campaigns were waged than to the difference in the bodily prowess of the Indians. When we had been in existence as a nation for a century the Modocs in their lava-beds and the Apaches amid their waterless mountains were still waging against the regulars of the day the same tedious and dangerous warfare waged against Harmar and St. Clair by the forest Indians. There were the same weary, long-continued campaigns; the same difficulty in bringing the savages to battle; the same blind fighting against hidden antagonists shielded by the peculiar nature of their fastnesses; and, finally, the same great disparity of loss against the white troops. During the intervening hundred years there had been many similar struggles; as for instance that against the Seminoles. Yet there had also been many struggles, against Indians naturally more formidable, in which the troops again and again

worsted their Indian foes even when the odds in
numbers were two or three to one against the whites.
The difference between these different classes of wars
was partly accounted for by change in weapons and
methods of fighting; partly by the change in the
character of the battle grounds. The horse Indians
of the plains were as elusive and difficult to bring to
battle as the Indians of the mountains and forests;
but in the actual fighting they had no chance to
take advantage of cover in the way which rendered
so formidable their brethren of the hills and the
deep woods. In consequence their occasional slaugh-
tering victories, including the most famous of all, the
battle of the Rosebud, in which Custer fell, took the
form of the overwhelming of a comparatively small
number of whites by immense masses of mounted
horsemen. When their weapons were inferior, as on
the first occasions when they were brought into contact with troops carrying breech-loading arms of
precision, or when they tried the tactics of down-
right fighting, and of charging fairly in the open,
they were often themselves beaten or repulsed with
fearful slaughter by mere handfuls of whites. In
the years 1867–68, all the horse Indians of the plains
were at war with us, and many battles were fought
with varying fortune. Two were especially noteworthy. In each a small body of troops and frontier
scouts, under the command of a regular army officer
who was also a veteran Indian fighter, beat back an
overwhelming Indian force, which attempted to
storm by open onslaught the position held by the
white riflemen. In one instance fifty men under

Major Geo. H. Forsyth beat back nine hundred warriors, killing or wounding double their own number. In the other a still more remarkable defence was made by thirty-one men under Major James Powell against an even larger force, which charged again and again, and did not accept their repulse as final until they had lost three hundred of their foremost braves. For years the Sioux spoke with bated breath of this battle as the "medicine fight," the defeat so overwhelming that it could be accounted for only by supernatural interference.[1]

But no such victory was ever gained over mountain or forest Indians who had become accustomed to fighting the white men. Every officer who has ever faced these foes has had to spend years in learning his work, and has then been forced to see a bitterly inadequate reward for his labors. The officers of the regular army who served in the forests north of the Ohio just after the Revolution had to undergo a strange and painful training; and were obliged to content themselves with scanty and hard-won triumphs even after this training had been undergone.

The officers took some time to learn their duties as Indian fighters, but the case was much worse with the rank and file who served under them.

Difficulties Experienced by the Officers. From the beginning of our history it often proved difficult to get the best type of native American to go into the regular army save in time of war with a powerful enemy, for the low rate of pay was not attractive, while the disciplined subordination of the soldiers to their offi-

[1] For all this see Dodge's admirable "Our Wild Indians."

cers seemed irksome to people with an exaggerated idea of individual freedom and no proper conception of the value of obedience. Very many of the regular soldiers have always been of foreign birth; and in 1787, on the Ohio, the percentage of Irish and Germans in the ranks was probably fully as large as it was on the Great Plains a century later.[1] They, as others, at that early date, were, to a great extent, drawn from the least desirable classes of the eastern sea-board.[2] Three or four years later an unfriendly observer wrote of St. Clair's soldiers that they were a wretched set of men, weak and feeble, many of them mere boys, while others were rotten with drink and debauchery. He remarked that men "purchased from the prisons, wheel-barrows, and brothels of the nation at foolishly low wages, would never do to fight Indians"; and that against such foes, who were terrible enemies in the woods, there was need of first-class, specially trained troops, instead of trying to use "a set of men who enlisted because they could no longer live unhung any other way."[3]

Doubtless this estimate, made under the sting of defeat, was too harsh; and it was even more applicable to the forced levies of militia than to the Federal soldiers; but the shortcomings of the regular troops were sufficiently serious to need no exaggeration.

[1] Denny's Journal, *passim*.

[2] For fear of misunderstanding, I wish to add that at many periods the rank and file have been composed of excellent material; of recent years their character has steadily risen, and the stuff itself has always proved good when handled for a sufficient length of time by good commanders.

[3] Draper Collection. Letter of John Cleves Symmes to Elias Boudinot, January 12, 1792.

Their own officers were far from pleased with the recruits they got.

To the younger officers, with a taste for sport, the life beyond the Ohio was delightful. The climate was pleasant, the country beautiful, the water was clear as crystal, and game abounded. In hard weather the troops lived on salt beef; but at other times their daily rations were two pounds of turkey or venison, or a pound and a half of bear meat or buffalo beef. Yet this game was supplied by hired hunters, not by the soldiers themselves. One of the officers wrote that he had to keep his troops practising steadily at a target, for they were incompetent to meet an enemy with the musket; they could not kill in a week enough game to last them a day.[1] It was almost impossible to train such troops, in a limited number of months or years, so as to enable them to meet their forest foes on equal terms. The discipline to which they were accustomed was admirably fitted for warfare in the open; but it was not suited for warfare in the woods. They had to learn even the use of their fire-arms with painful labor. It was merely hopeless to try to teach them to fight Indian fashion, all scattering out for themselves, and each taking a tree trunk, and trying to slay an individual enemy. They were too clumsy; they utterly lacked the wild-creature qualities proper to the men of the wilderness, the men who inherited wolf-cunning and panther-stealth from countless generations, who bought bare life itself only at the price of never-ceasing watchfulness, craft, and ferocity.

The regulars were certainly not ideal troops with

[1] State Dept. MSS., No. 150; Doughty's Letter, March 15, 1786; also, November 30, 1785.

which to oppose such foes; but they were the best attainable at that time. They possessed traits which were lacking in even the best of the frontier militia; and most of the militia fell far short of the best. When properly trained the regulars could be trusted to persevere through a campaign; whereas the militia were sure to disband if kept out for any length of time. Moreover, a regular army formed a weapon with a temper tried and known; whereas a militia force was the most brittle of swords which might give one true stroke, or might fly into splinters at the first slight blow. Regulars were the only troops who could be trusted to wear out their foes in a succession of weary and hard-fought campaigns.

The Regulars Superior to the Militia.

The best backwoods fighters, however, such men as Kenton and Brady had in their scout companies, were much superior to the regulars, and were able to meet the Indians on at least equal terms. But there were only a very few such men; and they were too impatient of discipline to be embodied in an army. The bulk of the frontier militia consisted of men who were better riflemen than the regulars and often physically abler, but who were otherwise in every military sense inferior, possessing their defects, sometimes in an accentuated form, and not possessing their compensating virtues. Like the regulars, these militia fought the Indians at a terrible disadvantage. A defeat for either meant murderous slaughter; for whereas the trained Indian fighters fought or fled each for himself, the ordinary troops huddled together in a mass, an easy mark for their savage foes.

The task set the leaders of the army in the Northwest was one of extreme difficulty and danger. Extreme Difficulty of the War. They had to overcome a foe trained through untold ages how to fight most effectively on the very battle-ground where the contest was to be waged. To the whites a march through the wilderness was fraught with incredible toil; whereas the Indians moved without baggage, and scattered and came together as they wished, so that it was impossible to bring them to battle against their will. All that could be done was to try to beat them when they chose to receive or deliver an attack. With ordinary militia it was hopeless to attempt to accomplish anything needing prolonged and sustained effort, and, as already said, the thoroughly trained Indian fighters who were able to beat the savages at their own game were too few in numbers, and too unaccustomed to control and restraint, to permit of their forming the main body of the army in an offensive campaign. There remained only the regulars; and the raw recruits had to undergo a long and special training, and be put under the command of a thoroughly capable leader, like old Mad Anthony Wayne, before they could be employed to advantage.

The feeling between the regular troops and the frontiersmen was often very bitter, and on several occasions violent brawls resulted. One The Feeling between the Regulars and Frontiersmen. such occurred at Limestone, where the brutal Indian-fighter Wetzel lived. Wetzel had murdered a friendly Indian, and the soldiers bore him a grudge. When they were sent to arrest him the townspeople sallied to his support. Wetzel himself resisted, and was, very properly, roughly handled in consequence. The interference of the townspeople was vigorously repaid in kind; they soon gave up the attempt, and afterwards one or two of them were ill-treated or plundered by the soldiers. They made complaint to the civil authorities, and a court-martial was then ordered by the Federal commanders. This court-martial acquitted the soldiers. Wetzel soon afterwards made his escape, and the incident ended.[1]

By 1787 the Indian war had begun with all its old fury. The thickly settled districts were not much troubled, and the towns which, like Marietta in the following year, grew up under the shadow of a Federal fort, were comparatively safe. But the frontier of Kentucky, and of Virginia proper along the Ohio, suffered severely. There was great scarcity of powder and lead, and even of guns, and there was difficulty in procuring provisions for those militia who consented to leave their work and turn out when summoned. The settlers were harried, and the surveyors feared to go out to their work on the range. There were the usual horrible incidents of Indian warfare. A glimpse of one of the innumerable dreadful tragedies is afforded by the statement of one party of scouts, who, in following the trail of an Indian war band, found at the crossing of the river " the small

Fury of the Indian Ravages.

---

[1] Draper MSS. Harmar's letter to Henry Lee, Sept. 27, 1789. Also depositions of McCurdy, Lawler, Caldwell, and others, and proceedings of court-martial. The depositions conflict.

tracks of a number of children," prisoners from a
raid made on the Monongahela settlements.[1]

The settlers in the harried territory sent urgent
appeals for help to the Governor of Virginia and to

Congress. In these appeals stress was laid
Difficulties
in Extend- upon the poverty of the frontiersmen, and
ing Help to their lack of ammunition. The writers
the Fron- pointed out that the men of the border
tiersmen.
should receive support, if only from
motives of policy ; for it was of great importance
to the people in the thickly settled districts that
the war should be kept on the frontier, and that the
men who lived there should remain as a barrier
against the Indians. If the latter broke through
and got among the less hardy and warlike people of
the interior, they would work much greater havoc ;
for in Indian warfare the borderers were as much
superior to the more peaceful people behind them
as a veteran to a raw recruit.[2]

These appeals did not go unheeded ; but there was
embarrassment in affording the frontier adequate
protection, both because the party to which the
borderers themselves belonged foolishly objected to
the employment of a fair-sized regular army, and
because Congress still clung to the belief that war
could be averted by treaty, and so forbade the taking
of proper offensive measures. In the years 1787,
'88, and '89, the ravages continued ; many settlers
were slain, with their families, and many bodies of

---

[1] State Dept. MSS., No. 71, vol. ii.   Letters of David Shepherd to
Governor Randolph, April 30, and May 24, 1787.

[2] Draper MSS.   Lt. Marshall to Franklin, Nov. 6, 1787.

immigrants destroyed ; while the scouting and rescue parties of whites killed a few Indians in return.[1] All the Indians were not yet at war, however; and curious agreements were entered into by individuals on both sides. In the absence on either side of any government with full authority and power, the leaders would often negotiate some special or temporary truce, referring only to certain limited localities, or to certain people ; and would agree between themselves for the interchange or ransom of prisoners. There is a letter of Boone's extant in which he notifies a leading Kentucky colonel that a certain captive woman must be given up, in accordance with an agreement he has made with one of the noted Indian chiefs ; and he insists upon the immediate surrender of the woman, to clear his " promise and obligation." [2]

The Indians watched the Ohio with especial care, and took their toll from the immense numbers of immigrants who went down it. After passing the Muskingum no boat was safe. If the war parties, lurking along the banks, came on a boat moored to the shore, or swept thither by wind or current, the crew was at their mercy ; and grown bold by success, they sometimes launched small flotillas of canoes and attacked the scows on the water. In such attacks they were often successful, for they always made the assault with the odds in their favor ; though they were sometimes beaten back with heavy loss.

The Indians Harry the Boats on the Ohio.

[1] Va. State Papers, iv., 357.
[2] Draper MSS., Boone Papers. Boone to Robert Patterson, March 16, 1787.

When the war was at its height the boats going down the Ohio preferred to move in brigades. An army officer has left a description [1] of one such flotilla, over which he had assumed command. It contained sixteen flat-boats, then usually called "Kentuck boats," and two keels. The flat-boats were lashed three together and kept in one line. The women, children, and cattle were put in the middle scows, while the outside were manned and worked by the men. The keel boats kept on either flank. This particular flotilla was unmolested by the Indians, but was almost wrecked in a furious storm of wind and rain.

The Federal authorities were still hopelessly endeavoring to come to some understanding with the Indians; they were holding treaties with some of the tribes, sending addresses and making speeches to others, and keeping envoys in the neighborhood of Detroit. These envoys watched the Indians who were there, and tried to influence the great gatherings of different tribes who came together at Sandusky to consult as to the white advance.[2]

Vain Efforts to Conclude Treaties of Peace.

These efforts to negotiate were as disheartening as was usually the case under such circumstances. There were many different tribes, and some were for peace, while others were for war; and even the peaceful ones could not restrain their turbulent young men. Far off nations of Indians who had never been harmed by the whites, and were in no

[1] Denny's Military Journal, April 19, 1790.
[2] State Department MSS., No. 150, vol. iii. Harmar's speech to the Indians at Vincennes, September 17, 1787. Richard Butler to the Secretary of War, May 4, 1788, etc.

danger from them, sent war parties to the Ohio; and the friendly tribes let them pass without inter- ference. The Iroquois were eagerly consulted by the western Indians, and in the summer of 1788 a great party of them came to Sandusky to meet in council all the tribes of the Lakes and the Ohio valley, and even some from the upper Mississippi. With the Iroquois came the famous chief Joseph Brant, a mighty warrior, and a man of education, who in his letters to the United States officials showed much polished diplomacy.[1]

The tribes who gathered at this great council met on the soil which, by treaty with England, had been declared American, and came from regions which the same treaty had defined as lying within the boundaries of the United States. But these provisions of the treaty had never been executed, owing largely to a failure on the part of the Americans themselves to execute certain other provisions. The land was really as much British as ever, and was so treated by the British Governor of Canada, Lord Dorchester, who had just made a tour of the Lake Posts. The tribes were feudatory to the British, and in their talks spoke of the King of Great Britain as " father," and Brant was a British pensioner. British agents were in constant com- munication with the Indians at the councils, and they distributed gifts among them with a hitherto unheard- of lavishness. In every way they showed their reso- lution to remain in full touch with their red allies.[2]

The In- dians Hold Great Councils.

[1] *Do.*, pp. 47 and 51.
[2] *Do.*, St. Clair to Knox, September 14, 1788 ; St. Clair to Jay, December 13, 1788.

Nevertheless, they were anxious that peace should be made. The Wyandots, too, seconded them, and addressed the Wabash Indians at one of the councils, urging them to cease their outrages on the Americans.[1] These Wyandots had long been converted, and in addressing their heathen brethren, said proudly: "We are not as other nations are—we, the Wyandots—we are Christians." They certainly showed themselves the better for their religion, and they were still the bravest of the brave. But though the Wabash Indians in answering spake them fair, they had no wish to go to peace; and the Wyandots were the only tribes who strove earnestly to prevent war. The American agents who had gone to the Detroit River were forced to report that there was little hope of putting an end to hostilities.[2] The councils accomplished nothing towards averting a war; on the contrary, they tended to band all the northwestern Indians together in a loose confederacy, so that active hostilities against some were sure in the end to involve all.

While the councils were sitting and while the Americans were preparing for the treaties, outrages of the most flagrant kind occurred. One, **Even the Far-Off Chippewas Make Forays.** out of many, was noteworthy as showing both the treachery of the Indians, and the further fact that some tribes went to war, not because they had been in any way maltreated, but from mere lust of blood and plunder. In July of this year 1788, Governor St.

---

[1] *Do.*, p. 267, Detroit River's Mouth, July 23, 1788.
[2] *Do.*, James Rinkin to Richard Butler, July 20, 1788.

Clair was making ready for a treaty to which he
had invited some of the tribes. It was to be held
on the Muskingum, and he sent to the appointed
place provisions for the Indians with a guard of
men.   One day a party of Indians, whose tribe was
then unknown, though later they turned out to be
Chippewas from the Upper Lakes, suddenly fell on the
guard.   They charged home with great spirit, using
their sharp spears well, and killed, wounded, or
captured several soldiers; but they were repulsed,
and retreated, carrying with them their dead, save
one warrior.[1] A few days afterwards they impru-
dently ventured back, pretending innocence, and six
were seized, and sent to one of the forts as prisoners.
Their act of treacherous violence had, of course,
caused the immediate abandonment of the proposed
treaty.

The remaining Chippewas marched towards home,
with the scalps of the men they had slain, and with
one captured soldier.   They passed by Detroit, telling the French villagers that " their father [the
British Commandant] was a dog," because he had
given them no arms or ammunition, and that in consequence they would not deliver him their prisoner,
but would take the poor wretch with them to their
Mackinaw home.   Accordingly they carried him on
to the far-off island at the mouth of Lake Michigan;
but just as they were preparing to make him run
the gauntlet the British commander of the lonely
little post interfered.   This subaltern with his party
of a dozen soldiers was surrounded by many times

[1] St. Clair Papers, ii., 50.

his number of ferocious savages, and was completely isolated in the wilderness; but his courage stood as high as his humanity, and he broke through the Indians, threatening them with death if they interfered, rescued the captive American, and sent him home in safety.[1]

The other Indians made no attempt to check the Chippewas; on the contrary, the envoys of the Iroquois and Delawares made vain efforts to secure the release of the Chippewa prisoners. On the other hand, the generous gallantry of the British commander at Mackinaw was in some sort equalled by the action of the traders on the Maumee, who went to great expense in buying from the Shawnees Americans whom they had doomed to the terrible torture of death at the stake.[2]

Under such circumstances the treaties of course came to naught. After interminable delays the Indians either refused to treat at all, or else the acts of those who did were promptly repudiated by those who did not. In consequence throughout this period even the treaties that were made were quite worthless, for they bound nobody. Moreover, there were the usual clashes between the National and State authorities. While Harmar was trying to treat, the Kentuckians were organizing retaliatory inroads; and while the United States Commissioners were trying to hold big peace coun-

---

[1] State Dept. MSS., No. 150, vol. iii.   William Wilson and James Rinkin to Richard Butler, August 4, 1788 ; Wilson and Rinkin to St. Clair, August 31, 1788.

[2] *Do.*, Rinkin to Butler, July 2, 1788 ; St. Clair to Knox, September 4, 1788.

cils on the Ohio, the New York and Massachusetts Commissioners were conducting independent negotiations at what is now Buffalo, to determine the western boundary of New York.[1]

All the while the ravages grew steadily more severe. The Federal officers at the little widely scattered forts were at their wits' ends in trying to protect the outlying settlers and retaliate on the Indians; and as the latter grew bolder they menaced the forts themselves and harried the troops who convoyed provisions to them. Of the innumerable tragedies which occurred, the record of a few has by chance been preserved. One may be worth giving merely as a sample of many others. On the Virginian side of the Ohio lived a pioneer farmer of some note, named Van Swearingen.[2] One day his son crossed the river to hunt with a party of strangers. Near a "waste cabbin," the deserted log hut of some reckless adventurer, an Indian war-band came on them unawares, slew three, and carried off the young man. His father did not know whether they had killed him or not. He could find no trace of him, and he wrote to the commander of the nearest fort, begging him to try to get news from the Indian villages as to whether his son were alive or dead, and to employ for the purpose any friendly Indian or white scout, at whatever price was set—

---

[1] *Do.*, Wilson and Rinkin to St. Clair, July 29, 1788. These treaties made at the Ohio forts are quite unworthy of preservation, save for mere curiosity; they really settled nothing whatever and conferred no rights that were not taken with the strong hand; yet they are solemnly quoted in some books as if they were the real sources of title to parts of the Northwest.

[2] State Dept. MSS., No. 150, vol. ii., Van Swearingen to William Butler, Washington County, Sept. 29, 1787.

he would pay it "to the utmost farthing." He
could give no clue to the Indians who had done the
deed ; all he could say was that a few days before,
one of these war parties, while driving off a number
of horses, was overtaken by the riflemen of the
neighborhood and scattered, after a fight in which
one white man and two red men were killed.

The old frontiersman never found his son ; doubtless the boy was slain; but his fate, like the fate of hundreds of others, was swallowed up in the gloomy mys-
tery of the wilderness. So far from being unusual,
the incident attracted no comment, for it was one of
every-day occurrence. Its only interest lies in the
fact that it was of a kind that befell the family of
almost every dweller in the wilds. Danger and
death were so common that the particular expression
which each might take made small impress on the
minds of the old pioneers. Every one of them
had a long score of slain friends and kinsfolk to
avenge upon his savage foes.

The subalterns in command of the little detachments which moved between the posts, whether they
The
Indians
Harass
the Regular
Troops.
went by land or water, were forced to be
ever on the watch against surprise and
ambush. This was particularly the case
with the garrison at Vincennes. The
Wabash Indians were all the time out in parties
to murder and plunder ; and yet these same thieves
and murderers were continually coming into town
and strolling innocently about the fort ; for it was impossible to tell the peaceful Indians from the hostile.
They were ever in communication with the equally

treacherous and ferocious Miami tribes, to whose
towns the war parties often brought five or six
scalps in a day, and prisoners, too, doomed to a
death of awful torture at the stake. There is no
need to waste sympathy on the northwestern Indians for their final fate; never were defeat and
subjection more richly deserved.

The bands of fierce and crafty braves who lounged
about the wooden fort at Vincennes watched eagerly
the outgoing and incoming of the troops, and were
prompt to dog and waylay any party they thought
they could overcome. They took advantage of the
unwillingness of the Federal commander to harass
Indians who might be friendly; and plotted at ease
the destruction of the very troops who spent much
of the time in keeping intruders off their lands. In
the summer of 1788 they twice followed parties of
soldiers from the town, when they went down the
Wabash, and attacked them by surprise, from the
river-banks, as they sat in their boats. In one instance, the lieutenant in command got off with the
loss of but two or three men. In the other, of the
thirty-six soldiers who composed the party ten were
killed, eight wounded, and the greater part of the
provisions and goods they were conveying were captured; while the survivors, pushing down-stream,
ultimately made their way to the Illinois towns.[1]
This last tragedy was avenged by a band of thirty
mounted riflemen from Kentucky, led by the noted
backwoods fighter Hardin. They had crossed the

---

[1] State Dept. MSS., No. 150, vol. iii. Lt. Spear to Harmar, June 2,
1788 ; Hamtranck to Harmar, Aug. 12, 1788.

Ohio on a retaliatory foray, many of their horses having been stolen by the Indians. When near Vincennes they happened to stumble on the war party that had attacked the soldiers, slew ten, and scattered the others to the winds, capturing thirty horses.[1]

The war bands who harried the settlements, or lurked along the banks of the Ohio, bent on theft
Dreadful Nature of the Warfare. and murder, did terrible deeds, and at times suffered terrible fates in return, when some untoward chance threw them in the way of the grim border vengeance. The books of the old annalists are filled with tales of disaster and retribution, of horrible suffering and of fierce prowess. Countless stories are told of heroic fight and panic rout; of midnight assault on lonely cabins, and ambush of heavy-laden immigrant scows; of the deaths of brave men and cowards, and the dreadful butchery of women and children; of bloody raid and revengeful counter stroke. Sometimes a band of painted marauders would kill family after family, without suffering any loss, would capture boat after boat without effective resistance from the immigrants, paralyzed by panic fright, and would finally escape unmolested, or beat off with ease a possibly larger party of pursuers, who happened to be ill led, or to be men with little training in wilderness warfare.

At other times all this might be reversed. A cabin might be defended with such maddened cour-

---

[1] Draper MSS. Wm. Clark Papers. N. T. Dalton to W. Clark, Vincennes, Aug. 23, 1788 ; also Denny, p. 528.

age by some stout rifleman, fighting for his cowering wife and children, that a score of savages would recoil baffled, leaving many of their number dead. A boat's crew of resolute men might beat back, with heavy loss, an over-eager onslaught of Indians in canoes, or push their slow, unwieldy craft from shore under a rain of rifle-balls, while the wounded oarsmen strained at the bloody handles of the sweeps, and the men who did not row gave shot for shot, firing at the flame tongues in the dark woods. A party of scouts, true wilderness veterans, equal to their foes in woodcraft and cunning, and superior in marksmanship and reckless courage, might follow and scatter some war band and return in triumph with scalps and retaken captives and horses.

A volume could readily be filled with adventures of this kind, all varying infinitely in detail, but all alike in their bloody ferocity. During the years 1789 and 1790 scores of Indian war parties went on such trips, to meet every kind of success and failure. The deeds of one such, which happen to be recorded, may be given merely to serve as a sample of what happened in countless other cases. In the early spring of 1790 a band of fifty-four Indians of various tribes, but chiefly Cherokees and Shawnees, established a camp near the mouth of the Scioto.[1] They first attacked a small new-built station, on one of the bottoms of the Ohio, some twenty miles from Limestone, and killed or captured all its fifteen inhabitants. They spared the lives of two of the captives, but forced the wretches

Deeds of a War Party.

---

[1] American State Papers, Indian Affairs, vol. i., pp. 87, 88, 91.

to act as decoys so as to try to lure passing boats within reach.

Their first success was with a boat going down-river, and containing four men and two unmarried girls, besides a quantity of goods intended for the stores in the Kentucky towns. The two decoys appeared on the right bank, begging piteously to be taken on board, and stating that they had just escaped from the savages. Three of the voyagers, not liking the looks of the men, refused to land, but the fourth, a reckless fellow named Flynn, and the two girls, who were coarse, foolish, good-natured frontier women of the lower sort, took pity upon the seeming fugitives, and insisted on taking them aboard. Accordingly the scow was shoved inshore, and Flynn jumped on the bank, only to be immediately seized by the Indians, who then opened fire on the others. They tried to put off, and fired back, but they were helpless ; one man and a girl were shot, another wounded, and the savages then swarmed aboard, seized everything, and got very drunk on a keg of whiskey. The fates of the captives were various, each falling to some different group of savages. Flynn, the cause of the trouble, fell to the Cherokees, who took him to the Miami town, and burned him alive, with dreadful torments. The remaining girl, after suffering outrage and hardship, was bound to the stake, but saved by a merciful Indian, who sent her home. Of the two remaining men, one ran the gauntlet successfully, and afterwards escaped and reached home through the woods, while the other was ransomed by a French trader at Sandusky.

Before thus disposing of their captives the Indians hung about the mouth of the Scioto for some time. They captured a pirogue going up-stream, and killed all six paddlers. Soon afterwards three heavily laden scows passed, drifting down with the current. Aboard these were twenty-eight men, with their women and children, together with many horses and bales of merchandise. They had but sixteen guns among them, and many were immigrants, unaccustomed to savage warfare, and therefore they made no effort to repel the attack, which could easily have been done by resolute, well-armed veterans. The Indians crowded into the craft they had captured, and paddled and rowed after the scows, whooping and firing. They nearly overtook the last scow, whereupon its people shifted to the second, and abandoned it. When further pressed the people shifted into the headmost scow, cut holes in its sides so as to work all the oars, and escaped down-stream, leaving the Indians to plunder the two abandoned boats, which contained twenty-eight horses and fifteen hundred pounds' worth of goods.

The Kentuckians of the neighborhood sent word to General Harmar, begging him to break up this nest of plunderers. Accordingly he started after them, with his regular troops. He was joined by a number of Kentucky mounted riflemen, under the command of Col. Charles Scott, a rough Indian fighter, and veteran of the Revolutionary War, who afterwards became governor of the State. Scott had moved to Kentucky not long after the close of the war with England ; he had lost a son at the hands of the savages,[1] and he delighted in war against them.

Harmar made a circuit and came down along the Scioto, hoping to surprise the Indian camp; but he might as well have hoped to surprise a party of timber wolves. His foes scattered and disappeared in the dense forest. Nevertheless, coming across some moccasin tracks, Scott's horsemen followed the trail, killed four Indians, and carried in the scalps to Limestone. The chastisement proved of little avail. A month later five immigrant boats, while moored to the bank a few miles from Limestone, were rushed by the Indians at night; one boat was taken, all the thirteen souls aboard being killed or captured.

Among the men who suffered about this time was the Italian Vigo; a fine, manly, generous fellow, of whom St. Clair spoke as having put the United States under heavy obligations, and as being "in truth the most disinterested person" he had ever known.[2] While taking his trading boat up the Wabash, Vigo was attacked by an Indian war party, three of his men were killed, and he was forced to drop down-stream. Meeting another trading boat manned by Americans, he again essayed to force a passage in company with it, but they were both attacked with fury. The other boat got off; but Vigo's was captured. However, the Indians, when they found the crew consisted of creoles, molested none of them, telling them that they only warred against the Americans; though they plundered the boat.

Misadventures of Vigo.

[1] State Dept. MSS., No. 71, vol. ii., p. 563.
[2] American State Papers, Indian Affairs, vol. i., Sept. 19, 1790.

By the summer of 1790 the raids of the Indians had become unbearable. Fresh robberies and murders were committed every day in Kentucky, or along the Wabash and Ohio. Writing to the Secretary of War, a prominent Kentuckian, well knowing all the facts, estimated that during the seven years which had elapsed since the close of the Revolutionary War the Indians had slain fifteen hundred people in Kentucky itself, or on the immigrant routes leading thither, and had stolen twenty thousand horses, besides destroying immense quantities of other property.[1] The Federal generals were also urgent in asserting the folly of carrying on a merely defensive war against such foes. All the efforts of the Federal authorities to make treaties with the Indians and persuade them to be peaceful had failed. The Indians themselves had renewed hostilities, and the different tribes had one by one joined in the war, behaving with a treachery only equalled by their ferocity. With great reluctance the National Government concluded that an effort to chastise the hostile savages could no longer be delayed ; and those on the Maumee, or Miami of the Lakes, and on the Wabash, whose guilt had been peculiarly heinous, were singled out as the objects of attack.

Prepara-tions to Attack the Indians.

The expedition against the Wabash towns was led by the Federal commander at Vincennes, Major Hamtranck. No resistance was encountered; and after burning a few villages of bark huts and destroying some corn he returned to Vincennes.

[1] American State Papers, Indian Affairs, vol. i. Innes to Sec. of War, July 7, 1790.

The main expedition was that against the Miami Indians, and was led by General Harmar himself.

Harmar's
Expedition
against
the Miami
Towns. It was arranged that there should be a nucleus of regular troops, but that the force should consist mainly of militia from Kentucky and Pennsylvania, the former furnishing twice as many as the latter. The troops were to gather on the 15th of September at Fort Washington, on the north bank of the Ohio, a day's journey down-stream from Limestone.

At the appointed time the militia began to straggle in; the regular officers had long been busy Poor
Quality of
the Militia. getting their own troops, artillery, and military stores in readiness. The regulars felt the utmost disappointment at the appearance of the militia. They numbered but few of the trained Indian fighters of the frontier; many of them were hired substitutes; most of them were entirely unacquainted with Indian warfare, and were new to the life of the wilderness; and they were badly armed.[1] The Pennsylvanians were of even poorer stuff than the Kentuckians, numbering many infirm old men, and many mere boys. They were undisciplined, with little regard for authority, and inclined to be disorderly and mutinous.

By the end of September one battalion of Pennsylvania, and three battalions of Kentucky, militia, The Army
Assembles. had arrived, and the troops began their march to the Miami. All told there were 1453 men, 320 being Federal troops and 1133 militia,

[1] American State Papers, Indian Affairs, vol. i., pp. 104, 105 ; Military Affairs, i., 20.

many of whom were mounted; and there were three light brass field-pieces.[1] In point of numbers the force was amply sufficient for its work; but Harmar, though a gallant man, was not fitted to command even a small army against Indians, and the bulk of the militia, who composed nearly four-fifths of his force, were worthless. A difficulty immediately occured in choosing a commander for the militia. Undoubtedly the best one among their officers was Colonel John Hardin, who (like his fellow Kentuckian, Colonel Scott), was a veteran of the Revolutionary War, and a man of experience in the innumerable deadly Indian skirmishes of the time. He had no special qualifications for the command of more than a handful of troops, but he was a brave and honorable man, who had done well in leading small parties of rangers against their red foes. Nevertheless, the militia threatened mutiny unless they were allowed to choose their own leader, and they chose a mere incompetent, a Colonel Trotter. Harmar yielded, for the home authorities had dwelt much on the necessity of his preventing friction between the regulars and the militia; and he had so little control over the latter, that he was very anxious to keep them good-humored. Moreover, the commissariat arrangements were poor. Under such circumstances the keenest observers on the frontier foretold failure from the start. [2]

---

[1] *Do.*, Indian Affairs, i., p. 104; also p. 105. For this expedition see also Military Affairs, i., pp. 20, 28, and Denny's Military Journal, pp. 343, 354.

[2] Am. State Papers, Indian Affairs, i. Jno. O'Fallan to the President, Lexington, Ky., Sept. 25, 1790.

For several days the army marched slowly forward. The regular officers had endless difficulty
The March with the pack horsemen, who allowed
to the their charges to stray or be stolen, and
Miami. they strove to instruct the militia in the
rudiments of their duties, on the march, in camp,
and in battle. A fortnight's halting progress
through the wilderness brought the army to a small
branch of the Miami of the Lakes. Here a horse
patrol captured a Maumee Indian, who informed his
captors that the Indians knew of their approach and
were leaving their towns. On hearing this an effort
was made to hurry forward; but when the army
reached the Miami towns, on October 17th, they
had been deserted. They stood at the junction of
two branches of the Miami, the St. Mary and the
St. Joseph, about one hundred and seventy miles
from Fort Washington. The troops had marched
about ten miles a day. The towns consisted of a
couple of hundred wigwams, with some good log
huts; and there were gardens, orchards, and immense
fields of corn. All these the soldiers destroyed, and
the militia loaded themselves with plunder.

On the 18th Colonel Trotter was ordered out
with three hundred men to spend a couple of days
Failure and exploring the country, and finding out
Defeat of a where the Indians were. After marching
Militia Ex-
pedition. a few miles, they came across two Indians.
Both were killed by the advanced horsemen. All
four of the field officers of the militia—two colonels
and two majors—joined helter-skelter in the chase,
leaving their troops for half an hour without a

leader.   Apparently satisfied with this feat, Trotter
marched home, having accomplished nothing.

Much angered, Harmar gave the command to
Hardin, who left the camp next morning with two
hundred men, including thirty regulars. **Defeat of a**
But the militia had turned sulky. They **Small De-**
tachment of
did not wish to go, and they began to **Troops.**
desert and return to camp immediately after leaving
it.   At least half of them had thus left him, when
he stumbled on a body of about a hundred Indians.
The Indians advanced firing, and the militia fled
with abject cowardice, many not even discharging
their guns.   The thirty regulars stood to their work,
and about ten of the militia stayed with them.
This small detachment fought bravely, and was cut
to pieces, but six or seven men escaping.   Their
captain, after valiant fighting, broke through the
savages, and got into a swamp near by.   Here he
hid, and returned to camp next day; he was so near
the place of the fight that he had seen the victory
dance of the Indians over their slain and mutilated
foes.

This defeat took the heart out of the militia.
The army left the Miami towns, and moved back a
couple of miles to the Shawnee town of **The Army**
Chilicothe.   A few Indians began to lurk **Begins its**
about, stealing horses, and two of the militia **Retreat.**
captains determined to try to kill one of the thieves.
Accordingly, at nightfall, they hobbled a horse with
a bell, near a hazel thicket in which they hid.   Soon
an Indian stalked up to the horse, whereupon they
killed him, and brought his head into camp, pro-

claiming that it should at least be worth the price of a wolf scalp.

Next day was spent by the army in completing the destruction of all the corn, the huts, and the belongings of the Indians. A band of a dozen warriors tried to harass one of the burning parties; but some of the mounted troops got on their flank, killed two and drove the others off, they themselves suffering no loss.

The following day, the 21st, the army took up the line of march for Fort Washington, having destroyed six Indian towns, and an immense quantity

A Detachment Sent Back to Attack Indians.

of corn. But Hardin was very anxious to redeem himself by trying another stroke at the Indians, who, he rightly judged, would gather at their towns as soon as the troops left. Harmar also wished to revenge his losses, and to forestall any attempt of the Indians to harass his shaken and retreating forces. Accordingly that night he sent back against the towns a detachment of four hundred men, sixty of whom were regulars, and the rest picked militia. They were commanded by Major Wyllys, of the regulars. It was a capital mistake of Harmar's to send off a mere detachment on such a business. He should have taken a force composed of all his regulars and the best of the militia, and led it in person.

The detachment marched soon after midnight, and reached the Miami at daybreak on October 22d. It

This Detachment Roughly Handled.

was divided into three columns, which marched a few hundred yards apart, and were supposed to keep in touch with one another. The middle column was led by Wyllys in person, and included the regulars and a few militia. The rest of the militia composed the flank columns and marched under their own officers.

Immediately after crossing the Miami, and reaching the neighborhood of the town, Indians were seen. The columns were out of touch, and both of those on the flanks pressed forward against small parties of braves, whom they drove before them up the St. Joseph. Heedless of the orders they had received, the militia thus pressed forward, killing and scattering the small parties in their front and losing all connection with the middle column of regulars. Meanwhile the main body of the Indians gathered to assail this column, and overwhelmed it by numbers; whether they had led the militia away by accident or by design is not known. The regulars fought well and died hard, but they were completely cut off, and most of them, including their commander, were slain. A few escaped, and either fled back to camp or up the St. Joseph. Those who took the latter course met the militia returning and informed them of what had happened. Soon afterwards the victorious Indians themselves appeared, on the opposite side of the St. Joseph, and attempted to force their way across. But the militia were flushed by the easy triumph of the morning and fought well, repulsing the Indians and finally forcing them to withdraw. They then marched slowly back to the Miami towns, gathered their wounded, arrayed their ranks, and rejoined the main army. The Indians had suffered heavily, and were too dispirited, both by their loss, and by their last repulse, to attempt further to harass either this detachment or the main army itself on its retreat.

Nevertheless, the net result was a mortifying failure. In all, the regulars had lost 75 men killed and 3 wounded, while of the militia 28 had been wounded and 108 had been killed or were missing. The march back was very dreary; and the militia became nearly ungovernable, so that at one time Harmar reduced them to order only by threatening to fire on them with the artillery.

Practical Failure of the Expedition.

The loss of all their provisions and dwellings exposed the Miami tribes to severe suffering and want during the following winter; and they had also lost many of their warriors. But the blow was only severe enough to anger and unite them, not to cripple or crush them. All the other western tribes made common cause with them. They banded together and warred openly; and their vengeful forays on the frontier increased in number, so that the suffering of the settlers was great. Along the Ohio people lived in hourly dread of tomahawk and scalping knife; the attacks fell unceasingly on all the settlements from Marietta to Louisville.

CHAPTER VIII.

THE SOUTHWEST TERRITORY, 1788–1790.

DURING the years 1788 and 1789 there was much disquiet and restlessness throughout the southwestern territory, the land lying between Kentucky and the southern Indians. The disturbances caused by the erection of the state of Franklin were subsiding, the authority of North Carolina was re-established over the whole territory, and by degrees a more assured and healthy feeling began to prevail among the settlers; but as yet their future was by no means certain, nor was their lot irrevocably cast in with that of their fellows in the other portions of the Union.

As already said, the sense of national unity among the frontiersmen was small. The men of the Cumberland in writing to the Creeks spoke of the Franklin people as if they belonged to an entirely distinct nation, and as if a war with or by one community concerned in no way the other[1]; while the leaders of Franklin were carrying on with the Spaniards negotiations quite incompatible with the continued sovereignty of the United States. Indeed it was some

Uneasiness in the Southwest.

---

[1] Robertson MSS. Robertson to McGillivray, Nashville, 1788. "Those aggressors live in a different state and are governed by different laws, consequently we are not culpable for their misconduct."

time before the southwestern people realized that after the Constitution went into effect they had no authority to negotiate commercial treaties on their own account. Andrew Jackson, who had recently taken up his abode in the Cumberland country, was one of the many men who endeavored to convince the Spanish agents that it would be a good thing for both parties if the Cumberland people were allowed to trade with the Spaniards; in which event the latter would of course put a stop to the Indian hostilities.[1]

This dangerous loosening of the Federal tie shows that it would certainly have given way entirely had the population at this time been scattered over a wider territory. The obstinate and bloody warfare waged by the Indians against the frontiersmen was in one way of great service to the nation, for it kept back the frontier, and forced the settlements to remain more or less compact and in touch with the country behind them. If the red men had been as weak as, for instance, the black-fellows of Australia, the settlers would have roamed hither and thither without regard to them, and would have settled, each man wherever he liked, across to the Pacific. Moreover the Indians formed the bulwarks which defended the British and Spanish possessions from the adventurers of the border; save for the shield thus offered by the fighting tribes it would have been impossible to bar the frontiersmen from the territory either to the north or to the south of the boundaries of the United States.

Fear of Indians Strengthens the Federal Bond.

[1] Tennessee Hist. Soc. MSS. Andrew Jackson to D. Smith, introducing the Spanish agent, Captain Fargo, Feb. 13, 1789.

Congress had tried hard to bring about peace with the southern Indians, both by sending commissioners to them and by trying to persuade the three southern States to enter into mutually beneficial treaties with them. A successful effort was also made to detach the Chickasaws from the others, and keep them friendly with the United States. Congress as usual sympathized with the Indians against the intruding whites, although it was plain that only by warfare could the red men be permanently subdued.[1]

The Cumberland people felt the full weight of the warfare, the Creeks being their special enemies. Robertson himself lost a son and a brother in the various Indian attacks. To him fell the task of trying to put a stop to the ravages. He was the leader of his people **Sufferings of the Cumberland People.** in every way, their commander in war and their spokesman when they sought peace; and early in 1788 he wrote a long letter on their behalf to the Creek chief McGillivray. After disclaiming all responsibility for or connection with the Franklin men, he said that the settlers for whom he spoke had not had the most distant idea that any Indians would object to their settling on the Cumberland, in a country that had been purchased outright at the Henderson treaty. He further stated that he had believed the Creek chief would approve of the expedition to punish the marauders at the Muscle Shell Shoals, inasmuch as the Creeks had repeatedly assured him that these marauders were refractory peo-

---

[1] State Dep. MSS., No. 180, p. 66; No. 151, p. 275. Also letters of Richard Winn to Knox, June 25, 1788; James White to Knox, Aug. 1, 1788; Joseph Martin to Knox, July 25, 1788.

ple who would pay no heed to their laws and commands. Robertson knew this to be good point, for as a matter of fact the Creeks, though pretending to be peaceful, had made no effort to suppress these banditti, and had resented by force of arms the destruction of their stronghold. [1]

Robertson then came to his personal wrongs. His quaintly worded letter runs in part: "I had the mortification to see one of my children **Robertson's** Killed and uncommonly Massacred . . . **Letters to** **the Creek** from my earliest youth I have endeavored **Chief** to arm myself with a sufficient share of **McGillivray** Fortitude to meet anything that Nature might have intended, but to see an innocent child so Uncommonly Massacred by people who ought to have both sense and bravery has in a measure unmanned me. . . . I have always striven to do justice to the red people; last fall, trusting in Cherokee friendship, I with utmost difficulty prevented a great army from marching against them. The return is very inadequate to the services I have rendered them as last summer they killed an affectionate brother and three days ago an innocent child." The letter concludes with an emphatic warning that the Indians must expect heavy chastisement if they do not stop their depredations.

Robertson looked on his own woes and losses with much of the stoicism for which his Indian foes were famed. He accepted the fate of his son **His Letter** with a kind of grim stolidity; and did not **to Martin.** let it interfere with his efforts to bring about a peace. Writing to his friend General Mar-

[1] Robertson MSS. Robertson to McGillivray. Letters already cited.

tin, he said: "On my return home [from the North Carolina Legislature to which he was a delegate] I found distressing times in the country. A number of persons have been killed since; among those unfortunate persons were my third son. . . . We sent Captains Hackett and Ewing to the Creeks who have brought very favorable accounts, and we do not doubt but a lasting peace will be shortly concluded between us and that nation. The Cherokees we shall flog, if they do not behave well."[1] He wished to make peace if he could; but if that was impossible, he was ready to make war with the same stern acceptance of fate.

The letter then goes on to express the opinion that, if Congress does not take action to bring about a peace, the Creeks will undoubtedly invade Georgia with some five thousand warriors, for McGillivray has announced that he will consent to settle the boundary question with Congress, but will do nothing with Georgia. The letter shows with rather startling clearness how little Robertson regarded the Cumberland people and the Georgians as being both in the same nation; he saw nothing strange in one portion of the country concluding a firm peace with an enemy who was about to devastate another portion.

Robertson was anxious to encourage immigration, and for this purpose he had done his best to hurry forward the construction of a road between the Holston and the Cumberland settlements. In his

[1] State Department MSS., No. 71, vol. ii. Robertson to Martin, Pleasant Grove, May 7, 1788.

letter to Martin he urged him to proclaim to possible
settlers the likelihood of peace, and guaranteed that
the road would be ready before winter.   It was
opened in the fall; and parties of settlers began to
come in over it.   To protect them, the district from
time to time raised strong guards of mounted riflemen to patrol the road, as well as the neighborhood of the settlements, and to convoy the immigrant
companies.   To defray the expenses of the troops,
the Cumberland court raised taxes.   Exactly as the
Franklin people had taken peltries as the basis for
their currency, so those of the Cumberland, in arranging for payment in kind, chose the necessaries
of life as the best medium of exchange.   They
enacted that the tax should be paid one quarter
in corn, one half in beef, pork, bear meat, and venison, one eighth in salt, and one eighth in money.[1]
It was still as easy to shoot bear and deer as to raise
hogs and oxen.

Robertson wrote several times to McGillivray,
alone or in conjunction with another veteran frontier

**McGilli-
vray's
Letter to
Robertson.**
leader, Col. Anthony Bledsoe.   Various
other men of note on the border, both
from Virginia and North Carolina, wrote
likewise.   To these letters McGillivray
responded promptly in a style rather more polished
though less frank than that of his correspondents.
His tone was distinctly more warlike and less con-
ciliatory than theirs.   He avowed, without hesitation, that the Creeks and not the Americans had
been the original aggressors, saying that " my nation

[1] Ramsey, p. 504.

has waged war against your people for several years past; but that we had no motive of revenge, nor did it proceed from any sense of injuries sustained from your people, but being warmly attached to the British and being under their influence our operations were directed by them against you in common with other Americans." He then acknowledged that after the close of the war the Americans had sent overtures of peace, which he had accepted—although as a matter of fact the Creeks never ceased their ravages,—but complained that Robertson's expedition against the Muscle Shoals again brought on war.[1]

There was, of course, nothing in this complaint of the injustice of Robertson's expedition, for the Muscle Shoal Indians had been constantly plundering and murdering before it was planned, and it was undertaken merely to put a stop to their ravages. However, McGillivray made adroit use of it. He stated that the expedition itself, carried on, as he understood it, mainly against the French traders, "was no concern of ours and would have been entirely disregarded by us; but in the execution of it some of our people were there, who went as well from motives of curiosity as to traffic in silverware; and six of whom were rashly killed by your men"[2]; and inasmuch as these slain men were prominent in different Creek towns, the deed led to retaliatory raids. But now that vengeance had been taken, McGillivray declared that a stable peace would be secured, and he expressed "considerable concern"

[1] State Department MSS., No. 71, vol. ii., p. 620. McGillivray to Bledsoe and Robertson; no date.
[2] McGillivray's Letter of April 17, 1788, p. 521.

over the "tragical end" of Robertson's slain kinsfolk. As for the Georgians, he announced that if they were wise and would agree to an honorable peace he would bury the red hatchet, and if not then he would march against them whenever he saw fit.[1] Writing again at the end of the year, he reiterated his assurances of the peaceful inclinations of the Creeks, though their troubles with Georgia were still unsettled.[2]

Nevertheless these peaceful protestations produced absolutely no effect upon the Indian ravages, which **Continu-** continued with unabated fury. Many in-**ance of the** stances of revolting brutality and aggression **Ravages.** by the whites against the Cherokees took place in Tennessee, both earlier and later than this, and in eastern Tennessee at this very time; but the Cumberland people, from the earliest days of their settlement, had not sinned against the red men, while as regards all the Tennesseans, the Creeks throughout this period appeared always, and the Cherokees appeared sometimes, as the wrong-doers, the men who began the long and ferocious wars of reprisal.

Robertson's companion, Bledsoe, was among the many settlers who suffered death in the summer of **Death of** 1788. He was roused from sleep by the **Bledsoe.** sound of his cattle running across the yard in front of the twin log-houses occupied by himself and

[1] *Do.* p. 625; McGillivray's Letter of April 15, 1788.

[2] Robertson MSS. McGillivray to Robertson, December 1, 1788. This letter contains the cautious, non-committal answer to Robertson's letter in which the latter proposed that Cumberland should be put under Spanish protection; the letter itself McGillivray had forwarded to the Spaniards.

his brother and their families. As he opened the door he was shot by Indians, who were lurking behind the fence, and one of his hired men was also shot down.[1] The savages fled, and Bledsoe lived through the night, while the other inmates of the house kept watch at the loop-holes until day broke and the fear was passed. Under the laws of North Carolina at that time, all the lands went to the sons of a man dying intestate, and Bledsoe's wealth consisted almost exclusively in great tracts of land. As he lay dying in his cabin, his sister suggested to him that unless he made a will he would leave his seven daughters penniless; and so the will was drawn, and the old frontiersman signed it just before he drew his last breath, leaving each of his children provided with a share of his land.

In the following year, 1789, Robertson himself had a narrow escape. He was at work with some of his field hands in a clearing. One man **Robertson** was on guard and became alarmed at some **Wounded.** sound; Robertson snatched up his gun, and, while he was peering into the woods, the Indians fired on him. He ran toward the station and escaped, but only at the cost of a bullet through the foot. Immediately sixty mounted riflemen gathered at Robertson's station, and set out after the fleeing Indians; but finding that in the thick wood they did not gain on their foes, and were hampered by their horses, twenty picked men were sent ahead. Among these twenty men was fierce, moody young Andrew Jackson. They found the Indians in camp, at day-

[1] Putnam, 298.

break, but fired from too great a distance; they killed one, wounded others, and scattered the rest, who left sixteen guns behind them in their flight.[1]

During these two years many people were killed, both in the settlements, on the trail through the woods, and on the Tennessee River, as they

Wrongs Committed by Both Sides. drifted down-stream in their boats. As always in these contests the innocent suf. fered with the guilty. The hideous border ruffians, the brutal men who murdered peaceful Indians in times of truce and butchered squaws and children in time of war, fared no worse than unoffending settlers or men of mark who had been staunch friends of the Indian peoples. The Legislatures of the seaboard States, and Congress itself, passed laws to punish men who committed outrages on the Indians, but they could not be executed. Often the border people themselves interfered to prevent such outrages, or expressed disapproval of them, and rescued the victims; but they never visited the criminals with the stern and ruthless punishment which alone would have availed to check the crimes. For this failure they must receive hearty condemnation, and be adjudged to have forfeited much of the respect to which they were otherwise entitled by their strong traits, and their deeds of daring. In the same way, but to an even greater degree, the peaceful Indians always failed to punish or restrain their brethren who were bent on murder and plunder; and the braves who went on the warpath made no discrimination between good and bad, strong and weak, man and woman, young and old.

[1] Haywood, 244.

One of the sufferers was General Joseph Martin, who had always been a firm friend of the red race, and had earnestly striven to secure justice for them.[1] He had gone for a few days to his plantation on the borders of Georgia, and during his visit the place was attacked by a Creek war party. They drove away his horses and wounded his overseer; but he managed to get into his house and stood at bay, shooting one warrior and beating off the others.

Among many attacks on the boats that went down the Tennessee it happens that a full record has been kept of one. A North Carolinian, named Attack on Brown, had served in the Revolutionary an Emi-War with the troop of Light-Horse Harry grant Boat. Lee, and had received in payment a land certificate. Under this certificate he entered several tracts of western land, including some on the Cumberland; and in the spring of 1788 he started by boat down the Tennessee, to take possession of his claims. He took with him his wife and his seven children; and three or four young men also went along. When they reached the Chicamauga towns the Indians swarmed out towards them in canoes. On Brown's boat was a swivel, and with this and the rifles of the men they might have made good their defence; but as soon as the Indians saw them preparing for resistance they halted and hailed the crew, shouting out that they were peaceful and that in consequence of the recent Holston treaties war had ceased between the white men and the red. Brown was not

---

[1] American State Papers, Indian Affairs, vol. i. Martin to Knox, Jan. 15, 1789.

used to Indians; he was deceived, and before he made up his mind what to do, the Indians were alongside, and many of them came aboard.[1] They then seized the boat and massacred the men, while the mother and children were taken ashore and hurried off in various directions by the Indians who claimed to have captured them. One of the boys, Joseph, long afterwards wrote an account of his captivity. He was not treated with deliberate cruelty, though he suffered now and then from the casual barbarity of some of his captors, and toiled like an ordinary slave. Once he was doomed to death by a party of Indians, who made him undress, so as to avoid bloodying his clothes; but they abandoned this purpose through fear of his owner, a half-breed, and a dreaded warrior, who had killed many whites.

After about a year's captivity, Joseph and his mother and sisters were all released, though at different times. Their release was brought

Sevier Secures Release of Prisoners.

about by Sevier. When in the fall of 1788 a big band of Creeks and Cherokees took Gillespie's station, on Little River, a branch of the upper Tennessee, they carried off over a score of women and children. The four highest chiefs, headed by one with the appropriate name of Bloody Fellow, left behind a note addressed to Sevier and Martin, in which they taunted the whites with their barbarities, and especially with the murder of the friendly Cherokee chief Tassel, and warned them to

---

[1] Narrative of Col. Joseph Brown, *Southwestern Monthly*, Nashville, 1851, i., p. 14. The story was told when Brown was a very old man, and doubtless some of the details are inaccurate.

move off the Indian land.[1] In response Sevier made
one of his swift raids, destroyed an Indian town on
the Coosa River, and took prisoner a large number
of Indian women and children. These were well
treated, but were carefully guarded, and were exchanged for the white women and children who
were in captivity among the Indians. The Browns
were among the fortunate people who were thus
rescued from the horrors of Indian slavery. It is
small wonder that the rough frontier people, whose
wives and little ones, friends and neighbors, were in
such manner rescued by Nolichucky Jack, should
have looked with leniency on their darling leader's
shortcomings, even when these shortcomings took
the form of failure to prevent or punish the massacre
of friendly Indians.

The ravages of the Indians were precisely the
same in character that they had always been, and
always were until peace was won. There
was the usual endless succession of dwellings burned, horses driven off, settlers slain
while hunting or working, and immigrant
parties ambushed and destroyed ; and there
was the same ferocious retaliation when opportunity
offered. When Robertson's hopes of peace gave out
he took steps to keep the militia in constant readiness to meet the foe; for he was the military commander of the district. The county lieutenants—
there were now several counties on the Cumberland
—were ordered to see that their men were well
mounted and ready to march at a moment's notice;

Efforts
of the
Settlers
to Defend
Them-
selves.

[1] Ramsey, 519.

and were warned that this was a duty to which they must attend themselves, and not delegate it to their subalterns. The laws were to be strictly enforced; and the subalterns were promptly to notify their men of the time and place to meet. Those who failed to attend would be fined by court-martial. Frequent private musters were to be held; and each man was to keep ready a good gun, nine charges of powder and ball, and a spare flint. It was especially ordered that every marauding band should be followed; for thus some would be overtaken and signally punished, which would be a warning to the others.[1]

The wrath of the Creeks was directed chiefly against the Georgians. The Georgians were pushing steadily westward, and were grasping the Creek hunting-grounds with ferocious greed. They had repeatedly endeavored to hold treaties with the Creeks. On each occasion the chiefs and warriors of a few towns met them, and either declined to do anything, or else signed an agreement which they had no power to enforce. A sample treaty of this kind was that entered into at Galphinton in 1785. The Creeks had been solemnly summoned to meet representatives both of the Federal Congress and of Georgia; but on the appointed day only two towns out of a hundred were represented. The Federal Commissioners thereupon declined to enter into negotiations; but those from Georgia persevered. By presents and strong drink they procured, and their government eagerly accepted, a large cession of land to which the two towns in question had no more title than was vested in all the others.

The Creeks and the Georgians.

[1] Robertson MSS., General Orders, April 5, 1789.

The treaty was fraudulent. The Georgians knew that the Creeks who signed it were giving away what they did not possess; while the Indian signers cared only to get the goods they were offered, and were perfectly willing to make all kinds of promises, inasmuch as they had no intention whatever of keeping any of them. The other Creeks immediately repudiated the transaction, and the war dragged on its course of dismal savagery, growing fiercer year by year, and being waged on nearly even terms.[1]

Soon after the Constitution went into effect the National Government made a vigorous effort to conclude peace on a stable basis. Commissioners were sent to the southern Indians. Under their persuasion McGillivray and the leading kings and chiefs of the Muscogee confederacy came to New York and there entered into a solemn treaty. In this treaty the Creeks acknowledged the United States, to the exclusion of Spain, as the sole power with which they could treat; they covenanted to keep faith and friendship with the Americans; and in return for substantial payments and guaranties they agreed to cede some land to the Georgians, though less than was claimed under the treaty of Galphinton. *McGillivray Signs a Treaty of Peace.*

This treaty was solemnly entered into by the recognized chiefs and leaders of the Creeks; and the Americans fondly hoped that it would end hostilities. It did nothing of the kind. Though the terms were very favorable to the Indians, so much so as to make the frontiersmen grumble, the Creeks scornfully repudi- *The Creeks Pay No Heed to the Treaty.*

[1] American State Papers, Indian Affairs, vol. i., p. 15.

ated the promises made on their behalf by their
authorized representatives. Their motive in going
to war, and keeping up the war, was not so much
anger at the encroachments of the whites, as the
eager thirst for glory, scalps, and plunder, to be won
at the expense of the settlers. The war parties
raided the frontier as freely as ever.[1] The simple
truth was that the Creeks could be kept quiet only
when cowed by physical fear. If the white men did
not break the treaties, then the red men did. It is
idle to dispute about the rights or wrongs of the
contests. Two peoples, in two stages of culture
which were separated by untold ages, stood face to
face ; one or the other had to perish ; and the whites
went forward from sheer necessity.

Throughout these years of Indian warfare the in-
flux of settlers into the Holston and Cumberland
Growth of regions steadily continued. Men in search
Immigra- of homes, or seeking to acquire fortunes by
tion. the purchase of wild lands, came more and
more freely to the Cumberland country as the settlers
therein increased in number and became better able
to cope with and repel their savage foes. The settlements on the Holston grew with great rapidity as
soon as the Franklin disturbances were at an end.
As the people increased in military power, they increased also in material comfort, and political
stability. The crude social life deepened and
broadened. Comfortable homes began to appear
among the huts and hovels of the little towns. The

---

[1] Robertson MSS., Williamson to Robertson, Aug. 2, 1789, and Aug.
7, 1790. American State Papers, Indian Affairs, i., 81. Milfort 131, 142.

outlying settlers still lived in wooden forts or
stations; but where the population was thicker, the
terror of the Indians diminished, and the people
lived in the ordinary style of frontier farmers.

Early in 1790, North Carolina finally ceded, and
the National Government finally accepted, what is
now Tennessee; and in May, Congress The South-
passed a law for the government of this western
Territory Southwest of the River Ohio, as Territory
they chose to call it. This law followed Organized.
on the general lines of the Ordinance of 1787, for
the government of the Northwest; but there was
one important difference. North Carolina had made
her cession conditional upon the non-passage of any
law tending to emancipate slaves. At that time
such a condition was inevitable; but it doomed
the Southwest to suffer under the curse of negro
bondage.

William Blount of North Carolina was appointed
Governor of the Territory, and at once proceeded to
his new home to organize the civil gov- Blount
ernment.[1] He laid out Knoxville as his Made
capital, where he built a good house with Governor.
a lawn in front. On his recommendation Sevier was
appointed Brigadier-General for the Eastern District
and Robertson for the Western; the two districts
known as Washington and Miro respectively.

Blount was the first man of leadership in the West
who was of Cavalier ancestry; for though so much is
said of the Cavalier type in the southern States it

---

[1] Blount MSS. Biography of Blount, in manuscript, compiled by one of
his descendants from the family papers.

was everywhere insignificant in numbers, and comparatively few of the southern men of mark have belonged to it. Blount was really of Cavalier blood. He was descended from a Royalist baronet, who was roughly handled by the Cromwellians, and whose three sons came to America. One of them settled in North Carolina, near Albemarle Sound, and from him came the new governor of the southwestern territory. Blount was a good-looking, well-bred man, with cultivated tastes; but he was also a man of force and energy, who knew well how to get on with the backwoodsmen, so that he soon became popular among them.

The West had grown with astonishing rapidity during the seven years following the close of the **Retrospect:** Revolutionary War. In 1790 there were **What had** in Kentucky nearly seventy-four thousand, **been Ac-** and in the Southwest Territory nearly **complished** **during the** thirty-six thousand souls. In the North- **Seven** west Territory the period of rapid growth **Years.** had not yet begun, and the old French inhabitants still formed the majority of the population.

The changes during these seven years had been vital. In the West, as elsewhere through the Union, the years succeeding the triumphant close of the Revolution were those which determined whether the victory was or was not worth winning. To throw off the yoke of the stranger was useless and worse than useless if we showed ourselves unable to turn to good account the freedom we had gained. Unless we could build

up a great nation, and unless we possessed the power
and self-restraint to frame an orderly and stable
government, and to live under its laws when framed,
the long years of warfare against the armies of the
king were wasted and went for naught.

At the close of the Revolution the West was
seething with sedition. There were three tasks before the Westerners; all three had to be accomplished, under pain of utter failure. It was their
duty to invade and tame the shaggy wilderness; to
drive back the Indians and their European allies;
and to erect free governments which should form
parts of the indissoluble Union. If the spirit of sedition, of lawlessness, and of wild individualism and
separatism had conquered, then our history would
merely have anticipated the dismal tale of the
Spanish-American republics.

Viewed from this standpoint the history of the
West during these eventful years has a special and
peculiar interest. The inflow of the teeming throng
of settlers was the most striking feature; but it was
no more important than the half-seen struggle in
which the Union party finally triumphed over the
restless strivers for disunion. The extent and
reality of the danger are shown by the numerous
separatist movements. The intrigues in which so
many of the leaders engaged with Spain, for the
purpose of setting up barrier states, in some degree
feudatory to the Spaniards; the movement in Kentucky for violent separation from Virginia, and the
more secret movement for separation from the United
States; the turbulent career of the commonwealth of

Franklin; the attitude of isolation of interest from all their neighbors assumed by the Cumberland settlers: —all these various movements and attitudes were significant of the looseness of the Federal tie, and were ominous of the anarchic violence, weakness, and misrule which would have followed the breaking of that tie.

The career of Franklin gave the clearest glimpse of what might have been; for it showed the gradual breaking down of law and order, the rise of factions ready to appeal to arms for success, the bitter broils with neighboring States, the reckless readiness to provoke war with the Indians, unheeding their rights or the woes such wars caused other frontier communities, and finally the entire willingness of the leaders to seek foreign aid when their cause was declining. Had not the Constitution been adopted, and a more perfect union been thus called into being, the history of the state of Franklin would have been repeated in fifty communities from the Alleghanies to the Pacific coast; only these little states, instead of dying in the bud, would have gone through a rank flowering period of bloody and aimless revolutions, of silly and ferocious warfare against their neighbors, and of degrading alliance with the foreigner. From these and a hundred other woes the West no less than the East was saved by the knitting together of the States into a Nation.

This knitting process passed through its first and most critical stage, in the West, during the period intervening between the close of the war for independence, and the year which saw the organization of the Southwest into a territory ruled under the laws, and by the agent, of the National Government. During this time no step was taken towards settling the question of boundary lines with our British and Spanish neighbors; that remained as it had been, the Americans never abandoning claims which they had not yet the power to enforce, and which their antagonists declined to yield. Neither were the Indian wars settled ; on the contrary, they had become steadily more serious, though for the first time a definite solution was promised by the active interference of the National Government. But a vast change had been made by the inflow of population; and an even vaster by the growing solidarity of the western settlements with one another, and with the Central Government. The settlement of the Northwest, so different in some of its characteristics from the settlement of the Southwest, had begun. Kentucky was about to become a State of the Union. The territories north and south of it were organized as part of the domain of the United States. The West was no longer a mere wilderness dotted with cabins and hamlets, whose backwoods builders were held by but the loosest tie of allegiance to any government, even their own. It had become an integral part of the mighty American Republic.

THE END OF VOL. III.

INDEX.

All Four Volumes Available in Bison Book Editions

THE WINNING OF THE WEST.

By THEODORE ROOSEVELT.